WITHOUT REGARD TO RACE

WITHOUT REGARD TO RACE

The Other Martin Robison Delany

Tunde Adeleke

UNIVERSITY PRESS OF MISSISSIPPI

JACKSON

www.upress.state.ms.us

The University Press of Mississippi is a member
of the Association of American University Presses.

11 10 09 08 07 06 05 04 03   4 3 2 1

∞

Library of Congress Cataloging-in-Publication Data
Adeleke, Tunde.
Without regard to race : the other Martin Robison Delany / by
Tunde Adeleke.
     p. cm.
Includes bibliographical references and index.
   ISBN 1-57806-598-4 (alk. paper)
1. Delany, Martin Robison, 1812–1885. 2. African
Americans—Biography. 3. African American intellectuals—Biography.
4. African American abolitionists—Biography. 5. African American
soldiers—Biography. 6. African Americans—Civil rights—
History—19th century. 7. Pan-Africanism—History—19th century.
8. Black nationalism—United States—History—19th century.
I. Title.
   E185.97.D4A34 2004
   973.7'092—dc21   2003010758

British Library Cataloging-in-Publication Data available

This book is dedicated to my daughter,
Chinyere "Chi-Chi" Adeleke (Honey!),
for the love, affection, and
immeasurable joy she brings into my life

CONTENTS

PREFACE

My initial introduction to Martin Delany occurred in 1977 during my senior year at the University of Ife (now Obafemi Awolowo University) in Nigeria. By some fortuitous circumstance, that year the history department chose for the mandatory honors "Special Paper" the course "Blacks in the New World." It quickly became my favorite course as I was both moved and captivated by the enormity of the tragedy and rupture of enslavement and transplantation and by the heroic and indomitable spirit of survival and resistance that slaves and free blacks demonstrated. I completed the course yearning for more knowledge and a deeper understanding of the African Diaspora. Fortunately, it was a time when in universities in Nigeria, and indeed in many other African universities, there was a growing demand for increased knowledge of the African Diaspora. In the 1970s, African universities increasingly began to offer courses and programs that emphasized the connections between Africans and blacks in the Diaspora. The prevailing conviction was that both constituted two sides of the same coin. Consequently, no understanding of African history was considered complete without an understanding of the history of blacks in the Diaspora, and vice versa. After my degree in African studies, it became logical for me to pursue postgraduate studies in African American history. In other words, I embarked upon a search for knowledge and understanding of the other side of the coin.

In Nigeria, our study of the black Diaspora focused attention on and illuminated certain themes, especially those relating to radical, anti-establishment, anti-imperial values and schemes. Hence, we spent more time on topics such as abolitionism, nationalism, Pan-Africanism, the civil rights movement, and Black Power. This was taking place within a broader historical context—the ascendance of postcolonial

African historiography, when African and Africanist scholars in Africa, Europe, and North America began deconstructing colonial historiography. Consequently, the emerging postcolonial African historiography assumed a combative character, which to a certain degree was reflected in the themes and values emphasized in the Diaspora courses. It should be noted that both the de-colonization movement in Africa and the civil rights movement in the United States offered participants on both sides the basis of confraternal engagements built upon shared values and experiences. The civil rights movement of the 1960s coincided with the ascendance of de-colonization in Africa. This historical coincidence enabled nationalist traditions and movements on both sides to share values and to influence each other. The Pan-African movement that began in the early twentieth century among blacks in Diaspora became a dynamic force in the anticolonial and anti-imperial struggles, helping to strengthen the bourgeoning nationalist movements in Africa. On the other hand, the independence of African states like Ghana and Nigeria and the appearance of black leaders in the United Nations constituted for black Americans moments of psychological emancipation and historical triumph. Watching African leaders participate in United Nations deliberations became a source of pride and an additional source of strength and inspiration. Malcolm X and Stokely Carmichael were among those who immediately advocated connecting the two struggles. In other words, they favored elevating the platform of the struggles on both sides into a unified transatlantic, Pan-African front.

This is, therefore, the broader historical context that influenced the growing interest in African universities in the black Diaspora and in issues of nationalism, Pan-Africanism, and historical linkages. One of the prominent historical actors highlighted in the studies as the exempla of the spirit of black nationalism and Pan-Africanism, and whose career embodied those values and traditions at their very best, was Martin R. Delany. He impressed many of us as an unusually strong-willed, ideologically consistent, and militant historical figure. He was presented to us as a man whose militancy and radical nationalism helped nurture Pan-Africanism and its basic tenets—black solidarity; the belief that Africans and blacks in Diaspora share historical, cultural, ethnic, and racial identity; and the use of these shared attributes as the foundation of, and rationale for, transatlantic nexus and unity against what was depicted as an ever-threatening global European imperialist thrust. Delany struck many of us as an unusually brave individual, for we read nothing other than materials that underlined his uncompromisingly militant, antiimperial, and antiestablishment ideas.

It should be noted, however, that there were no full biographical studies of Delany available to us in Nigeria at that time. We relied on a collection of articles, essays, and commentaries, most of them written by scholars and activists who were obviously sympathetic to his radical orientations and ideas. Consequently, the materials we read extolled his virtues, his unflinching devotion to the cause of black freedom, and his defense of African civilization, culture, and history. Most significantly, he was portrayed as someone who persistently and consistently stood in defense and furtherance of black interests, one who refused to sacrifice black interests on the alters of compromise or interracial cooperation. In fact, many portrayed him as a racial essentialist who neatly drew the racial boundary line and never crossed that line throughout his career. There were repeated references to his "Political Destiny" address to the National Emigration Convention in Cleveland in August 1854, in which he proclaimed what many describe as the classic racial essentialist creed of the century. He informed the delegates in unambiguous terms that the great challenge confronting the world was essentially racial—black and white. This racial struggle, he emphasized, mandated strict observance of the racial boundary line.

In combination, these materials stirred a yearning for more information on Delany. It was, therefore, with a determination to satisfy this growing, almost gnawing intellectual curiosity, that I began graduate studies in Canada. I wanted to know how he was able to maintain such ideological and schematic consistency, especially in a socioeconomic, political, and cultural milieu that was so oppressive, violent, and dehumanizing. Where did his strength and convictions come from? Why and how was he able to remain consistently radical, uncompromisingly antiestablishment, when blacks leaders around him seemed to be flip-flopping and vacillating between contending solutions and strategies? I yearned for more insights into the dynamics of his strength, convictions, and motivations.

I did not mention my interest in Delany to anyone until one cold Canadian morning sometime in the fall of 1981, when, during one of our weekly meetings, my faculty adviser, Craig Simpson, handed me a piece of paper on which he had scribbled the name "Martin Delany" and suggested I do some preliminary investigation as a possible dissertation subject. But he also quickly warned that he envisioned the publication of a book on Delany within the next two years. I left his office that morning amazed at his intuition and not quite sure what to make of his ambivalent suggestion, and for the next week or so I reflected on the risk of engaging a subject about whom a book seemed imminent.

My trepidation notwithstanding, I took Simpson's suggestion seriously and began preliminary research. My initial search turned up just three full biographical studies—Victor Ullman's *Martin R. Delany: The Beginnings of Black Nationalism*; Dorothy Sterling's *Martin R. Delany: The Making of an Afro-American*; and the authorized biography by Frank (Frances) Rollin, *Life and Public Services of Martin R. Delany*; two specialized studies on his nationalism—Cyril Griffith, *The African Dream: Martin R. Delany and the Emergence of Pan-Africanist Thought*, and Floyd Miller, *The Search for a Black Nationality: Black Emigration and Colonization*; and a host of books on black nationalism, black radicalism, and Pan-Africanism that assigned prominence and preeminence to Delany. These included the works of Sterling Stuckey, *The Ideological Origins of Black Nationalism*; Harold Cruse, *Crisis of the Negro Intellectual*; and Wilson J. Moses, *The Golden Age of Black Nationalism*. Although with different focuses and emphases, these studies underscore Delany's preeminence as a nationalist and Pan-Africanist. Most important, several affirmed his uncompromising militancy and unflinching devotion to the cause of black freedom and African liberation.

These studies, therefore, reinforced the knowledge and consciousness of Delany that I had in Nigeria. Further research, however, began to uncover radically different and contradictory images and portraits. One such was Theodore Draper's review article, "The Father of American Black Nationalism," in which he identified Delany as the ideological father of black nationalism. Most revealing to me, however, was Draper's contention that too much emphasis had been placed on a relatively brief and ideologically utilitarian phase of Delany's career (emigration/ nationalism) to the neglect of a far more potent and more significant integrationist phase. Draper suggested that had the integrationist phase of Delany's career been examined and illuminated as brilliantly as the nationalist, the excitement and accolade would have been subdued because of confrontations with his ambiguities, inconsistencies, and conservative and even reactionary values and themes. Finally, Draper struck what amounted to a telling blow on the nascent black nationalist tradition when he suggested that the nationalism historically associated with Delany was, in fact, superficial and functionally utilitarian. Delany and his emigrationist followers, he argued, were more interested in becoming fully American and embraced African nationality and identity only *after* being frustrated in their efforts. I read the angry reactions of the Delany aficionados and other scholars to Draper's work and the debates that ensued. Further research uncovered Bill McAdoo's scathing review of Delany's nationalism.

Exposure to these debates, angry exchanges, and the apparent inconsistencies of Delany's ideas launched me on the path of my own Delany investigation. I followed the trail of sources identified in the bibliographic sections of Ullman's and Sterling's works and was amazed by my initial findings, which suggested that indeed there may be some validity to the contentions of Draper and McAdoo, that we may in fact be dealing with a very complex individual, and that the dominant nationalist/Pan-Africanist historiography may have misrepresented and oversimplified a very complex historical figure. I reached this conclusion rather quickly after reading a few of Delany's own writing and speeches, where clearly and unambiguously he provided a self-definition and self-characterization that were anything but radical and ideologically consistent. For me, the critical challenge became trying to understand why some scholars emphasize and highlight his militancy and nationalism yet seem unaware of or uninterested in acknowledging and confronting crucial dimensions of his career that betray conservatism and inconsistencies. What constitutes the essential Delany? Is the key to the "essential Delany" in his nationalism and Pan-Africanism, as the dominant and prevailing historiography suggests, or could integration hold the key to the essential Delany, as Draper suggested? These are the questions and challenges at the heart of this book. As interesting and pathbreaking as is the work of the aficionados, I found myself questioning some of their interpretations, especially in the light of what Delany said about himself and his struggles. In other words,

I encountered discrepancies between the prevailing popular conception of Delany and Delany's own ideas and idiosyncrasies. Furthermore, I became convinced that the aficionados have only told one side of the Delany story. Further research reveals the ideological context of the works of the aficionados. My challenge was to balance the prevailing portrait of Delany with the other personality that pervades his writings and speeches, the one that has been rendered invisible by the dominance of what I call the instrumentalist context of his rehabilitation.

The Martin Delany that I encountered in Nigeria and early in graduate school was a militant black nationalist and Pan-Africanist. And he was real. However, in the course of further research and study, I have since encountered another Martin Delany who was conservative and accommodationist, who compromised when necessary, and who advocated and defended color-blind policies. And this other Delany was equally real. Unfortunately, overemphasis on the militant, nationalist, and uncompromising Delany had overshadowed and rendered invisible the other more pliable, conservative, and accommodating Delany. This work is conceived to correct this biographical anomaly. I assumed the challenge of bringing to light this other hidden and neglected Delany. There is nothing unusual about a black leader straddling varying ideological positions and boundaries. Recent scholarship in black biography has clearly established that black leaders in the nineteenth century were anything but ideologically consistent and doctrinaire. Forces and circumstances that compelled flexibility, complexity, and ambivalence very often influenced their ideas, actions, and choices. The tradition of compartmentalizing black leaders into rigid ideological categories is essentially political and now anachronistic. It does not adequately and accurately reflect and represent the true character and disposition of black leaders. It is therefore necessary to come to terms with the ambivalences and complexities of black leaders in history. There was nothing inherently saintly, angelic, or devilish about nineteenth-century black leaders. They were human beings who combined the human propensity for goodness, unpredictability, paradoxes, and ambivalence. The Delany in this study is not an aberrant personality but one whose ideas and choices mirrored dispositions that were characteristic of other black leaders, despite political divergences and differences.

ACKNOWLEDGMENTS

Martin Robison Delany (1812–1885) is a very interesting, engaging, and intriguing character to study. If there is one issue on which most scholars agree, it is that he was truly a complex human being. It is precisely this complexity that made studying and understanding his life challenging. But it is a challenge that I have enjoyed undertaking, one that has tremendously enriched my personal and intellectual life. What I now call my "Delany adventure" has consumed about two decades of my academic career. It has been a life-enriching experience, one that would most definitely have been otherwise but for the help and generosity of numerous individuals and institutions. They all deserve recognition. First, I could never thank my teacher and friend, Craig Simpson, enough for his intellectual guidance. I can only hope that this book reflects some degree of the intellectual excellence that he embodies. Next, I must pay homage to the Delany aficionados (Dorothy Sterling, Victor Ullman, Floyd J. Miller, and Cyril Griffith) for rescuing Delany from historical oblivion and for laying a solid foundation that made this and many other works on Delany possible. No serious interpretation or reinterpretation of Delany can occur without the benefits of the resources they garnered.

My desire to study and understand Delany's life and struggles has taken me to libraries and archives across North America. I will like to express my gratitude and appreciation to the staffs of the following for giving me unfettered access to the Delany papers and related documents and manuscripts in their collections: the South Caroliniana Research Library of the University of South Carolina in Columbia, especially its former director, Allen Stokes; the South Carolina Department of Archives and History in Columbia, for access to Delany's Freedmen's

Bureau Papers, Reconstruction correspondences, and the papers of the Reconstruction governors of the state; the South Carolina Historical Society in Charleston, for permission to publish Delany's "Trial and Conviction"; the Western Pennsylvania Historical Society, Pittsburgh; the Cross Cultural Learners' Center, London, Ontario, Canada; the Moorland-Spingarn Research Center, Howard University, Washington, D.C.; Hilton Head Island Public Library, Hilton Head, South Carolina; the Kent County Historical Society Library, Chatham, Ontario, Canada; the Carnegie Library, Pittsburgh; the War Records Office of the Library of Congress and the National Archives, Washington D.C.; Xenia Public Library, Xenia, Ohio; Wilberforce University Library, Wilberforce, Ohio; and the Amistad Research Center, Tulane University, New Orleans. The following deserve my gratitude for their prompt and generous responses to my solicitations for the Delany papers in their possessions: the Library Company of Philadelphia; the Boston Public Library; the American Antiquarian Society, Worcester, Massachusetts; the Western Reserve Historical Society, Cleveland; and the Francis A. Countway Library of Medicine, Harvard University. I must also acknowledge the invaluable and efficient services of the Interlibrary Loans Department of the Weldon Library, the University of Western Ontario, for keeping up with my incessant requests for Delany papers scattered in libraries, archives, and private collections across the world.

Two individuals deserve recognition for their contributions to the success of my research visits to South Carolina. First, Larry McDonnell who took a total stranger into his home and went out of his way to ensure that I lacked nothing. Larry made what would have been a hard and difficult research experience pleasurable and rewarding. Second, a chance encounter with a compatriot, Femi Olulenu, (Omo O'Dua, ire!) afforded me the comfort of a second home where, over sumptuous Nigerian dishes, with Fela Anikulapo Kuti, Ebenezer Obey, Sunny Ade, and other doyens of Nigerian music playing in the background, we reminisced about Nigeria. This, in fact, added a touch of cultural reawakening to my research visits. Femi remains a close friend.

I began serious reflections on Delany during the second phase of my teaching career at the University of Maiduguri, Nigeria (1985–1990).

I started by presenting my reflections and interpretations to students in my postgraduate seminar classes and to colleagues in the history and English departmental seminars. I gained immensely from their comments for which I am most grateful. I am also indebted to the faculty of the Department of Black Studies and the Center for African Studies of the Ohio State University, Columbus, especially Abiola Irele and Isaac Mowoe, for comments on a paper I presented at the Friday Lecture Series titled "Beyond Redemption: Martin R. Delany in African American Historiography." This paper, in fact, became the foundation for this study.

I must also not forget to acknowledge my Loyola-New Orleans history family (David Moore, Nancy Anderson, Bernard Cook, Maurice Brungard, Mark Fernandez, and Leo Nichol) for their support. The camaraderie and collegiality that permeate this department are unmatchable. Thanks y'all for allowing me to experience a working environment that most faculty only dream of! The work could not have been completed without the support of my colleagues in the history department of the University of Montana. My friend Mike Mayer (Mikeooo!) and his wife, Susie, deserve my gratitude for making my Montana experience warm, loving, and endearing. I am particularly appreciative of our (Mike and I) regular lunch sessions that also became occasions for discourses on Delany. Thanks, Mike, for the frequent intrusions of Delany into your "Eisenhower" thoughts! I am also most grateful to the anonymous reviewer for the University Press of Mississippi for insightful and constructive comments that revealed critical loopholes and shortcomings in the original draft.

My wife, Gloria, and children—Tosin, Toyin, and Chi-Chi—deserve recognition and appreciation. This could not have been done without their love and support. Thanks for everything, especially for keeping up with my "bookish" dispositions.

Finally, I must acknowledge the enduring influence of someone I last had contact with some forty years ago (1963)—Mr. Okoroye/Okolorie (not exactly sure of the spelling) who was my teacher in class five at the United Native Authority (UNA) Elementary School in Kaduna, Nigeria. If there was one moment in my life when the decision to become a historian was made, rather subconsciously, it was during one of his stirring and captivating history lessons. I can still hear his loud voice and visualize him agilely striding from one end of the classroom to another, with the class held in rapt attention, as he recaptured episodes and events in ancient and classical civilizations.

INTRODUCTION

Responding to an address Martin Robison Delany (1812–1885) delivered to the "Friendship Division No. 2 of the Philadelphia Order of the Sons of Temperance" on the 12th of May 1848, John I. Gaines of Cincinnati likened Delany to "the immortal, never-dying reformers of the sixteenth century—such as Melancthon, Zwingle, and Erasmus and Luther!"[1] Showering praises on Delany, Gaines expressed pride that someone "so well qualified both by nature and education . . . who has not a drop of Anglo-Saxon blood running in his veins" should represent the black cause.[2] It was important for Gaines to underline Delany's "unadulter-ated blackness," "for the simple reason that whenever a mind of a higher order is exhibited among us some gossip or goose is ready to attribute it to a little speck of white blood which is said to be coursing through our veins."[3] Gaines, in fact, spoke for many blacks. For Gaines and for many early-nineteenth-century black Americans, Delany had come to repre-sent the quintessence of blackness, to exemplify black capabilities at the very best.

In Delany's accomplishments, blacks found both ready answers to the prevailing racist questioning of black humanity, intelligence, and capability and evidence that negated the racist depiction of blacks as inherently inferior beings. Very early in his antislavery struggle, there-fore, Delany's unfeigned devotion to, and sacrifices for, the black cause, represented by his crusade for moral suasion, his fights against slavery and racism through the columns of his short-lived paper, the *Pittsburgh Mystery*, combined with his activities and accomplishments as coeditor and roving lecturer for the *North Star*, earned for him the reputation of a racial essentialist. He became the epitome of black pride and capabilities. This reputation grew stronger in the mid-nineteenth century when he was driven by the failure of moral suasion and the collapse of his integrationist aspirations, especially in the wake of political developments of the 1850s, to embrace and advocate emigration. The momentum he generated for emigration soon developed into a global Pan-African nationalism. The racial underpinnings of his emigration platform reinforced his growing image and perception as a racial essentialist. This reputation would eventually become the defining focus of his entire life and struggle.

The mention of the name Martin Delany today evokes militant nationalist and Pan-African consciousness among black Americans. In this period of increasing impoverishment of, and deepening consciousness of alienation among, black Americans, induced and exacerbated by recent attacks on and reversals of the gains of the civil rights movement in consequence of a resurging conservative agenda, black American protest thought has assumed a strong anti-American, countercultural, and counterestablishment character. Advocates of this countercultural consciousness and disposition have frequently invoked history as its legitimizing and dynamic force. In their quest for historical authentication, they often demonstrate preferences for historical actors and landmarks that are considered consistent with radical antiestablishment values. Few individuals have attracted the attention and admiration of the cultural nationalists and purveyors of the countercultural protest consciousness as Martin Delany, Marcus Garvey, and Malcolm X. Among this group of militant historical heroes, Delany is often distinguished as the granddaddy of them all, the one who set the tone and defined the values for subsequent generations of militant black nationalists and Pan-Africanists.

This radical and militant Delany, this antiestablishment hero whose career supposedly epitomized the notion of ontological blackness, has been the subject of countless books and articles on Black Nationalism. He is portrayed as a racial essentialist; a shining example of principled and uncompromising articulation and defense of black interests; and someone who maintained an uncompromisingly radical stand against what one critic termed "American apartheid" policy.[4] He is often contrasted with his famous contemporary, Frederick Douglass, whose ideas and programs are portrayed as exemplifying accommodation, compromise, and racial inconsistency. This portrait of Delany, which has shaped and defined scholarly and popular perceptions and understandings of him, emanated from the instrumentalist projection of black American historiography. This historical tradition, which assumed dominance in the 1960s, specifically mandated a utilitarian (that is, instrumental) construction of black history designed not for scholarship per se but essentially as an intellectual weapon for the advancement of the black struggle.[5] The consequence for black biography, and for black history in general, has been the construction of historical and biographical narratives that are often reflections of the narrow sociopolitical and ideological imperatives of the black struggle, to the neglect, sacrifice, and at times outright misrepresentation of historical facts. Unfortunately, the resultant one-dimensional portrait of Delany as a militant nationalist represents only a dimension of his career and character-a small aspect of his idiosyncrasies that is lifted from a one-decade period (1852–1862) in a life-long struggle and career that spanned almost five decades. Why the Delany historiography is defined by the ideological orientation of a single decade will be explained shortly. For the greater part of his life and career, Delany represented very complex, diverse, and ambivalent values and idiosyncrasies that underscore an equally complex and much more pragmatic personality, radically different from and often diametrically opposed to the militant nationalist that modern scholars highlight and exalt. Put differently, there was another "Martin Delany" deeply buried and forgotten beneath the debris of instrumentalist historiography.

The unraveling of this other side and personality, this neglected and forgotten personality, is the subject of this book. My underlying objective is to illuminate the other critical dimension of Delany. While underscoring a much more conservative and pragmatic personality, I seek to compel a reassessment of his place in, and legacy to, the black American life and struggle.[6] His life brightly illuminates the limitations of ideological pigeonholing of black leaders. Developments in black biographical studies in the last two decades clearly emphasize the historical dominance of a black leadership typology that was less ideological and much more pragmatic. Those black leaders hitherto conceived within ideologically constricted frameworks are now reexamined in their complexities as leaders who harbored conflicting ideological values and perspectives and who often changed their choices and values as the prevailing circumstances dictated. The same person often combined radical and conservative strategies and solutions. Delany was no exception. Unfortunately, for reasons to be discussed below, he has been misrepresented as an ideological militant and an uncompromising nationalist. His career and accomplishments are paraded and glamorized as radical signposts and guiding lights. His ideas have selectively been invoked, often out of historical context, and offered as dynamic utilitarian guides in the advancement and prosecution of the black struggle and as inspirational values to younger generations of would-be radical black nationalists.

This study challenges the dominant intellectual genre by focusing on and illuminating the "other Delany." In several of his writings and speeches, Delany himself provided ample evidence of and insights into the complexities of his mind-set and personality. This evidence clearly suggests a much more complex, and less ideologically inclined, character. But more revealing and compelling is Delany's own poignant self-definition contained in a definitive letter he wrote to Frederick Douglass in which he described the essential focus of his life and struggle as a strong commitment to the pursuit and advancement of a color-blind struggle, one that de-emphasized old party lines and alliances. This commitment, he informed Douglass, so enraged radicals (black and white alike) that they subsequently conspired to victimize him.[7] A strong dedication to a biracial struggle and society defined the very essence of his postbellum career in South Carolina, at precisely the critical historical moment when other black leaders felt the need, and imperative, for race-based alliances and politics.

In fact, from the time Delany jettisoned emigration in 1863 and joined other blacks in the pursuit of integrationist goals to the end of Reconstruction in 1877, he unambiguously articulated ideas that challenged and disregarded orthodox lines of race, color, and politics. At a time when other black leaders, apprehensive of the hostile and unrepentant dispositions of former slave owners and in gratitude to the Republican Party for facilitating freedom and political empowerment, chose to strengthen and consolidate old party ties and loyalty, Delany embarked upon a contrary course, one that de-emphasized race, color, and old party allegiances and alliances in favor of the appeasement of and reconciliation with the former slave masters. The Civil War and the reforms of Reconstruction seemed to deracinate him, almost completely eradicating from his consciousness the racial and Black Nationalist ethos that had defined his thoughts and propelled his actions during the emigrationist phase. His membership in the Republican Party early in Reconstruction was, therefore, analogous to putting a square peg in a round box. For about a decade he remained, rather uncomfortably, within the party to fight an uphill battle for a politics that de-emphasized race and old party ideology. Frustrated by the rejection of his views and subjected to political victimization and isolation, Delany gradually began the momentous strides that would eventually take him into the fold of the state conservatives. He felt more at ease among the conservatives, but as he would later discover, this feeling was not reciprocal. The conservatives did not really feel comfortable with him. Paradoxically, by abandoning the Republican Party for the Democratic, Delany seemed to contradict his professed commitment to a color-blind society and platform, because the party and platform he embraced, and proceeded to propagate and defend, in the judgment of most blacks and corroborated by historical and subsequent developments, exemplified the politics of race and color at its worst.

I choose the phrase "without regard to race" as the defining basis of this study precisely because Martin Delany would have felt comfortable with it. After all, this was exactly how he described his life-long struggle. Regardless of how contemporaries felt about or perceived him, even in the heyday of his emigrationist crusade, when he seemed frustratingly alienated from America, Delany never regarded himself as racially driven and motivated but, on the contrary, as someone of universalistic motivations, engaged in a broader struggle to achieve racial reconciliation and the unity of humankind. As this study will show, he imbibed this universalistic orientation and conviction from his ideological mentors in Pennsylvania very early in his antislavery career; this universalism remained indelibly ingrained in his consciousness, although at times subdued by, and subsumed under, the nationalist ideology of emigration. Even when he seemed to be advocating racially limited ideas and values or drawing the racial boundary lines, there was a broader dimension that inhered universalistic values. Delany himself would later confide in Frederick Douglass that in both the antebellum and postbellum phases, his thoughts and struggles were driven by universalistic, color-blind convictions. As he boldly told Douglass, "With the same faithful adherence to the cause of universal liberty as in ANTE BELLUM days, shall I continue to advocate the rights of the whole people of the state, *without regard to race, color, or politics*" (emphasis added).[8]

Yet despite Delany's unambiguous self-characterization as a moderate and ample evidence and records of his actions in furtherance of a color-blind society, he has persistently been depicted as a racial essentialist who exemplified militant black consciousness, separatism, and identity. He has thus been appropriated by the militant and radical generation of the 1960s as their ideological mentor and guru. The result has been the relegation of the integrationist and interracial aspects of his life and struggle to insignificance, while elevating the "racialist Delany" to historical dominance. This skewed perspective has resulted in an equally skewed and narrow understanding and appreciation of his ideological values and legacies. He seemed frozen in an ideological twilight that foreclosed the possibility of discovering and appreciating the wealth, diversity, and complexities of his thought and personality. This study is thus about this neglected side of Delany and seeks to provide a counterbalance to the more dominant militant and uncompromising nationalist perspective. That Delany chose the path of reconciliation during Reconstruction and espoused values that diametrically contradicted not only the prevailing and dominant disposition among blacks but also the ideas, values, and schemes that he had once popularized and defended in the antebellum period, especially during his brief emigration crusade, affirms the pragmatism of his character and nature. Although there were certainly ample reasons and excuses to continue on a path of racial antagonism, many blacks, among them Delany, came to the realization that the realities of the Civil War and Reconstruction mandated shifts away from the previous politics of confrontation and racial and political alliances that had fought and won the war. Delany chose to de-emphasize the racial, color, and party loyalty that had defined his mid-nineteenth-century career. In other words, he veered away from the very framework within which twentieth-century radical black nationalists have studied, analyzed, conceptualized, and understood him—emigration and nationalism—to adopt and defend a very strong integrationist platform.

This study, therefore, focuses on the integrationist phases of Delany's career, aspects that have been neglected and obscured by the dominance of instrumentalist historiography. The objective is to provide a more balanced understanding of his personality, motivations, choices, and legacy. Overemphasis on the nationalist and Pan-Africanist dimensions of his career has so overshadowed and dominated scholarship as to leave the impression that Delany was essentially a radical black nationalist. Many have been too quick to represent this "militant" personality as "the essential Delany" and have then built a cultic figure around him to the extent that a mention, or even a hint, of any aspect or characterization of Delany that is contrary to this cultic militant personality, or one that attempts to negate or qualify the militant image in any shape or form, is strongly resisted, questioned, and doubted. At a recent black studies conference, one respondent to my paper, "Demythologizing Martin Delany," questioned the veracity of my thesis. However, when confronted with incontrovertible historical evidence, facts and sources, this particular critic and "Delany scholar" quickly invoked classic instrumentalist response—that black Americans are still very much under siege (the nature of which he did not clearly explain) and, consequently, a mythologized hero such as Delany is needed to continue to inspire and invigorate the youth. My paper, he argued, was a negative and destructive attempt to pull the rug from under a black hero and undermine the struggle. I responded that as a historian, I did not consider my preoccupation therapeutic and that my primary consideration is not in creating heroes or engaging in selective and isolative profiling designed to satisfy and advance extra-academic considerations but in facilitating historical understanding of the careers of black leaders, exploring every available historical dimension, seeing them in their totalities, embracing all the complexities and nuances. This study is, therefore, deconstructive in nature, aimed at representing "the other Delany," the one who has been ignored and overshadowed by the instrumentalist tradition. It is only by juxtaposing the many dimensions of the life of "this most extraordinary and intelligent Blackman," as President Abraham Lincoln once described him, that one can hope to better appreciate him and determine the very nature of his historical legacy, his place in American history, and his ideological location in black leadership tradition.[9]

The thrust of this study, therefore, is on the postbellum phase, 1865–1885. Much of present-day knowledge of Delany comes from the antebellum phase, especially the ten-year emigration decade, 1852–1862. His reputation as a militant nationalist, antiestablishment, and counter-cultural hero that the militant generation of the 1960s and cultural nationalist scholars and critics embrace derives largely from this relatively brief period of his life. The postbellum phase seems to present ideological problems and challenges to those accustomed and socialized to a one-dimensional, monohermeneutical conception of Delany, derived and built solely upon the emigration/nationalist era. There has been a tendency to avoid confronting and deconstructing the complexities and challenges of the latter phase of his life. Even books that fall within the biographical and quasi-biographical genres simply utilize the postbellum phase to reinforce the militant nationalist thrust of the antebellum era, and, in the process, the very complex and enigmatic personality of the postbellum era escapes critical engagement and analysis.

The study consequently shifts the Delany historiography beyond instrumentalism and in the direction of confronting the less instrumentally noble but equally significant aspects of the man. It is therefore not a full biography but an attempt to complement existing biographical and specialized studies by highlighting a critical but neglected dimension of his personality and career. This will provide the basis for a holistic understanding of the complexities of the man. Although this may not advance the instrumentalist need for a hero, it does facilitate understanding of the historical as opposed to the mythologized Delany. It reveals a personality that was different from, and diametrically opposed to, the ideologized hero of instrumentalist fame. There was a complex historical personality that has been systematically ignored by the militant tradition. The Delany of instrumentalist tradition was narrowly conceived to build a certain image for a specific social function. While this may have served the social function it was designed for, it remains, historically, an inaccurate representation of the man, his disposition and legacy. This study does not seek to denigrate or depreciate Delany's place in history but, on the contrary, to facilitate understanding of the complexities of his career and struggles.

Delany himself provided the framework for probing into and understanding these critical but neglected aspects of his struggle in two epic letters written in the 1870s addressed to someone he held in high esteem, someone he reverently addressed "Honorable Frederick Douglass." Written five years apart, these two letters, "A Political Review" (1871) and "Trial and Conviction" (1876) (see Appendixes A and B) provide insights into Delany's conservatism, revealing its very nature, defining elements and essence, underlying principles and values, the reactions of blacks, and the crises it provoked in his life. The two letters underscore his integrationist ideas and convictions, and, most critically, his self-definition and self-characterization within the larger traditions of black leadership during Reconstruction. The letters serve as the bedrock and springboard for the analysis of the neglected but perhaps most crucial conservative phase of his career—the post–Civil War years.[10] This might be the most critical phase of his entire life, and yet it remains the least critically examined. This study undertakes this reexamination utilizing these two critical letters in which Delany laid bare, in unambiguous terms, the very nature, character, and dimensions of his complexities. Focusing on the letters, and the reactions and responses of his contemporaries provides valuable insights not only into his own self-definition but also how his contemporaries perceived him. This is, therefore, a search for Delany in the context of his times, away from the instrumentally constructed context of mid-twentieth-century black American historiography. The letters provide convenient focal points for unraveling the nature, dynamics, and complexities not only of his ideas and schemes but also of those of the black leadership cadres during Reconstruction.

These letters outline and describe in detail, his conservative leanings, values, and, most significantly, his disdain for radicalism (a movement he has erroneously been associated with) and the price he paid for his antiradical crusade. They illustrate, according to him, his victimization in the hands of radicals. Delany clearly identified himself with the conservatives. He preached moderation toward and reconciliation between blacks and their former slave masters. He caricatured and ridiculed Northern philanthropists and Republican politicians (the very constituents blacks had embraced, the ones who had helped them secure freedom). He objected strongly to the political empowerment of blacks. He deemed the exercise of political power by blacks premature and troubling. He preferred to see, and seemed more comfortable with, white politicians in positions of political authority. Most critically, he persistently blamed blacks and their Radical Republican friends for exacerbating racial tensions in the South.

Perhaps a major explanation for Delany's antiradical disposition was his refusal to acknowledge the need for a Radical Reconstruction program. He perceived federal involvement in Reconstruction in the South as unnecessary intrusion in the internal affairs of the region, an intrusion that he blamed for, among many other faults, straining the relationship between blacks and the former slave masters. In his analysis, therefore, Radical Reconstruction was a negative intervention in what would otherwise have been an amicable working relationship between two hitherto hostile forces. Had Delany had his way, blacks would most certainly have been abandoned to the tender mercies of "ole massa." He expressed preference for the political leadership of the Old South and, at times, acknowledged white superiority, urging blacks to concede superior positions to whites and be contented with lower-level municipal positions that were supposedly less challenging and required little intelligence.

Despite their separation in 1849, induced by growing ideological conflict over the state of black America, with each embarking upon different paths and strategies, Delany and Douglass retained mutual respect for each other. At the height of Delany's emigrationist crusade in 1863, Douglass complimentingly described him as the "intensest embodiment of black nationality to be found anywhere outside of the valley of the Niger."[11] On the other hand, Delany publicly proclaimed his admiration and respect for Douglass on numerous occasions. In one of such displays of humility and deference, he wrote to Douglass,

> It would be useless here for me to state the estimate that I set upon your talent and ability as a man among us. I have often announced that with pen

and voice, and have ever felt proud that we had so noble a specimen of our oppressed and enslaved brethren, who, with a righteous indignation, cursed the slaveholder, spurned slavery, and, with the power of Hercules had riven the contemptible fetters that bound his manly form, dashing them to atoms, and walked forth untrammeled as nature had designed him, a god-like nobleman.[12]

Though separated by growing disagreement over the course of the black struggle, neither doubted the other's commitment to the black cause. The separation that lasted from 1849 to the outbreak of the Civil War was soon healed by the war itself, as both found themselves in the same camp, advocating and working for black enlistment. Both sought and found audience with President Lincoln on the subject of making emancipation a war strategy. Their relationship, in fact, goes back to 1846, when Douglass visited Delany in Pittsburgh and sought his help in founding the *North Star*. Both shared a vision and strategy. They believed in the American Dream and its attainability. They both embraced moral suasion as a reform strategy, believing strongly that by assuming direct responsibility for defining and articulating their problems and interests and by cultivating habits of thrift, industry, and moral uprightness, blacks would advance and accelerate the cause of integration. This underlying shared conviction led to the founding of the *North Star* in 1847. On the invitation of Douglass, Delany relocated to New York and became co-editor and roving lecturer for the paper.

Between 1847 and 1849 Delany took his crusade for moral suasion, under the auspices of the *North Star*, to numerous black communities in the North. In his lectures, he condemned slavery, highlighting its evil nature and character. He also drew the attention of the black communities to several strategies for overcoming poverty and degradation. His lectures and activities had positive impacts on blacks, as evidenced by the commendations he garnered. The *Cincinnati Herald* gave the following account of Delany's lecture,

The address of Dr. R. Delany, (one of the editors of the North Star), Rochester, a colored man, on the subject of slavery, on Monday evening last in the Sixth Congregational Church, was an extraordinary production in more than one respect. Apart from its being a well arranged discourse, clear, distinct, and forcible, from one of a proscribed and disenfranchised race, it was a most bold and manly denunciation of the religious and political hypocrisy of the times.[13]

Another appreciative comments from one "M.C." in York, Pennsylvania read: "My present purpose in writing to you, is to say, that the people in this part of the vineyard have been invigorated by a discourse, long, eloquent and argumentative, by your manly and distinguished co-laborer, M. R. Delany. His subject was the present condition of the colored people, and he did ample justice to it, occupying the major part of three evenings in delivering it. . . . The Dr. speaks well, clear, distinct, and to the point."[14] Unfortunately, these commendations could not seal the developing cracks in the relationship of Delany and Douglass. By 1849, the co-editors and colaborers had begun to drift apart due largely to conflicting responses to the state of the black struggle. Delany had come to a pessimistic crossroads, and saw no further basis for hope and faith in integration. He described his pessimism exhaustively in a scathing commentary on "American Civilization." As he concluded, rather disappointingly,

> Not a place is there in the United States of America, whether city, town, village, or hamlet, in which a colored person resides or has ever been, or may go, that they are not continually subject to the abuse, more or less or the whites—if not adults, the children faithfully keep up the persecution. And though at times this abuse may not be corporeal or physical, yet it is at all times an abuse of the feelings, which in itself is a blasting outrage on humanity, and insufferable to the better senses of man and womanhood.[15]

Underscoring the depth of racism and the breadth and scope of the racist culture, he averred, "There appears to be a fixed determination on the part of the oppressors of this country, to destroy every vestige of self-respect, self-possession, and manly independence left in the colored people. . . . This appears to be simultaneous in all parts of the country."[16] Though equally disillusioned, Douglass was not quite willing to give up on America. Their paths consequently diverged, as Delany proceeded to spearhead emigration in the following decade, while Douglass continued to pursue integrationist strategies and ends. Despite their ideological separation, however, Delany retained tremendous respect for Douglass. There was also the compelling consideration that Douglass soon attained national influence and prominence. In Delany's judgment, Douglass was the most prominent black leader of the epoch, if there was one to identify, and hence someone in position to intervene at critical moments in the saga of black Americans.

These two letters, therefore, provide the framework for understanding the complexities of Delany's postbellum career and the dynamics of the conservatism that defined this crucial phase of his life. This is not to suggest that he manifested complexities and paradoxes/conservatism only in the postbellum era. In fact, he began his antislavery career in the 1830s as a conservative, in an era when black leaders generally embraced conservative solutions and strategies of reform. He spent almost the first two decades of his struggle, like his contemporaries, experimenting with moderate and conservative strategies for change. His "militant" and "uncompromising" ideas and values came in the aftermath of the frustrations, and disappointments he felt over the failures of moderate conservative efforts to bring about radical changes in the black American situation. This shows that Delany started out a conservative who believed strongly in the promises of the American Dream and who pursued moderate strategies of achieving full integration. This early conservative phase also provides a strong qualification to his antiestablishment and uncompromising reputation.

The conservative essence of the early phase of Delany's career has escaped the notice of his modern biographers and critics. He did not start out a black nationalist, his radical nationalist reputation notwithstanding. He started out a committed and patriotic American nationalist who believed in the possibility of the American Dream and in the perfectibility of the American order. In other words, he strongly believed that blacks would eventually realize full integration on the basis of full equality in America and considered it his prime responsibility to help blacks understand what he termed the "Mystery" of their predicament and the solution to it. The first phase of his abolitionist career, therefore, preoccupied him with unraveling this "Mystery" and helping blacks overcome it in order to become fully integrated into America. Delany thus began his antislavery career, like other black leaders of his time, as a strong advocate of integration, compromise and accommodation. It was only after the disappointing end of his first integrationist epoch that he embarked upon the nationalist phase (1852–1862), distinguished by frustration, alienation, anger, and a strong anti-American national consciousness. It was, therefore, frustration and alienation over the betrayal of his first integrationist dream that gave birth to Delany the "radical" black nationalist and Pan-Africanist, Delany of instrumentalist historiography, the one that became the dominant personality. Yet several scholars have highlighted this brief, intermediate, ten-year nationalist phase, when he was compelled by alienation and frustration to seek his identity elsewhere, as the defining moment of his life, ignoring the first and the last two integrationist phases of his life. This is perhaps because confronting these three integrationist phases not only negates the radical and militant personality of the instrumentalist genre but also reveals the ambiguities that defined the character and idiosyncratic complexity of Delany; that is, those "unruly" dimensions of his life that would definitely have contradicted the heroic and mythical images and qualities with which he has been associated.

Historically, therefore, there was a deracinated Martin Delany, a color-blind American who persistently fought against attempts by other blacks to uphold and defend racial and old party allegiances. This personality was most prominent in postbellum South Carolina and stood in direct opposition to the "race and color conscious Delany" of the 1850s who had angrily and frustratingly drawn the racial boundary line in order to justify emigration, and who condemned other blacks who refused to embrace his emigration scheme as shortsighted and misguided. This study hopes not only to illuminate this neglected deracinated personality, but also to attempt a reconciliation with the instrumentalist, for they are not necessarily irreconcilable. The instrumentalist Delany, therefore, was not the historically dominant personality. There was indeed another Delany buried beneath the heap of instrumentalist tradition who did not always embrace militant uncompromising ideas and schemes. There was another Delany who, like most of his contemporaries, sought compromises whenever prudence dictated but who also embraced militant antiestablishment strategies whenever they seemed appropriate. This other Delany did not cringe at self-criticism, including the criticism of fellow blacks, regardless of the consequences, including political victimization and social ostracism. This work attempts to resurrect this other Delany, to bring him to historical attention in order to shed lights upon, and provide access to the complexities and paradoxes that informed his entire life and struggle. Most important, the study goes beyond illuminating the multidimensionalities to providing the basis for reconciling the dualities and paradoxes of his life. As recent changes in the historiography of black biography show, it was possible for a black leader to straddle conflicting ideological spaces. Acknowledging the conservative dimensions of Delany would help us both better appreciate him, and the breadth of his ideological influence and legacy, for he was not just the "granddaddy" of militant black nationalists such as Malcolm X and Marcus Garvey but also that of compromisers and accommodationists such as Booker T. Washington and, in our time, Justice Clarence Thomas.

WITHOUT REGARD TO RACE

ONE

Black Biography
From Instrumentalism to Functionalism

EARLY IN 1970, Theodore Draper published an article in the *New York Times Review of Books* titled "The Father of American Black Nationalism."[1] The theme of this article, which developed from a larger study, is a critical review of Martin R. Delany's nationalist ideas and programs. Draper raised serious doubts about the depth of Delany's commitment to black nationalism. Delany, according to Draper, saw himself first as an American and, like most black nationalists of his epoch, sought the realization of his American citizenship and identity much more than anything else. Draper characterized black nationalism as the consequence of a frustrated American nationalism. Given a choice, he further contended, Delany would undoubtedly have chosen his American nationality over his African. Finally, he portrayed Delany as an integrationist who spent the greater part of his life in search of the American Dream. Draper goes on to observe the inordinate attention scholars had given to Delany's emigrationist and nationalist aspirations and the contradictions that marked significant phases of his career. According to Draper, "the consistently emigrationist portion of his life filled only about ten years. After 1861 he went further and further away from the cause to which he owes his fame, and for almost a quarter of a century he represented reconciliation far more than emigration. His entire life was filled with contradictions and dualities."[2] He accused black nationalist scholars of being interested only in the brief emigrationist phase of Delany's career,

3

avoiding confrontation with the contradictions and dualities of the broader dimensions of his life. Underscoring the ephemeral and utilitarian character of Delany's nationalism, Draper pointed out correctly that Delany "went to Africa as an explorer, not as a settler. Once the Civil War offered some hope of emancipation, he could not restrain his impulse to throw himself into the thick of it. Then he more or less made peace with the country that he once said had bade him be gone and had driven him from her embraces."[3] Delany's reaffirmation of faith in America in the aftermath of the Civil War would, Draper argued, lead him ultimately into making decisions and choices that "indirectly helped restore white rule in South Carolina." Draper described this as the final contradiction, "the ultimate duality of his life and public service."[4]

The article unleashed a heated debate on the legacy and place of Delany in the black American struggle. Several respondents took exception to Draper's conclusions, questioning his qualification to write and pass commentaries on the black experience.[5] (Draper is white.) One respondent suggested that Draper was dabbling into "documents produced by people he does not understand, and whose thought he does not respect."[6] However, the most vitriolic reaction came from Floyd Miller, who was then a graduate student at the University of Minnesota. Miller described Draper's essay as marked by "polemical peroration which apparently motivated the flimsy scholarship of his biographical effort" and accused him of shallow, arrogant, and shoddy juxtaposition.[7] Draper, of course, fired back, underlining what he saw as the racial undertones of the angry reactions to his article. According to him,

> I strongly suspect that the trouble is something else. The real aim is to make Black Studies, including the history of black nationalism, a black and especially a black nationalist monopoly. The real danger is a black nationalist party line imposed on work in this field, particularly in our schools. In effect, black nationalists wish all of us to accept the premise that they are the only ones who can understand the history of black nationalism or who have the right to write about and teach it.[8]

Since the publication of the article coincided with increased scholarly interests in Delany, knowledge of the sociopolitical context of the period is relevant to understanding the hostile reactions. The civil rights movement of the 1960s, and the ascendant nationalist upsurge, drew the attention of scholars to Delany, who seemed to have espoused values dear to the hearts of black militants. In fact, 1970 was a year of great anticipation. Many eagerly awaited new publications on Delany. The civil rights movement inspired demands for a new black history designed to redeem, rehabilitate, and reconstruct the careers of black leaders who supposedly embodied values pertinent to the needs and aspirations of blacks. Martin Delany was quickly identified as one such individual. Victor Ullman and Dorothy Sterling were working independently on biographies of Delany. At the University of Minnesota, Floyd J. Miller was completing his dissertation on Delany and the emigration movement. Another student, Cyril Griffith, was doing a similar study at Michigan State University. Collectively, they all constituted, in Sterling's judgment, the "Delany *aficionados.*"[9]

Draper's article, therefore, could not have escaped public attention and scrutiny, and his conclusions were guaranteed to provoke controversy. The article highlighted an existential contradiction within a context that seemed intentionally sardonic—here is the father of an ideological movement, Draper seemed to be saying, who maintained a relationship that was anything but close to that movement. In Draper's view, Delany was simply using black nationalism as a weapon with which to advance a nationalism of greater import—American nationalism. Delany's attachment to black nationalism and Pan-Africanism was, therefore fragile, circumstantial, and short-lived.[10] In essence, Draper raised doubts about Delany's commitment and devotion to black nationalism and Pan-Africanism, ideas and movements that he helped create and for which he became legendary. Draper, it appeared, was both trying to counteract the growing perception of Delany as a militant nationalist and also caution against the mistaken projection of black nationalism as his very essence and defining character. His objective was to suggest that Delany's nationalism was just one among his many attributes and idiosyncrasies. It is unclear if Draper was deliberately looking for confrontation. Nevertheless, his attempt to erode the force of Delany's nationalism constituted a telling blow on the dominant instrumentalist historiography.

The anger and controversy that Draper's article provoked should therefore have been anticipated, given the state of black American historiography, especially the field of black biography. Black biography had inherited much of the instrumentalist and militant thrust of the civil rights historiography. The civil rights movement was not confined to socioeconomic and political issues. It was also a revolt against Eurocentric and hegemonic scholarship. As black Americans struggled for civil and political rights, they also sought a positive and usable historical tradition, one that could be mobilized in the service of the struggle. There was strong demand for a new black history—"Applied Negro History," as the late Earl Thorpe termed it—a demand that set the stage for the creation and institutionalization of black studies.[11] Essentially, this was a demand for a history that emphasized practical utilitarian application as opposed to the narration of events and recording of factual information. Historical events and facts were perceived as raw materials in the making of a new history designed specifically for the advancement of the black struggle. The roots of this utilitarian projection of history in fact go back decades earlier to the scholarly efforts of Carter G. Woodson and the New Negro history movement that he inspired at the beginning of the twentieth century, and to the works of W. E. B. Du Bois. Collectively, they laid the foundation for the radical turn in black historiography. In fact, many would contend that the advent of the New Negro history movement in the early twentieth century heralded the emergence of trained professional historians who truly deserved the title "intelligentsia."

Woodson published profusely on different aspects of the black Diaspora experiences. His publications emphasized, inter alia, the contributions of blacks to American national development, the role of racism in the shaping of the black American experience, and the pivotal contributions of Africa to the march of world civilization. Woodson's most enduring contribution, which won for him the appellation "father of Negro history," was the creation of the organizational framework for encouraging research into and study of the African and black historical experiences. Convinced that the experiences were rich, diverse, vibrant, and worthy of serious scholarly attention, Woodson launched the Association for the Study of Negro Life and History in 1915 (ASNLH, now

Association for the Study of African American Life and History). This was followed by the founding of the *Journal of Negro History, Negro History Bulletin,* and the celebration of Black History Week. Woodson described the crowning achievement of the first decade of the ASNLH as that of making "the world see the Negro as a participant rather than as a lay figure in History."[12] He indeed deserves the title "father of Negro history." Though black history has a long tradition that predates him, Woodson created the organizational structure that not only brought that history fully to the surface but also set it on the path of recognition and legitimacy.[13] Woodson's initiatives inspired the emergence of a cadre of protégés and young scholars—Alrutheus A. Taylor, Rayford Logan, and Benjamin Brawley, to name a few—who took up the challenge of researching, popularizing, and thereby earning credibility for the black historical experience. Brawley was a graduate of Morehouse College and Harvard University. He later taught at Morehouse, Howard, and Shaw Universities. His scholarship extolled the black historical experience, noting the contributions of blacks as historical actors. Rather than being an object, blacks were depicted as nation-builders and heroes, whose presence enhanced the American nation—politically, economically, socially, and culturally.[14]

Du Bois's research and publications, in the estimation of many, signaled the advent of scientific black historiography. He was a trained historian who paid careful attention to sources and whose interpretation compelled attention and respect.[15] A graduate of Fisk and Harvard Universities who later taught at Atlanta University and the University of Pennsylvania, Du Bois has been described as an intellectual par excellence. He not only wrote in defense of the historicity of blacks but also boldly took on the "propaganda of history" defended by some of the leading aristocratic historians of the epoch—William A. Dunning, James Ford Rhodes, John W. Burgess, Walter Fleming, James Pike, Ulrich B. Phillips, and Claude G. Bowers—whose works had misrepresented and negated the contributions of blacks to American national growth.[16] Collectively, these historians nurtured the dominant racist and segregationist aristocratic culture by providing it with historical legitimacy. Du Bois's book *Black Reconstruction in America, 1860–1889* boldly contested the claims of aristocratic historians who attempted to defend a lily-white account of Reconstruction in America, and in the process he not only rehabilitated blacks but exposed the depth of intellectual racism in America.[17] Collectively, according to Du Bois, the works of the above historians sustained an intellectual orthodoxy that completely misrepresented the role of blacks in America during Reconstruction. As he put it,

> In order to paint the South as a martyr to inescapable fate, to make the North the magnanimous emancipator, and to ridicule the Negro as the impossible joke in the whole development, we have in fifty years, by libel, innuendo and silence, so completely misstated and obliterated the history of the Negro in America and his relation to its work and government that today it is almost unknown. This may be fine romance, but it is not science. It may be inspiring, but it is certainly not the truth. And beyond this it is dangerous. It is not only part foundation of our present lawlessness and loss of democratic ideals; it has, more than that, led the world to embrace and worship the color bar as social salvation and it is helping to range mankind in ranks of mutual hatred and contempt, at the summons of a cheap and false myth.[18]

In combination, the efforts of Woodson, Brawley, and Du Bois coalesced into a movement by the early twentieth century. Spearheaded and represented by the New Negro history movement, black history thus acquired more visibility and respectability, especially because of the presence of trained historians who paid careful attention to research methods. That is, writings about the black experience became much more "scientific," attracting more scholars. Among the next generation of black historians who derived much inspiration from the efforts of Woodson were Benjamin Quarles and John Hope Franklin. Emerging to prominence in the 1940s, both went on to establish themselves among the outstanding historians of American history. Quarles and Franklin, and other historians of the epoch, emphasized the contributions of blacks to the American experience. They used their writings to appeal for and advocate a much more inclusive society by highlighting the positive and contributory dimensions of black history.[19] This was not new. A strong desire for inclusion and integration has propelled black history from its beginnings. Free blacks pioneered this tradition in the early nineteenth century. These pioneers included William Wells Brown,

James W. C. Pennington, William Cooper Nell, William Still, and George Washington Williams, individuals who overcame impeding adversity and brutal force to gain literacy and who then quickly mobilized their intellectual resources for the services and advancement of the cause of black integration by providing historical counterpoints to prevailing racist thoughts and policies.[20] As critical and condemnatory as they were of the racist establishment, their writings combined rehabilitationist and appellate themes. They sought to rescue blacks from historical oblivion, while appealing for acceptance and integration. The overarching theme in their works was that of optimism in the eventual perfectibility of the American order.

Collectively, the accomplishments of these historians and scholars laid the groundwork for the foundation of black studies. The thrust of their combined scholarship was to rehabilitate and redeem black history. They all used scholarship to establish the historicity of the black and African experiences and to stake a strong claim for the integration of blacks into American society. Since the dominant historical tradition had been used to justify black subordination and marginalization, they sought to use history to argue for black integration. Their efforts won recognition and respectability for black history and inspired many scholars to begin serious and sustained research in the field.

By the 1960s, however, there were new demands on black history. Redeeming the black experience and history primarily for integration was no longer an end itself. Scholar-activists of the civil rights era, such as Vincent Harding and Sterling Stuckey, forcefully advocated a new black history, one that jettisoned the redemptionist focus of the old. They urged the adoption of an instrumentalist focus, one that pushed black history beyond the traditional advocacy and appellate thrust to a much more combative antiestablishment posture.[21] Harding contended that the founders of black history had so much faith in America that it enabled them to write with so much optimism, ignoring the glaring contradictions and problems. As he argued, "They believed because they had internalized America and its 'promise.' They believed and wrote out of belief because they had come so far through 'clanking chains and melting prayers' that they could not afford to consider unbelief as a live option. Essentially America was a great land, and one day its greatness would overwhelm it, partly as a result of black struggle, partly because of 'well-meaning' whites."[22] Advocating a new black history, Harding rendered a clear articulation of the challenge of writing *black* as opposed to *Negro* history. As he explained it:

> We who write Black history cannot track our "bleeding countrymen through the widely scattered documents of American history" and still believe in America. We cannot see luster when we must glimpse it through the ocean of tears. We cannot—do not wish to—write with detachment from the agonies of our people. We are not satisfied to have our story accepted into the American saga. We deal in redefinitions, in taking over, in moving to set our own vision upon the blindness of American historiography. Black history is that plunge which refuses to fall prey to the American dream, which is romanticism and childlike avoidance of tragedy and death.[23]

Harding's distinction is very clear. Historians of black history would inevitably become alienated from America. It is not possible to write about the ugly realities of the black experience and remain optimistic and enthusiastic. "Black History looks upon America with little of the affection and admiration which was obviously carried by our Negro History Fathers," he contended.[24]

In his own criticism, Stuckey basically agreed with Harding, accusing "[h]istorians of the Negro history movement" of failing to "condemn America for her crimes against black people. So strong was racism in American life that almost all of those involved in this movement concentrated their efforts on using history to prove the black man's humanity and to demonstrate to the larger society that their people were Americans entitled to the rights and privileges of all other Americans."[25] Their stress on progress, he argued, ignored the tragedies of black American life. The violence of the 1960s, according to him, exposed the failure of the optimistic perspective. He urged a new direction for black scholarship, contending, "Only from radical perspectives can the necessary new questions and answers come to consciousness. As we move away from 'integrating' blacks into American history, we must concern ourselves increasingly with examining that larger society which arrogantly calls itself the mainstream. White institutional and personality development must be subjected to the most careful scrutiny."[26] Merely redeeming the careers of black leaders was no longer an end in itself. History became endowed with a higher purpose. It became an instrument for ideological propagation, for a radical critique of the mainstream, and for the advancement of the black struggle. The switch to instrumentalism was undoubtedly induced and strengthened by the cultural-nationalist slant of the black struggle, particularly, the rejectionist, antiestablishment, anti-European, and, ipso facto, anti-colonial character of black nationalism, coupled with a strong affirmation of blackness and ethnicity that became pronounced in the 1960s.

The relevance of the new history was measured by its adaptability to the struggle, that is, its capacity to advance the black struggle. Put differently, this is a history induced by the exigencies of a social revolution. In order for this history to effectively execute its revolutionary and social raison d'être, it had to be very critical and condemnatory of and judgmental vis-à-vis mainstream society. "Applied Negro History" sought the reinterpretation of the past in the light of the experiences of blacks, utilizing their own frame of reference and taking due cognizance of the peculiar needs of their struggles. This is history with a mission, one specifically designed for immersion in the struggle. In fact, the scholar-activists became critical of the traditional redemptionist focus of African American historiography that they perceived as overly integrationist to the extent of compromising too much. They wanted a history that is strongly antiestablishment. This is a clear rejection of the New Negro history and its emphasis on progress as a means of appealing to whites and making a case for integration. The scholar-activists of the 1960s called for a new history from a radical perspective, one that zeroed in on the mainstream society, critical and condemnatory of its institutions and values. Stuckey, however, traced the beginning of this new combative historiography to the publication of Du Bois's *Black Reconstruction*.[27] The need for a socially focused and utilitarian history therefore set the guidelines for historical studies. The scholar-activists reached into the past, both remote and immediate, in search of resources for this new combative history, propelled by the twin objectives of reshaping the past in the militant image of the present and using that past in the service of the revolution. The field of black biography was particularly susceptible, given, first, the preeminence of leadership in the black struggle and second, the prevailing tradition in mainstream American scholarship of denying and denigrating the performance, contributions, and accomplishments of black leaders.

The search for, and rehabilitation of, the careers of notable black leaders who would serve as inspirations for the militant generation of the 1960s became the focus of black biography. The dominant trend was to search in the past for leaders whose values conformed to the canons of the instrumentalist genre. Consequently, portraits and depictions of black leaders were predictably self-fulfilling. They all seemed to satisfy the criteria of relevance and adaptability. Put differently, they represented and espoused values that satisfied the instrumentalist demand. The methodology of black biography betrayed what one critic described as a "selective perception syndrome," that is, biographical studies were built upon a narrow and often biased selection process in which only data and information that were deemed capable of positively impacting the black struggle were utilized.[28] This resulted, very often, in an equally skewed biography. This kind of biography was not meant to present a holistic understanding of the subject, underscoring his or her essence as a human being, that is, a person capable of committing judgmental errors. The goal was to produce heroes whose stories of triumph over adversity often defy rational expectations. This is the context that nurtured the historical rehabilitation of Martin Delany.

Because black nationalism in the 1960s assumed a militant, antiestablishment character, both within the United States and in the global context of decolonization, its nineteenth-century antecedent was erroneously presumed militant and equally antiestablishment, antiEuropean, and antiwhite. Martin Delany, identified as the nineteenth-century's most vocal advocate of black nationalism and the emigration movement, was lionized, and he became an icon to the militant generation of the 1960s, indeed the reference personality, the one who set the standard against which contemporaries and future militants were measured. Consequently, studies of Delany, both biographical and specialized, portrayed him as a radical leader, an uncompromising black nationalist, someone who refused to compromise with whites, one who prioritized principles and ideological convictions over practical/pragmatic

considerations. This is the image and personality of Delany that is popularized in modern historiography. Although modern scholars and critics
such as Victor Ullman, Dorothy Sterling, and Vincent Harding acknowledged a certain ambiguity in Delany's thoughts and actions, they handled
these ambiguities in a manner that suggested that they were neither
significant nor essential to understanding Delany. For example, though
Ullman rightly observed that Delany could not be classified with "either
the good guys or the bad guys," thereby acknowledging a certain complexity, he nevertheless insisted on depicting him as an ideologically consistent and uncompromisingly militant leader.[29] In his own
study, Harding regretted Delany's support for governmental policies
that seemed to undermine and deny the aspirations of blacks during
the early phase of Reconstruction after the Civil War. Nevertheless,
Harding proclaimed Delany the granddaddy of militant black nationalism and a successor to the revolutionary traditions of David Walker
and Nat Turner.[30] Several other critics of Delany have equally represented him as the quintessence of radicalism.

The attempts by scholars to advance a lopsided portrait of Delany, as
someone with a consistency of purpose, satisfied the demands of instrumentalist historiography. Biographical and critical studies of his career
sustain this militant image, and consequently, as Draper rightly noted,
we know more about Delany's nationalism, emigrationism, and Pan-
Africanism than about any other aspects of his career.[31] It becomes
obvious, therefore, why Draper's article provoked such angry responses.
He had taken on an icon of the black experience. He questioned precisely those aspects of Delany's career that had endeared him to the militant generation—nationalism and Pan-Africanism. It was also clear
that the mood of the time was not receptive to any "Delany" other than
the one conceived in instrumentalist terms. This also explains the
treatment accorded an earlier critique of Delany's nationalism. In 1966
Bill McAdoo published a scathing indictment of Delany in an article
titled "Pre-Civil War Black Nationalism."[32] He descried Delany as a
reactionary nationalist, a Zionist, and an imperialist whose objective
was to exploit, rather than advance, the interests of black Americans
and Africans. As he put it, "The dominant form of reactionary black
nationalism, arising between 1830 and 1860, was black Zionism.

Martin R. Delany . . . was one of the chief spokesmen and prime movers of black Zionism."[33] Underscoring the imperialist and anti-Africa nature of Delany's nationalism, McAdoo wrote, "The black Zionists had designs on Africa, but they were not in the spirit of a 'long lost' descendant returning to his ancestral home (after two centuries of oppression) to live among 'his own' in peace and harmony . . . they were returning to possess and exploit Africa in accordance with their black capitalist aspirations."[34] Few acknowledged this article. It was met with what amounted to a conspiracy of silence. There were no attempts to address the critical issues raised by McAdoo that suggested a certain complexity to nineteenth-century black nationalism. In fact, as discussed above, my first encounter with Delany occurred also in the context of what I now describe as the mythologized perspective. The first "Delany" I encountered as I began preliminary research into his career was the militant, uncompromising, antiestablishment black nationalist. It did not take long, however, for me to discover discrepancies in his values and idiosyncrasies that directly contradicted the mythologized hero. I soon encountered a far greater and dominant conservative and pragmatic side to Delany that, in my judgment, represented a far more accurate depiction of him.

Black biography has generally been susceptible to utilitarian usages. When the militant generation of the 1960s reached into the past for reference personalities and heroes to inspire them, they sought individuals of almost saintly disposition, leaders with impeccable character whose lives and careers reflected the anger, frustrations, alienation, and antiestablishment mood of the 1960s. In other words, they looked for mirror images of themselves. There was thus a tendency and disposition to create those images where they did not exist, to enlarge small ideological and often ephemeral and transient ideological values into permanent and larger-than-life dimensions in order to create an ideological personality that fit the instrumentalist hero they were looking for. Methodologically, this entailed a selective and isolative process whereby only those aspects of the individual's career that mirrored radical and militant idiosyncrasies were carefully highlighted. All other aspects to the contrary were either ignored or handled in a manner that de-emphasized their significance. For example, some of the early biographies of Frederick Douglass by Philip Foner and Benjamin Quarles tended to highlight the progressive aspects of Douglass's career, often ignoring or overshadowing his complexities and paradoxes. An acknowledgment of Douglass's contradictions, one writer contends, would have entailed encounters with the "unruly" dimensions of his career, dimensions that would not only have cast Douglass in a bad light but also would have negatively impacted, or even subverted, the social function his biography was meant to advance.[35] In other words, a tendency to "resolve the problem of human unruliness . . . by avoiding it, characterized black biographical methodology."[36]

The imperative of moving black biography beyond instrumentalism became evident as black American history began to gain a foothold in the academy and as the issues of respectability and intellectual validation became important. Scholars began to reexamine critically the careers of black leaders who had hitherto been conceived within the instrumentalist framework, raising critical questions about how black leaders actually "functioned" in history—questions that entailed engaging and acknowledging both the rational and unruly aspects of their lives with a view to attaining a much broader understanding of their careers, ideologies, and legacies. This revisionist thrust is still very much in progress in black biography. The last two and half decades have witnessed an outpouring of revisionist studies of black leaders who were previously conceived within the instrumentalist framework. Reflective of a methodological change in black biography, more recent biographies of Frederick Douglass present a much more complex individual whose choices and decisions changed as the contexts and circumstances changed.[37]

From about the mid-1970s to the early 1980s, black biography witnessed a gradual abandonment of instrumentalist historiography, which was replaced by a functionalist perspective, one that de-emphasizes the social function of biography while highlighting the intersection of complex historical, geo-political, social, economic, and cultural factors and how these factors shape the responses, choices, and decisions of black leaders. Within this complex milieu, the individual performed as a member of a wider community—a very complex community in which the values espoused by such an individual, and the decisions made, reflect the complexity of that community. The subject of a biography is, therefore, perceived as someone whose actions entailed a delicate balancing act between complementary and often conflicting interests.

The concept "functionalism" thus assumes a relationship of interdependence. The individual is a constituent part of a system, whose functionality depended on the degree to which each and every member balances his or her interests against those of others. The act of balancing presupposes some degree of cooperation, not necessarily compromise, even though it does not completely preclude compromise. The functional framework enables us to better understand human complexity and to be able to appreciate and come to terms with the unruly dimensions of human behavior. Black leaders had much less room to assume consistently dogmatic and doctrinaire postures. They exhibited a complex range of behavioral and idiosyncratic tendencies. As recent studies establish, there were radicals who often found it prudent to accommodate and compromise, just as there were accommodationists who at times found radical strategies attractive and logical.

Collective biographical studies of the performance of black leaders during Reconstruction heralded the emergence of critical black biography. Beginning with the seminal works of Du Bois, Woodson, and Taylor, to name a few, scholars were concerned not only with neutralizing the racist content of American historiography but also with critically ascertaining why blacks failed to hold on permanently to the opportunities brought about by freedom and political enfranchisement following the Civil War. The main preoccupation of these scholars, one that remains a focus of scholarly research, is to ascertain the extent to which blacks could be held accountable for what happened during Reconstruction. Du Bois, Taylor, Brawley, and Woodson all underscore the positive accomplishments of black leaders. Although Du Bois was very critical of the bourgeois inclinations of black leaders, the thrust of his study of Reconstruction, like that of the others, was redemptionist and rehabilitationist, that is, to redeem the careers of blacks whose contributions and accomplishments had been denied and systematically denigrated. Black American history maintained this redemptionist focus until the advent of the civil rights movement, when the instrumentalist tradition assumed dominance.

The ascendance of functionalist biography in the 1980s focused attention on the still unresolved question of the performance of blacks during Reconstruction. This time, however, a more critical approach to the subject prevailed. The new studies underscore the complex nature of the choices, interests, and values that permeated the socioeconomic, cultural, and political contexts of black leadership development and performance. Included in this group are the works of Thomas Holt, David Rankin, Edmund Drago, and Howard Rabinowitz.[38] Holt, for example, zeroed in on the ideological division within the black leadership ranks in South Carolina and the divergence in interests and aspirations between the black political leadership and the masses. His findings are revealing and significant given the strategic importance of South Carolina. In his anthology, Rabinowitz brings together some of the best examples of revisionist historiography.[39] These articles, authored by some of the leading scholars in the black biographical genre, illuminate the complexities of black leaders throughout history. Collectively, they reveal that black leaders were less ideological and more compromising and pragmatic. Their values, policies, and choices often changed with changing circumstances. It is clear that they rarely maintained consistently ideological positions; if there was anything consistent and predictable about black leaders, it was their ability and propensity to compromise whenever the situation warranted. August Meier, a leading advocate of the "functional" perspective, provides this apt characterization of black leadership in the nineteenth century,

> Overall, the typical late nineteenth-century black political leader in the South was a moderate. All were practical men who saw the necessity of compromise. They were also ambitious men who needed white support to advance themselves and the interest of their black constituents. Even the most militant spokesmen . . . found astute compromise essential to obtain the benefits desired either personally or for the race. The intersection of personal rivalries among blacks, class cleavages, the activities of whites—both Democrats and Republicans—and the very nature of the American Political system made inevitable the emergence of a typically moderate political type.[40]

A critical examination of Delany's activities in South Carolina during Reconstruction reveals a dimension that Holt did not fully explore. The prevailing view that black political leaders emphasized political rights and power to the detriment of economic elevation, while accurate, assumes a certain degree of consensus among blacks that did not exist in practice. Not all black politicians in South Carolina upheld or prioritized political rights. From the onset of Reconstruction, a vocal minority, Delany among the most prominent, stood vehemently opposed to black political rights and power, advocating the prioritization of economic power instead. Political power was, in Delany's estimation, akin to the epic Trojan horse, designed to lure blacks into a false sense of security and bury them deeper in the dungeon of degradation and misery. In fact, he was among those who popularized the image of the Northern carpet-bagger as a political and economic predator. He did not believe that, left alone, blacks would have demanded political rights. He blamed Northern radicals and the Republican Party for miseducating and misleading those he termed ignorant and gullible black leaders. He consequently launched a one-man crusade against Radical Reconstruction, the black political leadership, and its ally, the Republican Party. According to him, blacks needed economic elevation, a condition that was attainable only through a policy of reconciliation with, and appeasement toward, the former slave owners. And since these former slave owners remained indomitably opposed to black political rights, Delany lectured the black political leadership on the wisdom of surrendering political power. This concession, he believed, would break down barriers to economic elevation. Delany's ideas provoked bitter conflict with the Republican Party and with other black leaders, a conflict that punctuated the entire Reconstruction era in South Carolina, leading ultimately to his decamping to the Democratic Party in the crucial election of 1876. Contemporaries perceived Delany as a traitor to his race, an accommodationist and compromiser. In South Carolina, therefore, we encounter a radically different Delany from the one popularized in instrumentalist historiography. Delany's activities in South Carolina during Reconstruction clearly identified him as a perfect prototype of a functionalist leader. An examination of his career within a functionalist framework reveals a multidimensional personality, a far cry from the militant, principled, and uncompromising hero of instrumentalist genre.

TWO

Delany Historiography

"I AM AN invisible man . . . I am a man of substance, of flesh and bone, fiber and liquids—and I might even be said to possess a mind. I am invisible, understand, simply because people refuse to see me. Like the bodiless heads you see sometimes in circus sideshows, it is as though I have been surrounded by mirrors of hard, distorting glass. When they approach me they see only my surroundings, themselves, or figments of their imagination—indeed, everything and anything except me," laments the hero in Ralph Ellison's epic novel *Invisible Man*.[1] This characterization aptly captures the larger invisibility that defined the fate of blacks in American history. As historian Idus Newby brilliantly articulates, for decades leading American historians persistently de-emphasized, and at times completely ignored, the presence and contributions of blacks to the historical and national development of America.[2] He identifies the "invisible perspective" as among several negative historical paradigms that shaped American scholarly representations of the black experience.[3] In nineteenth-century black American history, Martin Delany exemplified the perfect prototype of the invisible man. His invisibility was two-fold. First, he did not begin to receive due scholarly recognition and respect until the late 1960s and early 1970s. He shared this late recognition along with many other black leaders. Second, and perhaps more important, he exemplified the Ellisonian invisibility model. Even when he began to receive attention, he remained largely misunderstood and misrepresented. When modern critics looked back at him, it appeared they saw every other thing around him but himself. His real personality often evaded recognition. More often than not, what they saw and projected was the product of their own ideological imagination and construction. Despite his visibility, and even notoriety, and in spite of his prominence in the forefront of the nineteenth-century black struggle, Delany was soon forgotten, and he quickly disappeared from historical memory. Like so many of his contemporaries, he was buried beneath the weight of aristocratic historiography. Consequently, until the black awakenings of the 1960s, very little was known of him. According to one authority, "with the exception of the stray and occasional references that have slipped into scholarly publications," very little was done to refurbish the image of Delany.[4] Writing for the *Pittsburgh Courier*, over half a century ago, W. E. B. Du Bois lamented Delany's obscurity. "His was a magnificent life, and yet how many of us heard of him?" Du Bois inquired, rather disappointingly.[5] To explain Delany's obscurity, one has to understand the culture of the late-nineteenth-century New South Movement with its emphasis on sectional harmony. The New South ideology watered the soil that would later germinate and nurture the aristocratic historiography and the accompanying nullification of the historical heritage and experience of blacks. Just at the time when blacks clamored for and needed democratic reforms, the North, according to one authority, suddenly developed an innate love and respect for southern aristocratic values and traditions. As the heroism of the southern soldier assumed mythic dimension in the North, northern sentiments began to concede that the South was right just about everything else, including the definition of the status of blacks in American society. Blacks, and their historical memory and accomplishments, were sacrificed to consecrate the national meeting of minds.[6]

By the turn of the century, the New South ideology and emergent segregation stabilized a status quo of black subordination. The achievement and efforts of black leaders such as Delany, Frederick Douglass, Henry H. Garnet, and Henry McNeal Turner, to name but a few, were deliberately misrepresented and de-emphasized with a view to underscoring their irrelevance to national historical development. The Delany that almost single-handedly bore the mantle of the emigrationist crusade in the 1850s; the same Delany whose spirited and fiery speeches sent shock waves through the planter community of South Carolina in the early phase of the Civil War; the first combat black major to be commissioned into the Union Army; the one Frederick Douglass referred to respectfully as "the intensest embodiment of black nationality"; the one who allegedly always thanked "God for making him a Black man"; the one who John Gaines of Cincinnati referred to as the quintessence of blackness simply vanished from historical memory.

By the first decade of the twentieth century, Delany, along with prominent nineteenth-century blacks, had almost been totally erased from historical memory. Historical writings of leading American historians simply relegated blacks to oblivion. Blacks were treated in books as invisible or negative objects with marginal effects on American history. This is reflected in the writings of several American historians who developed and nurtured the aristocratic ideals.[7] Historical scholarship became a vehicle for black subordination. The net result sustained what Samuel DuBois Cook characterizes as "a tragic conception" of the black experience premised on a persistent and institutionalized negation of black meanings and values.[8] This aristocratic historiography that produced history from the white perspective remained dominant until the emergence of Woodson and the New Negro History Movement, which sought to reverse the debilitating impact of aristocratic history and restore blacks to their rightful place in the historical narrative and memory of America. Carter G. Woodson and W. E. B. Du Bois contributed to building and nurturing a countervailing historical tradition and scholarship in opposition to the dominant hegemonic scholarship. Their efforts, as already argued, unleashed a surge of interests in, and a determination to unearth and illuminate, the positive and counter-Samboic dimensions of the African and black Diaspora historical experiences.[9] The resultant scholarship progressed from a rehabilitationist and integrationist framework to the instrumentalist perspective of the civil rights context. Renewed interest in, and efforts to rehabilitate the career of, Martin Delany occurred in the latter context.

Delany's authorized biography and his other publications marked him out as a perfect candidate for instrumentalist history. He seemed to embody a complex mix of ideas that endeared him to radical groups.

In the authorized biography, Frank (Frances) Rollin presented Delany as a man who "conformed to no conservatism for interest's sake, nor compromises for the sake of party or expediency. . . . His sentiment partaking of the most uncompromising radicalism."[10] She portrayed him as a resolute and consistently radical fighter in the forefront of the black struggle. Rollin's contentions may be accurate given that her biography did not extend beyond 1868, just as Radical Reconstruction was getting under way, the inauguration, arguably, of the most controversial phase of Delany's career. Yet some seventeen years later, at a memorial for Delany, Rev. Theodore J. Holly of the Episcopal Church of Haiti echoed precisely the same sentiments as Rollin. He characterized Delany as "manly and independent," someone "who refused to play second fiddle to whites on issues relating to the black struggle . . . his devotion to his race was such that he would not compromise with whites, always preferring to 'be himself', alone in 'solitary grandeur' against republican radicalism, corruption, evincing foresight that enabled him anticipate the demise of reconstruction."[11] Rev. Holly affirmed the imperative of illuminating and highlighting only those aspects of Delany's career that are positive and could serve both as an inspiration for future generations and standards against which past, present, and future generations of black leaders could be measured. As he put it, "Thus in time, Dr. Delany, by the high distinctive principles of his life and character, has given us the standard of measurement of all the men of our race, past, present and to come, in the work of Negro elevation in the United States of America."[12] Many scholars have since followed the admonition of Rev. Holly not to "cite anything except what was good in the lives and characters of those thus gone before" and have focused almost exclusively on the positive dimensions, projecting these as guiding lights and standards for present and future generations.[13] It thus seems that the mandate to isolate Delany's memory within the narrow confine of instrumentalism came as early as his memorial.

The ascendance of Black Power and militant black nationalism, especially the demand by some black leaders (for example, Malcolm X and Stokely Carmichael) for the forging of a transatlantic nexus of the black struggle, further pushed Delany into prominence. It was discovered that he had endorsed a similar nexus in his seminal publications in the 1850s. The race riots that exploded in the urban ghettoes in the 1960s exposed the limitations of the reformist strategies of the integrationist mainstream and fueled race consciousness. Reminded of Du Bois's classic turn-of-the century declaration that the "problem of the twentieth century is the problem of the color line," some blacks criticized the integrationist aspirations and strategies of the National Association for the Advancement of Colored People (NAACP) and Martin Luther King Jr.'s nonviolent tradition for de-emphasizing and ignoring racism. Delany's insistence on black self-determination caught the attention of this group.[14] It was also discovered that he had not only advanced both cultural-nationalist and racialist solutions but also had in fact anticipated Du Bois's essentialist construction of race in his presidential address before the National Emigration Convention in Cleveland (August 1854), in which he unambiguously advanced race as the essential dynamics of human relations. As he warned the delegates, "It would be duplicity longer to disguise the fact that the great issue, sooner or later, upon which must be disputed the world's destiny, will be the question of black and white, and every individual will be called upon for his identity with one or the other."[15] Furthermore, throughout the 1850s, Delany's emigrationist and Pan-Africanist ideas and schemes were premised on a strong affirmation of the notion of ontological blackness.

Delany, therefore, seemed a perfect candidate for instrumentalist history. He espoused nationalist, Pan-Africanist, and even separatist ideas. These images spurred further interest in him. Those who took up the challenge of studying him, therefore, did so within a sociocultural environment that demanded adherence to the twin objectives of reshaping the past in the militant image of the present and of using that past in the service of the struggle. Studies of his career appear to defer to these objectives. Many critics perceived him as someone who pioneered black cultural nationalism, separatistism, and Pan-Africanism, one who led the struggle for black empowerment and nationhood in the nineteenth century.

The exaltation of Delany as a racial essentialist and Pan-Africanist hero led to a corresponding de-emphasizing of his conservatism, complexities, and ambiguities in modern biographical and critical studies.

Modern scholars emphasize his emigrationism, nationalism, and supposedly radical orientation. They portray Delany as a consistently radical crusader for black freedom. Portions of his writings are carefully selected to reflect this radical image. Those portions that betray ambiguities and conservatism are either carefully avoided or, if confronted at all, are handled in a manner underscoring their superficiality and remoteness.

Theodore Draper's article "The Fantasy of Black Nationalism" (1969), and his follow-up "The Father of American Black Nationalism" (1970) and *The Rediscovery of Black Nationalism* (1970), seemed to have pioneered the movement to rescue Delany from historical oblivion.[16] Draper emphasized the nationalistic ideas of Delany, whom he defined as the ideological father of black nationalism, even as he underlined Delany's "dualities." Acknowledging that "the story of his life has been strangely neglected," Draper proceeded to explore in details the nationalist career of Delany, depicting him as "the outstanding advocate of the new black nationalism" (that is, emigration), underlining the complexities and ambivalences that characterized his entire life.[17] Numerous other articles and books on black nationalism have assigned a place of prominence to Delany. In fact, it is almost inconceivable for any new book on black nationalism or on the careers of more recent nationalists such as Henry M. Turner and Marcus Garvey not to acknowledge Delany's pioneering efforts. On balance, therefore, we know more about his nationalism today than we do of any other phase of his career. This is not surprising considering that the decade of the 1960s, when critical responses to Delany began, has gone down in history as the apogee of African nationalism. The emigrationist and nationalist emphasis of modern scholars is, therefore, a product of the vigorously Pan-Africanist orientation that black American liberation politics assumed in the 1960s and the linkages drawn between nationalism and the challenges of contemporary black America. What seems obvious is that because Delany's rediscovery coincided with the militant phase of the 1960s and also with the instrumentalist slant of black historiography, interpretations of him are colored by the radical predisposition of the time and also by the utilitarian underpinnings of black history. The nationalist aspirations of the past were then linked to those of the present and projected as the continuum of an antihegemonic tradition. Hence, those who espoused nationalism in the past became ideological leaders of the present struggle, models of ideological and practical strategies to be highlighted and emulated. The emphasis on emigration and nationalism has, however, tended to obscure the other, and perhaps more significant, side of Delany—his integrationism. As Draper acknowledged, emigration occupied only a relatively small part of Delany's career. Another reason that partly explains the strong emphasis on his nationalism is the fact that it is perhaps easier to sustain the aura of consistent radicalism that is built around him by simply looking at his emigrationist ideas. To focus on his integrationism is to confront his ambiguities. Little wonder then that few scholars have risked ventures into this area.

Sterling Stuckey discusses Delany's nationalism extensively in his writings, concluding that "no recognized ideologist of black nationalism has placed as much emphasis as he on the need for black people to have a land set aside for the purpose of establishing their own nation outside the boundaries of America."[18] Victor Ullman's and Dorothy Sterling's works, both published in 1971, represent the only available full biographical studies of Delany. As already established, both works, especially Ullman's, which was more tailored toward an academic audience, while Sterling's appeared directed more at a juvenile audience, fail to capture the complexities of Delany, leaving one with the strong impression of Delany as a one-dimensional, radical, uncompromising leader in the vanguard of the black struggle.[19] There have been specialized studies that focus on Delany's nationalist and Pan-Africanist career. Cyril Griffith's book deals with the Pan-African dimensions of Delany's ideas. He traces the ideological origins of modern Pan-Africanism to the African themes and projects in Delany's works.[20] Floyd J. Miller, in his own study, deals exhaustively with the centrality of Delany to the emigrationist and colonizationist movement.[21] In their writings, both Griffith and Miller solidify Delany's place and legacy as a nationalist and Pan-Africanist. Following these studies, numerous other scholars have written articles and commentaries on Delany's militant and radical nationalist ideas and programs.

Wilson J. Moses, a leading scholar of the black nationalist genre, historian Nell I. Painter, and historian-theologian Vincent Harding are among the leading scholars in solidifying Delany's reputation as a nationalist and Pan-Africanist. Painter acknowledges Delany's elitism in her contribution to an anthology on nineteenth-century black leaders. This elitism, she contends, became a distinguishing mark of his career, particularly its nationalist phase. Significantly, Painter acknowledges the ideological context of Delany's rediscovery. As she put it, underscoring the utilitarian and instrumentalist context of Delany's rediscovery, "Delany reemerged as a symbol of Black Nationalism but transmogrified to fit the tastes and politics of the mid-twentieth century. Because the black nationalism of the 1960s and 1970s was egalitarian and democratic, inspired by anti-imperialism and emphasizing self-determination for ordinary black people in the United States and Africa, many assumed that as a black nationalist Delany must also have held ordinary black people in high regard. Few of his twentieth-century admirers realized that his nineteenth-century black nationalism was an elitist, not democratic, creed."[22]

Painter discusses the contradictions and ambiguities of Delany's post-bellum career, albeit sketchily. She acknowledges and draws attention to these paradoxes without exhaustive and detailed analysis of their implications for his leadership style, typology, legacy, and ideological place in the broader tradition of black leadership. An exhaustive and detailed analysis is necessary if Delany is to be fully understood in his complexity and accorded his rightful place in the black leadership tradition and in black American historiography.

Painter clearly recognizes the need to confront the ultimate paradox of Delany's career, what Draper aptly termed, the "duality of all dualities"—Delany's support for the Democrats in 1876. Yet she seems reluctant to probe deeper its broader dynamics and implications. In another article on Delany's nationalism, Painter underscores even more forcefully his dual historical character and the dualistic contexts within which he could be examined.[23] First, there was the chronological and historical Delany; a personality entwined with major episodes of American history—"American and trans-Atlantic abolitionism, the Civil War, Reconstruction, redemption, and business Republicanism." She identifies this as Delany's horizontal context. Second, there was the "vertical dimension," the "transmogrified" Delany, product of a one-dimensional, racial essentialist construction of identity. The latter characterizes the 1960s context. Here again, Painter does underline the lack of congruence between the "transmogrified" Delany of the 1960s and the Delany of the nineteenth century.[24]

In modern black nationalist historiography, Delany is almost completely subsumed under a racial essentialist paradigm that has made it difficult to fully grasp the idiosyncratic complexities of the nineteenth-century horizontal context of his career. Painter calls for appreciating a black leader such as Delany "in two kinds of times, the vertical and horizontal, as historic/symbolic figures in our times and as actors in their own."[25] Here one senses a rationalization or justification and authentication of the "historical/symbolic subjectivity" factor as both necessary and authentic. The "historical/symbolic subjectivity" is, however, a mark of twentieth-century cravings for black heroes who would function as biographical pillars and markers upon whom to balance the modern radical nationalist phase of the struggle. And as Painter rightly observes, the "symbolic/subjective" perspective serves to illuminate the functional purpose of black leadership "in mid-twentieth-century Afro-American History."[26] Yet this historic/symbolic subjectivity and its illumination of Delany's relevance to twentieth-century black American history have undermined or foreclosed the possibility of understanding the other equally pertinent horizontal/historical and chronological Delany. One shares Painter's desire to see "Afro-American history in terms that are broader than race, for containing Delany's thought within racial categories limits him to one kind of time."[27]

Vincent Harding also highlights the radical dimensions of Delany's life and thought in his works. Harding, a leading participant in the civil rights movement, strongly believes in the instrumentalist construction of black history. His works fall within the intellectual tradition of using history to effect social change and portraying the black historical development in the most positive light. He emphasizes the black radical tradition and classifies Delany among the principal representatives of radicalism. In this regard, he places Delany in a direct line of succession from Nat Turner and David Walker.[28] In his own study, Harold Cruse strongly condemns modern black intellectuals for their integrationist aspirations. He faults them for failing to recognize that the only productive strategy for black elevation and empowerment was a combination of racial solidarity, racial distinctiveness, and cultural nationalism. He portrays Delany's brand of black nationalism and racial solidarity as the most effective and appropriate ideological strategy, which black leaders and intellectuals unfortunately ignored. Had they embraced Delany's strategy, Cruse suggests, the racial problem in the United States would have long been resolved.[29] Whether this is true is debatable. However, in Cruse's judgment, Delany offered the most appropriately radical alternative to what he regards as the conciliatory strategy of the integrationists.

In a brief article on Delany's political philosophy, Robert Khan offers the rather jaundiced suggestion that Delany's abandonment of emigration in the 1860s was consistent with his earlier political ideas. "Without sounding like an apologist of inconsistency," Khan writes, "one can argue that Delany's earlier principles are compatible with his later life as a political activist."[30] Khan's conclusion derives solely from two of Delany's publications, *The Condition, Elevation, Emigration, and Destiny of the Colored People of the United States* (1852) and "Political Destiny of the Colored Race on the American Continent" (1854), works that do not adequately capture the wealth and complexities of Delany's political ideas. Had Khan availed himself of Delany's other political writings and speeches, he would have recognized the complexities, divergences, deviations, and inconsistencies that characterized Delany's life and thought.

Contributing to the rehabilitation of Delany, Louis Rosenfeld identifies Delany's greatest contribution to American life and black history as his "defiant blackness." He depicts Delany as "America's first black nationalist" and the intense embodiment of black pride."[31] According to Rosenfeld, "Delany was the most outspoken advocate of cultural black nationalism among 19th century Afro-Americans. After decades of neglect . . . he has emerged as the most prominent historical model for black consciousness and pride."[32] Concurring, Mike Sajna writes, "Though any black man who had worked himself into the position of a publisher almost two decades before the Civil War had to be an extraordinary person, the attitude of Delany was nothing less than revolutionary. Instead of trying to hide his color and deferring to whites, as blacks were generally expected to do even by people in the North, Delany looked upon himself as superior."[33]

Mia Bay offers perhaps the most recent reconstruction of Delany within the narrow confines of instrumentalist historiography. Although not in the biographical genre, her book offers affirmative and categorical conclusions and generalizations about Delany's life and struggle, narrowly construed from a selection of his writings and speeches, including his authorized biography and the works of the Delany aficionados (Ullman, Sterling, Miller). The main thrust of her book is an examination and critical analysis of African American conceptions of whites between 1830 and 1925. According to Bay, enslaved and free blacks unambiguously rejected the notion of black racial inferiority and in consequence "redefined the character of both races."[34] There was, however, a certain complexity to African American responses to the racial ideology of the dominant society. The black intellectual class, with which Martin Delany is associated, rejected and deconstructed white racial ideology essentially by "creating their own version of ethnology—the nineteenth century science of the races."[35] To effectively negate the white hegemonic ideology, they had to construct their own ethnological theories and paradigms and, in the process, adduced a "revisionist account of both races (that) went beyond upholding the equity of the races to argue that the character of the Anglo-Saxon compared unfavorably with the better nature of their own race."[36] Illuminating the "barbarous" and negative character and qualities of Anglo-Saxon heritage enabled free blacks to more effectively challenge and debunk white racial values by counterpoising a glowing rendition of their own history and heritage, suggesting "that the racial character of black people more than equaled that of white people, and they frequently predicted a racial redemption in which 'the destined superiority of the Negro' would at long last be recognized."[37]

Bay describes Delany as a leading black intellectual combatant in this African American assault against Anglo-Saxon racial ideology, whose work served as ethnological counterthesis to the dominant ideology of white supcriority. She refers to Delany as "practically a black supremacist" and "an enthusiastic advocate of black separatism and emigration *for most of his life*."[38] She quotes selectively from three of Delany's major writings and relies totally, and rather uncritically, on the works of the aficionados for validation of her narrow conceptualization of Delany as a racial critic of white society and civilization and an indomitable and uncompromising advocate and defender of African history and civilization. She interprets Delany's last major publication, *The Principia of Ethnology: The Origins of Races and Color*, as a statement of his antagonistic "case against the white race" and a book that made the most "unambiguous argument for the existence of permanent distinctions between the races by any nineteenth-century African-African [*sic*].[39] In this book, according to Bay, Delany advanced perhaps his most effective deconstruction of Anglo-Saxon racial ideology and his most powerful defense and exaltation of the African heritage. His rejection of "pluralism," she contends, clearly mirrored Delany's alienation from Anglo-Saxon culture.

The problem with Bay's interpretation of Delany stems from her over-reliance on very few of Delany's writings and on the instrumentally slanted writings of the aficionados, thus limiting herself to their own narrow interpretative focus. Only an interpretation of Delany derived from such a narrow, ideologically skewed perspective would lead one to conclude that he was a "black supremacist," separatist, and emigrationist "for most of his life." There are hundreds of Delany's unpublished letters and speeches scattered in libraries and archives across the nation. A definitive study that makes categorical statements and conclusions about an individual's life and career should, at the very least, have consulted more than just a select few of that person's writings. What Bay accomplishes is to reinforce and perpetuate a historical myth—this one-dimensional portrait of Delany. Had she consulted Delany's other writings, she would have been alerted to the possibility of a much more complex personality, and this would have enriched her analysis and interpretation of the man and his ethnographic book. Delany's *Principia of Ethnology* was indeed his intellectual response and contribution to the prevailing ethnological debates of his times. Whites used ethnological science to argue for black inferiority and separatism, and Delany offered his book, as Bay rightly argues, to negate claims of black inferiority. This notwithstanding, the book did not absolutely reject pluralism, as Bay suggests. In fact, as will be demonstrated later in this study, the book emphatically staked claims for a pluralistic integrative social order.

There appears to be reluctance on the part of most modern critics to acknowledge and come to terms with the ambiguities of Delany's career. It is inconceivable to balance their portraits of a radical and ideologically doctrinaire person with obvious and glaring instances of compromises, conservatism, and, sometimes, in the judgment of his contemporaries, acts of deliberate sabotage of black aspirations. Because Delany espoused black nationalist aspirations in the nineteenth century, it was assumed that he had to be radical and militant in the tradition of twentieth-century militant and radical black nationalism. Since his nationalist ideas at times sounded militant and uncompromising, these aspects so captured the imagination and fascination of the twentieth-century militant generation as to warrant a complete jettisoning of other vital aspects of his career. What seems obvious is that because Delany's rediscovery coincided with the militant phase of the 1960s, and also with the instrumentalist construction of black history, interpretations of him have been colored by the radical predisposition and inclinations of the era.

Robert S. Levine's critical study presents perhaps the most exhaustive attempt thus far to unravel the complexities of Delany. Fundamentally, the book deals with the relationship between Douglass and Delany. Focusing on some of their writings, Levine analyzes the complexities of their thoughts, showing areas of divergence and convergence. Levine's study challenges prevailing binary interpretation of the two as ideologically opposed and irreconcilable leaders. He goes beyond any previous study in revealing Delany's complexities, while underscoring the problematic of ideological compartmentalization.[40] Nonetheless, the book remains steeped in the nationalist genre, for it affirms Delany's reputation as a black nationalist even as it underscores the changing dynamics of his ideas and leadership style. A major problem, however, is Levine's subscription to the racial essentialist construction of Delany. Even at the height of his emigrationist/nationalist crusade, Delany was never consistent on the issue of race. He may have reproached Douglass on his marriage to a white woman and on numerous occasions may have publicly espoused racial essentialist ideas, yet his personal life and public policies underscore ambiguity and a much more complex attitude toward race. First, there was Delany's marriage to a woman who was a mulatto, despite his often-quoted pride in not having a drop of white blood coursing through his veins. Second, to read racial essentialism into Delany's *Principia of Ethnology*, as Levine and Bay do, is to misunderstand and misrepresent Delany's central message.[41] The book in fact represents Delany's conflicting, and even confusing, responses to the racist climate and realities of the post-Reconstruction era. It combines racial, universalistic, and amalgamationist ideas.[42] Levine again errs in advancing a binary interpretation of the ideas and values of two of the leading figures in Delany's formative years—Lewis Woodson and William Whipper, his mentors. He erroneously depicts the two as advocates of opposing strategies. It is true that both seemed to disagree and that Woodson at times appeared critical of Whipper's universalism. However, both men in fact shared a lot in common. For instance, they shared an enduring faith in moral elevation and reforms. The "racial separatism" that Woodson allegedly advocated has to be understood in the context of his overall faith in America and moral elevation.[43] Furthermore, Levine wrongly interprets Woodson's complementary values as criticism and rejection of Whipper's integrative platform. Also he narrowly, and mistakenly, interprets Woodson's ideas by focusing on and highlighting one aspect (separatism) in isolation from the broader corpus of integrationism that Woodson advanced. He characterizes Woodson as a black separatist and equates his "internal emigration" proposal with advocacy of "black nation" within the United States. According to Levine,

> Woodson proposed a plan to bring about black elevation in ways quite different from Whipper: through racial separatism. He explained, "I would have them (free blacks) leave the cities where they are now 'scattered' and 'mixed' among the whites, whose prejudices exclude them from equal privileges in society, churches and schools, and settle themselves in communities in the country, and establish society, churches and schools of their own." In doing so, arguably, blacks would constitute their own "nation" within U.S. national borders.[44]

To suggest from the above that Woodson envisaged the creation of a black nation within the United States is erroneous. When Woodson advised black to go "West," he did not envisage separation from mainstream America. The move was simply a search for an open and conducive environment where blacks would grow and develop their potentialities. It was not a call for a permanent internal black state. His ultimate goal was black integration, not separatism. In fact, a broader understanding of the debate on moral suasion during this period reveals that even among the identified "radical" group, separatism was more of a temporary strategy designed to achieve integration. When Woodson advised those blacks residing in racist environments to migrate to the West, he suggested places he deemed open, places with abundant resources and opportunities for blacks to realize their potentialities. In other words, he suggested relocation to environments where they would have unimpeded opportunities to elevate themselves and, at the same time, establish beyond any shadow of doubt the imperative for integration.[45] Despite Levine's forceful articulation and analysis of Delany's complexities, his study relies too much on a racial essentialist construction that derives largely from a misreading and misinterpretation of Delany's writings and those of his mentors. In this respect, Levine's book falls far short of illuminating the ideological character and implications of the complexities and contradictions he underscores.

Scholars are not the only ones trumpeting and celebrating the instrumentalist qualities of Delany. Politicians have since joined the bandwagon. The afternoon of Saturday, May 11, 1991, was a memorable day in Pittsburgh. At the corner of Third and Market Streets, Mayor Sophie Masloff, the Pennsylvania Historical and Museum Commission, and the Black History Advisory Committee unveiled a state historical marker in memory and honor of Martin Delany at a spot close to where he had published the *Mystery*.[46] This marker was the fifty-fourth in Allegheny County and the thirtieth in the state honoring black Americans.[47] This event, in fact, marked the culmination of developments some trace to 1944 when, through some fortuitous circumstances, a Wilkinsburg resident, Charles W. Bower, discovered a copy of the *Mystery* in the trash and immediately took it to the

Carnegie Library, where it has since been preserved. The following year, at the commemoration of the Great Fire of 1845, it was discovered that the only existing eyewitness account of that tragedy was in the pages of the *Mystery*.[48] This chance discovery of the paper, according to local historians, brought Delany to the limelight and launched scholarly interest in him, resulting in numerous publications. It also gave recognition to Pittsburgh as the birthplace of black nationalism. As one writer put it, "Never doubt it. Truth cannot be obliterated forever from the pages of history . . . and as fate would have it, the *Mystery* came to light, and since then scholars have written many articles and at least four books about Delany."[49] Furthermore, according to the above writer, the unveiling of the marker was the fulfillment of an aspiration "Augustine" expressed in 1835 that we leave "a monument of our existence behind to beckon our children on to higher moral improvement."[50] It therefore represented a monumental tribute to "one of the greatest patriots and achievers who ever lived in Pittsburgh."[51] Even in the 1990s, with the benefit of almost two decades of scholarship on Delany and the growing challenges to instrumentalism, the dominant perceptions of Delany and the dominant hermeneutical lens remain the nationalist, militant, and racial essentialist, whose "great contribution to American life and black history stems from his defiant blackness. He was America's first 'Black Nationalist' and the intense embodiment of black independence . . . he always identified with the black experience and its place in history."[52] In the Pittsburgh of the 1990s, therefore, Delany was still nothing other than the militant black nationalist—uncompromising and quintessentially racial. The marker indeed symbolized the solidification of Delany in the folklore of western Pennsylvania as a hero whose stay in Pittsburgh led to immense positive contributions that included, among others, his laudable services to the city during the cholera epidemic of 1849 when he unselfishly, and without regard to race or economic background, rendered services to all in need, a feat that won a certificate of appreciation from the City Council and the Board of Health.[53] His stay in the city also enabled Pittsburgh to lay claim to being the seedbed of black nationalism. As one Pittsburgher claims, "Today . . . historians agree that the roots of black nationalism can be traced back to the efforts of black Pittsburghers in the mid-19th century. And in particular to Martin Delany."[54]

Why has there been this reluctance to confront, illuminate, and deconstruct the complexities of Delany? Why this almost schizophrenic disinclination to confront the "total Delany" as opposed to the "transmogrified Delany"? The answer perhaps lies in what the late Nathan Huggins identified as a dominant theme in African American historiography—the search for a black American narrative history that would "serve emotional needs as well as purely rational ones—(one intended to) contribute to one's sense of identity."[55] As Huggins explained, "Quite understandably, many want to find heroes and great men in the past with whom black people—especially children—can identify. In addition, they want to use a new history to exercise a sense of righteous rage at the oppression of their people and to collar their white contemporaries with the responsibility and the guilt of historical racism."[56] He described such history as "moralistic hero worship" and, consequently, bad and self-defeating.[57] Those who persist in construing Delany within the instrumentalist framework believe strongly in the need for heroes and heroines to advance what many still see today as an existential struggle. They are searching for individuals whose heroic accomplishments would instill a sense of worth in and inspire present and future generations of blacks. Confronting or revealing the "unruly" dimensions of these heroes would only dampen and undermine, rather than advance, the struggle. There is, therefore, almost an unending need for these heroes, whose careers are jealously guarded against possible damage or discrediting.

In a strongly worded article that explores "the limits of history as a social instrument," the renowned historian Louis Harlan draws attention to the "nonprofessional but intensely interested black militants who want to use history as an instrument to promote group solidarity, or a more optimistic self-image, or in some cases racial revolution or nationalism."[58] He cautions against "the new distortions that would come from a propagandistic use of history to promote Negro cultural nationalism and separatism."[59] The main thrust of his brilliant analysis is advocacy of the necessity of moving beyond redemption and instrumentalism to a study of the black American past in all its richness, diversity, and complexity. This calls for a perspective that captures and mirrors the diversities and complexities of the black experience. Since the late 1970s, many have responded to the demand for a functionalist perspective and framework for studying black leaders. This has yielded significant revisionist studies in black biography, especially in the last two decades. The conclusions of these studies illuminate the inherent shortcomings of instrumentalist historiography.[60] Black leaders functioned in a very fluid and unstable environment that dictated adjustments and flexibility. Group biographical portraits also reveal the complexity of the ideas, programs, and responses of black leaders. The present state of black biography, therefore, confirms August Meier's hypothesis about the complexity of the typical late-nineteenth-century black political leader.[61] Delany was indeed a prototype of this leadership.

In contemporary radical black nationalist historiography, to juxtapose the name Delany with conservatism immediately creates tension, for the two are deemed so diametrically opposed and distant as to render such correlation, under any circumstances, improbable if not utterly stupendous. Martin Delany is today acclaimed, and has been since the early 1970s when sustained scholarly interests in his career began, as the nineteenth-century exemplar of militant black nationalism, the ideological granddaddy of contemporary black nationalists. He is often singled out as the precursor of twentieth-century militant, countercultural, and counterestablishment traditions of Black Power, Malcolm X, and Marcus Garvey. In black American historiography, Delany occupies an exalted place in the militant nationalist genre; his militancy and supposedly uncompromising stance often contrasted with the conservative and accommodating tradition of Frederick Douglass. Delany's militancy, according to Victor Ullman, left no room for compromise with whites. He was indomitably and uncompromisingly opposed to the injustices of American society.

Unfortunately, this instrumentalist portrait of Delany was the product and reflection of the epoch that launched the rehabilitation of his career. Since at some point in the nineteenth century he spearheaded the nationalist and emigrationist movement that derived from deep alienation from America and represented rejection of American values and institutions, Delany appeared in the specter of a hero, among the earliest of black leaders to confront and challenge historical circumstances and problems similar to those of twentieth-century black Americans. He quickly became the archetype of everything ideological that modern-day black militants espoused and cherished. He has since been crowned the ideological precursor of militant black nationalism. Yet this image, upon which subsequent scholars have built the militant portrait of Delany, is derived narrowly from the nationalist and emigrationist phase of his career, a brief ten-year period, 1852–1862, a period sandwiched between three broader, longer, and more significant epochs that embody certainly the most defining elements of his career—integration/conservatism (1830–1850, 1863–1874, and 1875–1880). His conservative ideas and values are encapsulated in these three dominant integrationist phases of his career. It is, therefore, on these phases that this study is focused in order to fully unravel the neglected, but fundamental, dimensions of his life and struggle.

What we know of Delany today, of his philosophy and legacy, is unfortunately narrowly constructed from the middle phase of his career, which as Theodore Draper rightly contends, was the least significant, for there was a certain superficiality and shallowness to the nationalism and alienation, upon which so many have relied in advancing Delany as a militant, antiestablishment hero. Few are willing to confront and acknowledge the fact that he harbored conservative ideas and inclinations and that he was more of an integrationist, precisely because such an acknowledgment would undermine, or reflect negatively on, that instrumentally constructed hero whose accomplishments and values are projected as shining examples and guiding lights for present and future generations of black activists and nationalists. Yet the changes in black biographical studies in the last two decades, heralded by the outpouring of revisionist studies of black leaders, many of whom were hitherto conceived within the instrumentalist genre, underscore much more complex individuals and personalities who defy ideological compartmentalization—leaders who exhibited tendencies that suggested that they were less ideological than hitherto presumed. The result is the recognition of these leaders as persons who combined many ideological traditions and inclinations, leaders who often straddled conflicting ideological spaces and are propelled by circumstantial and utilitarian considerations. The line separating a conservative from a radical was indeed a thin one, and very often blurry. These studies continue to reveal very complex personalities and caution against too rigid classification of black leaders along ideological categories. Unfortunately, despite the increasing attention that black leaders have attracted in the last two decades and the revisionist thrust of black biography, Martin Delany remains confined to the instrumentalist tradition. As already suggested, even the most recent studies of Delany do not adequately confront the critical biographical problematic of his historiography— neglect of the conservative dimensions of his life and thought. Paradoxically, Delany himself recognized, and in fact affirmed, the imperative of understanding and appraising black leaders not just in the context of the needs and demands of specific historical moments, however critical, but also on the basis of much broader, historically credible framework. He acknowledged this clearly in his eulogy to the Reverend Fayette Davis. According to him,

> To faithfully record the life and history of a good and virtuous man, requires more than the fleeting reflections of a moment . . . Had I have the time necessary for the undertaking, the data and memoranda before me, when considering the person of the subject now under consideration. I feel myself inadequate to do justice; but how much more so, when, without the proper source of references, and in possession of but an impartial account, upon which to lay the foundation of our subject.[62]

The above consideration alone, if for no other reason, requires that Delany be accorded in death that critical historical context that he so eloquently underscored in life. It is therefore time to shift the focus away from the nationalist phase of Delany's career (the one to which he owed his reputation, the one that modern scholars and activists continue to highlight) to the equally fundamental and, in fact, much more pervasive and domineering integrationist phases, for it is within the latter neglected aspect that Delany's true character and personality are illuminated. The nationalist phase lasted just a decade, sandwiched between three dominant integrationist epochs that are not only of much longer duration but also of more significance in illuminating and unraveling his true character and personality. Although this study is focused on the postbellum integrationist phases, it is necessary to visit the first integrationist phase of his career, for it serves as a background to understanding the forces and individuals that nurtured Delany's formative years and whose ideas shaped his life thereafter. This phase is also significant in that it demonstrates the depth of his conservatism and provides a much broader historical basis for understanding his place in the ideological spectrum of black leadership and his legacy to the black historical experience.

THREE

First Integrationist Phase
Moral Suasion, 1830–1849

MARTIN DELANY HAD the "good fortune" of belonging to the "free" black community through the fortuitous circumstance of being born of a "free" mother on May 6, 1812, in Charlestown, Virginia (now in West Virginia). Being free, however, brought little comfort, for it conferred no special distinguishing privilege or status. In this respect, Delany exemplified the curious paradox of "free blacks" in early-nineteenth-century America. To be "free" and "black" juxtaposed two inherently contradictory qualities. The two in fact mocked each other, for freedom represented an existential value, the want of which defined the essence of being black. And, as several scholars have pointed out, the attainment of freedom by a black person was often the beginning of a sustained struggle that itself underscored the emptiness and sterility of the freedom.[1]

Although born free, Delany's experience was in no fundamental way different from that of a slave. He therefore shared with other free blacks the fate of having no fundamental experiential advantage over those in bondage. Consequently, from his birth, Delany's experiences were too negative to inspire any positive and endearing consciousness of America. Like other free blacks, he grew up frustrated and alienated, perhaps even angry, at the misery and degradation that defined black lives in America. As a young boy growing up in Jeffersonian Virginia, he had only negative, alienating childhood experiences. Blacks were denied education. In 1793 free blacks were barred in Virginia. In 1806 the Virginia General Assembly passed a law ordering emancipated slaves not to reside in the state beyond twelve months or risk reenslavement. Free blacks were subjected to a series of regulations that emphasized their inferiority. They were denied the franchise and were required to register every three years to renew their certificates of freedom. They were taxed excessively and frequently arrested for vagrancy.[2]

These negative experiential markers clearly formed the elements of Delany's socialization. As a young child, he saw the deep scar on his father's face inflicted by slaveholders determined to destroy his sense of manhood.[3] He could not have missed the fright and horror in his mother's face as she spirited him and his brothers to safety in Chambersburg, Pennsylvania, secure from the clutches of Virginian authorities who were bent on prosecuting her for no other cause than that her children had somehow gained literacy.[4]

It was a crime in Virginia, as in other slaveholding states, for blacks to be educated. Perhaps most painfully, he saw opportunities for education closed to him even in Chambersburg. It was not until 1834, the year the free schooling law was enacted in Pennsylvania, that public schools system began in Chambersburg.[5] But Delany would not be deterred, nor would his aspirations be stunted by legal barriers. He had come to the realization of the significance of education and enlightenment to the future of his people. He was thus compelled, at a very youthful age of nineteen, to take the momentous decision to relocate to Pittsburgh in 1831 in search of education. His experience in Pennsylvania became central to his ideological development. There he encountered a black community excited and agitated by Nat Turner's abortive insurrection in Southampton, Virginia. Though it failed, the episode took on mythic proportions among blacks. The heroic act of Turner and his group emboldened blacks, not necessarily to strike violently at slavery but to intensify efforts at eradicating slavery and racism. The black community Delany immersed himself in, therefore, was one actively engaged in antislavery activity. Coming from different backgrounds, these blacks were united by a determination to further the cause of black liberation.

In the 1830s Pennsylvania was regarded as the "Mecca" of the black struggle. Its long tradition of liberalism attracted blacks from all over the country. According to Du Bois, immigrants made up almost 50 percent of the black population of Philadelphia. Indeed, the leading men in the black struggle in the whole state had almost all migrated from other Northern or Southern states.[6] Their collective goal was to make Pennsylvania a model state. Many were imbued with a deep sense of responsibility and driven by the conviction that the fate of the enslaved depended very much on how free blacks utilized their freedom. It was in this context, and among these motivated blacks, that Delany, recalling the humiliating experiences of his background, "consecrated himself to freedom, and registered his vows against the enemies of his race."[7] This vow, however, would not be a vow to confront head-on the oppressive and dehumanizing institution of slavery and racism. The vow would not mandate any confrontational attempts or strategies to overthrow the oppressive system.

It was indeed a vow conceived in the womb of early-nineteenth-century reformism. The early 1800s was, in fact, an optimistic age in American history. To many, it was the age of reform. The period witnessed the emergence of reform organizations associated with the evangelical movement and the Second Great Awakening. Religious revivalist traditions swept through the middle and western states and New England. Religious evangelicals such as Charles G. Finney, William E. Channing, and Lyman Beecher focused on the moral capacity of the individual to effect change for the good of society. The reformers emphasized social reforms, prison reforms, peace, temperance, and the abolition of slavery.[8] The plethora of reform activities illuminated perhaps one of the greatest paradoxes of America, the enthusiasm for reform in a context that sustained two contradictory experiences—freedom and slavery. The surge for reform awakened and energized blacks. The challenges they confronted made the reform efforts all the more important and relevant—oppression, slavery, discrimination, the denial of citizenship rights and privileges. To blacks, America was a nation of contradictory experiences and forces: slavery-freedom, oppression-oppressors, superior-inferior—and the dividing line was color.

But the reform initiatives, and the entire culture of what historians refer to as "Jacksonian Democracy," tended to obscure this racial reality, for when blacks looked around, they saw whites actively engaged in and spearheading the reform initiatives; they heard whites talk about the moral imperative of change, and they heard whites advocate universal humanity and the reform of society for the good of all. Consequently, while the socioeconomic and political structures and realities underlined race, the reform initiatives tended to obscure race and thus encourage blacks to embrace the prevailing optimistic culture and immerse themselves in the reform initiatives. This experience convinced many blacks to de-emphasize race, believing that their predicament stemmed from the moral failures of individuals. Therefore, they sought solution in a moral crusade targeted at appealing to the moral conscience of the nation. Believing strongly in the perfectibility of the American order and in the ultimate redemptive power of the American Dream, black leaders, most prominently Frederick Douglass, Henry H. Garnet, William Whipper, Rev. Lewis Woodson, and Martin Delany, joined whites and embraced the reformist and optimistic outlook of the era, invoking standard American middle-class values and solutions and underscoring faith in their future as Americans. As the "Address" of the Second Negro National Convention in Philadelphia underscored,

> We yet anticipate in the moral strength of this nation, a final redemption from those evils that have been illegitimately entailed on us as a people. We yet expect by due exertions on our part, together with the aid of the benevolent philanthropists of our country, to acquire a moral and intellectual strength, that will unshaft the calumnious darts of our adversaries, and present to the world a general character, that they will feel bound to respect and admire.[9]

Believing strongly in the human capacity for self-improvement through rational moral choices, blacks, in consonance with the prevailing reformist and optimistic outlook of early-nineteenth-century America, projected themselves collectively as a people capable of positively changing their conditions. It was this conviction that inspired William Hamilton of New York, president of the Fourth National Negro Convention in New York, to "recommend earnestly that you [that is, blacks] press upon our people the necessity and advantage of moral reformation. It may not produce an excess of riches, but it will produce a higher state of happiness, and render our circumstances easier."[10]

This moral imperative, this faith in the human capacity for self-improvement, this confidence in a person as an agent of change and in the malleability of the American order, instilled in the black community of Pennsylvania a sense of hope and optimism in the ultimate redemptive capacity of American democracy. Many blacks, therefore, did not see the American political culture as inherently bad but, on the contrary, as inherently progressive and propelled by liberal ideas and values that, unfortunately, had been undermined by the moral failures, selfishness, and evil intensions of human beings. Changing this corrupted human disposition through indirect appeals to its presumed moral conscience became the preoccupation of leading blacks of Delany's generation. The key to black salvation, and to the ultimate perfectibility of the American order, they believed, lay in moral suasion, an appeal to the moral conscience of the nation.[11]

Moral suasion thus became the prevailing and dominant abolitionist creed of the black community of Pennsylvania into which young Delany immersed himself in the early 1830s. The organization that spearheaded the moral suasion efforts was the American Moral Reform Society, established at the 1835 Negro National Convention in Philadelphia. According to Howard Bell, "The aims and aspirations of the new organization were comprehensive. The members planned to emphasize education, temperance, economy, and universal liberty. They had no use for distinctions of color or complexion, and they chose to disregard geographical boundaries in their efforts to elevate the entire human race through Christian example and persuasion."[12]

Certain key elements became the defining focus of moral suasion. As McCormick underscored, "The rallying points of such a general effort at moral reform would be education, temperance, economy, and universal liberty. By practicing these virtues, the free colored population would be elevated and objections to immediate emancipation would be nullified."[13] As a young and quite impressionistic boy, Delany could not have escaped the pervasive influence of moral suasion, for his mentors in Pittsburgh, Lewis Woodson and William Whipper, were two of the leading moral suasion advocates of the epoch, who engaged each other, and blacks from other parts of the nation, in a spirited debate on the efficacy of moral suasion as a reform strategy.

Both Woodson and Whipper, arguing from different but often complementary perspectives, deprecated violence and radical/militant confrontational strategies in preference for self-reliance, industry, Christian
character, economy, and temperance as the means to the ultimate eradi-
cation of the twin evils of slavery and racism. In Pittsburgh, Delany continued his education under the tutelage of Woodson at the African
Methodist Episcopal Church Cellar School. The school was founded by
Woodson and another Pittsburgh black, "Daddy" Ben Richards, a wealthy
butcher and real estate agent, whose daughter Delany would later marry.
It was necessary for blacks to establish their own school since they
were not allowed into the public school system. There is no doubt that
Woodson greatly influenced Delany, a fact already acknowledged by
many scholars.[14] Both Woodson and Whipper profoundly shaped Delany's
moral suasionist convictions. It was largely through their influences
that he, too, adopted moral suasion as a philosophy and guiding principle
as he matured and began to take a more active and independent role in
the black struggle. The early 1830s also coincided with the beginning
of an organized black abolitionist crusade. This movement began in
Philadelphia in 1830, and for the next five years, through the Convention
movement, leading blacks from different parts of the country met annu-
ally to deliberate on strategies for achieving the goal of full integration
into American society. Almost from the start, they proclaimed moral
suasion as the philosophical underpinning of their struggle.[15]

The progressive rendition of American political culture and institutions by blacks is exemplified by their invocations of both the Constitution and the Declaration of Independence in justification of their
claims to American citizenship. They perceived the two as documents
infused with progressive ideals and values that could, and should,
appropriately be extended to blacks. This meant that blacks attributed
the shortcomings and corruption of American democracy to the moral
failures of individuals. They perceived American political culture as
inherently democratic. Returning this corrupted and perverted culture
to its original and intended democratic character entailed reforming the
moral character of individuals, particularly those who were both responsible for and benefiting from the perverted culture. Improving the moral
conscience of these individuals through moral suasion would facilitate

the integration of blacks into what was inherently a liberal and progressive political culture.[16] Moral suasion thus eroded the force of race and ethnicity as essential factors, for blacks were convinced that their disabilities had little to do with race and more with their condition. Changing the condition through moral suasion would appeal favorably to the moral conscience of whites. Moral suasion instilled a certain universalism that accounted for the early universalistic platform of the early black abolitionist crusade as evidenced in the first five national conventions, which witnessed the attendance of white abolitionists, the formation of the American Moral Reform Society in 1835, and the dominance of moral suasion as black abolitionist philosophy throughout the 1830s and 1840s.[17] Delany was a product of this integrative and moral suasionist acculturation, and as he matured, he took it upon himself to cultivate and advance moral suasionist values as the guiding principles of his own life and the keys to the salvation of blacks.

To appreciate the context of Delany's socialization in Pittsburgh, it is necessary to become acquainted with some of the leading blacks who helped shape his ideological orientation. One of the most prominent was John Vashon, in whose house Delany lived briefly, sharing a room with his son, George. John Vashon's lucrative barber business and his ownership of the city baths made him one of the most economically successful blacks in Pittsburgh. The Vashon home was the nerve center of antislavery activities among blacks in Pittsburgh. A mulatto originally from Virginia, Vashon was a dedicated Garrisonian and served as Pittsburgh agent of the *Liberator*.[18] The Garrisonians were supporters of the abolitionist movement organized and spearheaded by the white abolitionist William Lloyd Garrison of Boston, who founded the New England–based American Anti-Slavery Society in the early 1830s and whose movement became closely associated with nonviolence and moral suasion. The fundamental components of his philosophy became collectively known as Garrisonism. They included "belief in effecting emancipation through the use of moral suasion, his belief in peace . . . and his belief that the human family constituted one species."[19] His paper, the *Liberator*, was one of the earliest and most radical abolitionist papers. Garrison won the respect and admiration of blacks, and many of them joined his movement and patronized his paper.

Delany also met several other blacks, including John Peck, Abraham D. Shadd, Charles Lenox Remond, and Robert Purvis. John Peck was a successful barber and wigmaker. Abraham Shadd, originally from Wilmington, Delaware, was a shoemaker by profession and was also very wealthy. He participated actively in the early Negro Convention movement, and held the distinction of being "one of the five blacks to serve on the Board of Managers of the American Anti-Slavery Society at its founding meeting in 1833."[20] Shadd also served briefly as agent of the *Emancipator*, the official organ of the American Anti-Slavery Society. He developed a reputation as an ardent antislavery advocate and supporter of the Underground Railroad, whose homes in Wilmington, Delaware, and West Chester County, Pennsylvania, provided safe havens for fugitives.[21] Shadd moved to Canada West in the 1850s, where he achieved another distinction of becoming the "only black to hold elective office prior to the Civil War."[22] Charles Remond hailed from a wealthy New England background and led the struggle against segregation in the railroads in Massachusetts. An eloquent antislavery lecturer, he toured England and Ireland, delivering antislavery lectures. A dedicated Garrisonian, Remond was for many years an agent of the American Anti-Slavery Society.[23] Robert Purvis was a mulatto son of a white South Carolina merchant and a Moorish-Jewish woman whose mother had been a slave. Of wealthy background, Purvis was educated in private schools in Philadelphia before completing his education at Amherst College. After college, he immersed himself in the abolitionist crusade, becoming a founding member of the American Anti-Slavery Society and a dedicated follower of Garrison.[24] These were all economically successful men who constituted the vanguard of the black community of Pennsylvania. Most important, they were men who embraced the pacifist, nonviolent tradition of Garrison and whose individual triumph over adversity, particularly economic poverty, inspired a sense of hope and optimism and the conviction that other blacks could equally attain economic elevation if the right strategies and values were observed and pursued. This faith led them to embrace the reformist culture of the age and to project themselves and blacks in general, individually and collectively, as viable agents of change.

Since the two individuals with the most profound impact on Delany were his mentors, Woodson and Whipper, their ideas are worth exploring in greater detail. Delany first met Lewis Woodson at the Vashon's. A fugitive from Virginia, Woodson participated actively in antislavery activities. Although an immigrant, he succeeded economically, owning several barbershops. As already indicated, he collaborated with another black, "Daddy" Ben Richards, to establish a school for black children.

Woodson became one of the ideological leaders of the black struggle. He published extensively on a wide range of issues—moral reform, education, economic elevation, Christian virtue, and nonviolence. The conviction that the problems confronting blacks were largely the result of their degraded moral and economic conditions led him to recommend and strongly endorse internal reform initiatives among blacks. He believed that racism would diminish as blacks improved their condition.[25] Convinced that Jacksonian America was fundamentally an open society, Woodson admonished blacks to cultivate moral virtues, education, and business skills as prerequisites for acceptance and integration.[26] He publicly stressed the importance of business enterprises, attributing black poverty and underdevelopment to the low level of business initiatives. Economic elevation and moral uprightness would, in his judgment, mitigate and overcome prejudice. He offered his own experience as evidence that a good man of moral virtue and economic standing could live under, and overcome, bad laws. He urged blacks to fight racism with moral reform.[27] He believed that any man of moral purity would escape the worst excesses of racism. Writing under the pseudonym "Augustine," Woodson underlined the openness, possibilities, and opportunities that were available to resourceful and industrious blacks in America. He identified deficiencies in the condition, rather than racial intolerance, as the chief cause of prejudice.[28] Woodson advised those blacks living in extremely racist environments to emigrate to the "West," which he defined as comprising Ohio, Indiana, Illinois, Wisconsin, and Pennsylvania, where, according to him, they would find great opportunities for realizing their potentialities, unimpeded by racism.[29] The "West" could prove to be the "Promised Land" if only blacks developed two critical qualities—high moral virtue and business skills.

William Whipper also provided strong ideological mentoring and leadership to Delany and other blacks. Whipper, like Woodson and Vashon, was wealthy, owning a lucrative lumber business in Columbia,

Pennsylvania. In 1834 he opened a free labor and temperance store in Philadelphia, and for over thirteen years, according to a source, he contributed $1,000 annually to the antislavery cause. He also owned a fleet of streetcars.[30] As a founding member of the American Moral Reform Society, he advocated, and strongly believed in, the notion of universal humanity, love, and peace. According to one authority, "Whipper's preoccupation with moral reform became more evident at the 1832 convention, in which he played a large role. He secured the unanimous adoption of a resolution: 'That the Convention recommend to the people of color throughout the United States, the discontinuance of public processions on any day. We considering them highly prejudicial to our interests as a people.'"[31] Another of his resolutions recommending "the formation of societies for the promotion of Temperance, on the plan of total abstinence from the use of ardent spirits" was also adopted.[32] Whipper exercised influence in the early Negro convention movement. The eventual formation of the American Moral Reform Society in 1835 signaled the triumph of his ideas and values and a testimony to his influence within the convention movement.[33] For the next decade, he propagated the Society's guiding principles, which included the advancement of temperance, economy, moral virtue, thrift, and the universal brotherhood and sisterhood of humankind. Perhaps most significantly, these values and principles clearly underline situational deficiencies (condition), rather than color (race), as the underlying dynamics of the black experience. Whipper's universalism offended those who wanted the color line clearly drawn. The representative of the *Colored American* to the First Annual Moral Reform Convention in Philadelphia condemned universalism in favor of racially exclusive strategies.[34] Although the paper advocated a narrowing of the focus of the black struggle, it, too, accepted the notion that condition, not color, was responsible for black degradation.[35] Late in 1837 Whipper ran a series on "Non-violence to Offensive Aggression," where he argued, among others, that violence was ungodly. He literarily asked blacks to turn the other cheek rather than respond violently to any acts of aggression.[36]

These are the men into whose circle Delany entered in the 1830s. Some were from wealthy backgrounds. Others had to work their way up from poverty. They all belonged to the emerging black middle class and shared a common conviction in the potency of the economically self-made individual. They considered business knowledge and enterprise as the solution to black poverty. They also strongly believed in the necessity for moral and character reforms. Their voices, visions, and strategies were fundamentally integrationist and conservative. But there was a certain radical dimension to their goal—they all sought the transformation of blacks into full-fledged American citizens. To achieve this, however, they invoked standard American middle-class values and strategies. These were the men whose lifestyles, ideas, and values influenced Delany. It was among them that he came across the *Liberator* and David Walker's *Appeal To the Colored Citizens of the World*, documents that inspired and reinforced his abolitionist inclinations, and, very soon, he found himself in the web of the reform initiatives.

Barely a year after he arrived in Pittsburgh, Delany participated in a meeting chaired by John Vashon, with Rev. Woodson as secretary. They convened to discuss the denial of educational access to blacks and decided to create the African Education Society of Pittsburgh, whose objective was to provide education for blacks.[37] As already indicated, Delany's own education began under the tutelage of Woodson at the Cellar School. When he outgrew this school, Delany concentrated on independent efforts with other youths. He helped found the Theban Literary Society for improvement in the literary and intellectual endeavors of blacks. By 1834 he was an active member of the Pittsburgh moral suasion reform efforts, secretary of the Temperance Society of the People of Color of Pittsburgh, and a founding member of the Young Men's Moral Reform Society of Pittsburgh.[38]

The black community and struggle that Delany embraced in the 1830s, therefore, did not really draw the racial/ethnic line. Though drawn together by shared experiences of deprivation and subordination, these blacks, many of them fugitives and migrants from other states, subscribed to the mainstream Protestant work ethic and middle-class values. Lewis Woodson and John Vashon ran successful barber establishments. "Daddy" Ben Richard became wealthy as a butcher and real estate agent. William Whipper ran a lucrative lumber business and also owned a fleet of streetcars. These men had all attained some measure of economic power through sheer personal efforts and believed very strongly that others could do the same. A certain faith in the flexibility and openness of Jacksonian society shaped their ideological outlooks. They manifested optimism, convinced that through hard work and perseverance blacks would ultimately attain the moral capacity to induce positive reforms. Therefore, they did not see the need for racially exclusive and antagonistic reform strategies. In fact, they welcomed several whites—including Rev. S. S. Jocelyn, William Lloyd Garrison, Arthur Tappan, and Benjamin Lundy—to the first Annual Negro Convention of 1831 in Philadelphia. As already suggested, many leading blacks had links with Garrison's American Anti-Slavery Society and shared his enduring faith in moral suasion.

The adoption of moral suasion by leading blacks such as Whipper and Woodson underscored their acceptance of biracial reform strategy. Implicit in moral suasion is the identification of situational deficiency (that is, condition), rather than racial intolerance (racism) as the more critical reason blacks were disadvantaged. Change and improve the condition through industry, thrift, education, and moral reform (that is, temperance), many reasoned, and the walls of racism would come tumbling down. Faith in the potency of moral suasion, therefore, rendered racially exclusive reform strategies unnecessary. Whipper, perhaps the most forceful defender of moral suasion, insistently and persistently advocated the universal solidarity of humanity. In his judgment, the problems and challenges that blacks confronted were not racially determined; consequently, he assigned responsibility for dealing with the challenges and solving the problems to humanity in general.[39] Thus Whipper objected strongly to any solutions or strategies that tended to divide people along racial/ethnic lines. This belief in a monolithic humanity strengthened his optimism in the possibilities of Jacksonian society.

Delany's antislavery career, therefore, took shape in an environment strongly infused with universalistic and integrative ideological values. That he learned his lessons well became apparent as he assumed a more active role in antislavery activities. He began by becoming fully involved in the many activities organized by blacks in Pennsylvania to advance the cause of moral elevation through education, industry, temperance, and self-reliance. As a resident of Pittsburgh, he actively supported the efforts of local blacks to generate community support for moral improvement. He began his short-lived newspaper, the *Mystery*, in 1843. The twin objectives of the paper were to expose and condemn the evils of slavery and racism, and to enlighten blacks on the "Mystery" of their condition—that is, means of elevation. Only two copies of the paper exist. Subscriptions sold for $1.50 a year, and the initial issues sold over a thousand copies in Pittsburgh alone. Delany had agents in twenty-seven towns and cities of Pennsylvania. He had eighteen repre- sentatives in Ohio and five each in Indiana, Massachusetts, New York, and Illinois. He also had agents in Virginia and Iowa. Delany undertook periodic lecture tours to promote the paper. The *Mystery* became a potent antislavery medium, and it won the admiration and support of the black communities of Pennsylvania.[40] Delany advocated adherence to the prevailing middle-class values of the dominant society—hard work, thrift, and temperance. His solution betrayed faith in mainstream moral suasionist doctrine and the belief that a change in the condition of blacks was all that mattered.

It was, however, his collaboration with Frederick Douglass in co-editing the *North Star* from 1847–1849 that catapulted Delany to prominence as a national crusader for moral suasion—an integrative posture. Douglass arrived in Pittsburgh in 1846 and solicited the help of Delany in starting his paper, the *North Star*. Delany agreed and relocated to Rochester, New York, and became co-editor and roving lecturer for the paper. In the capacity of roving lecturer, he had to travel to free black communities in the North to organize meetings and deliver anti- slavery lectures and, most important, to inform blacks on the means to elevation and integration.

Delany's objective, as he repeatedly declared, was to educate blacks on how to transform their wretched condition to one that would inspire the respect and admiration of whites and compel concessions of the rights and privileges of blacks. He traveled extensively through Northern free black communities unfurling the banners of antislavery and moral suasion. He neither defined nor presented black problems in racial/ethnic terms that would have suggested hostility toward, or alienation from, white liberals and abolitionists as agents of change. In fact, the desire to see blacks emulate mainstream values, especially materialism and capitalism, propelled his antislavery lectures.

One theme dominated his antislavery lectures as he journeyed through Pennsylvania, Ohio, Delaware, Michigan, and New York—the indispensability of moral suasion. Though he acknowledged, wherever possible, evidence of black industry (individual and collective), he was equally careful to underline the grim reality of mass poverty among blacks. In certain parts of Ohio, for example, he deplored the very low level of economic wealth among black residents, a condition he attributed to the neglect of capitalism. Blacks were simply not subscribing to the spirit of the age—capitalism.[41] He presented wealth accumulation and industry as the potent factors that would lead blacks to economic independence and eventual integration into American society. He also found disheartening situations in Wilmington, Delaware. Though a majority of the 2,000 colored citizens appeared to be "quite and industrious and laboring people," they remained ill-adapted to "the higher incentives of life" and continued to exhibit slavish characteristics.[42] However, in parts of Columbus, Cincinnati, and Chillicothe, Ohio, and in black communities in other states, Delany witnessed ample evidence of black industry. He encountered several black carpenters, bricklayers, shoemakers, painters, and realtors. Some black business establishments even had white employees. He applauded this development, because it signified the ultimate potentiality of moral suasion—racial cooperation and harmony.[43] What we see here is Delany's subscription to, and search for, black integration in classic American middle-class values. In his lectures, Delany offered philosophical explanations for what he characterized as the "objectionable relations" existing between blacks and whites. He attributed white dominance largely to their cultivation of the habits of industry and economy, and he offered these same values to blacks for emulation.[44]

His moral suasion lectures focused on what he identified as the key question—"What shall we do to better our condition?" His answer was simple—industry, that is, the accumulation of wealth, the attainment of economic power through trade, commerce, and agriculture.[45] "Our people must become mechanics and farmers—producers instead of consumers, if we ever expect to be elevated on a level with those who now predominate and rule over us," he insisted.[46] Just as his ideological mentor Rev. Woodson had earlier done, Delany suggested that abundant opportunities existed for industrious and enterprising among blacks. "Go, brethren," he urged, "go, young men and women, to the level lands of the West—go to the beautiful plains of Michigan, Iowa or Wisconsin, lands in themselves, promised by God and blessed of heaven—lands which now lie suffering for the healing hand of the skillful cultivator."[47] He dismissed as absurd the notion of "prejudice against color" (racism). What blacks perceived as prejudice against color was in reality, he argued, "prejudice against condition."[48] Change the condition and prejudices would cease. As he opined,

> You can scarcely imagine the effect it would have over the pro-slavery feeling in this slave holding country, if, in addition to the few business men we have, there were in New York city, Philadelphia, Boston, even Baltimore, Richmond, Norfolk, Washington city, and all other ports of entry where colored men are permitted to trade, and Buffalo (which has one colored mercantile house), Cleveland, Detroit (which has another), Milwaukee, Chicago, Cincinnati, and Pittsburgh, and many other places, but one shipping house, wholesaler or retail store, the proprietor or proprietors or which were colored men, and one extensive mechanic of any description and trade. Such indisputable evidence as this of the enterprise and industry of the colored man, compared with that of the white, would not admit of controversy. It would bear with it truths as evident as self-existence—truths placed beyond the shadow of a doubt.[49]

The belief that industry and moral purity would undermine racism was pervasive among leading blacks of Delany's generation, Frederick Douglass included. Delany's antislavery lectures were, therefore, double-edged swords. Though in his criticisms of slavery he accused the white establishment of responsibility for the wretchedness of blacks, he equally blamed blacks for being oftentimes unconscious accomplices in the making of this wretchedness.

Delany attributed black culpability largely to religion and ignorance. Years of enslavement exposed blacks to certain "egregious errors"— values that were both emotionally and psychologically crippling and self-abnegating. The source of these errors was a certain theological indoctrination designed specifically to discourage any consciousness of self-determination. Slavocrats, according to him, taught blacks that slavery and segregation were divinely instituted and that there was little anyone could do to change the existing situation. The black religious leadership swallowed this fallacy hook, line, and sinker and encouraged blacks to endure their earthly pains like stoics. This earthly suffering was considered the stepping-stone to the kingdom of God.[50] He ridiculed the notion of "standing still" for the salvation of God or waiting prayerfully for the heavenly kingdom. This was, in his judgment, a misleading and "false impression made by erroneous religious doctrines at the instigation of our oppressors, and continued by us through ignorance."[51] He urged blacks to abandon this debilitating religious worldview for one that focused their attention on the injustices of the world and how to work actively toward eradicating them.[52] In this, he encountered the hostility of many black churches and religious leaders, who viewed his materialist conceptualization of moral suasion as too this-worldly and potentially distractive to the religious duties and responsibilities of blacks.[53]

The black church, therefore, did not stand solidly behind the anti-slavery cause. Delany experienced difficulty, at times open hostility, in attempts to elicit church endorsement of his antislavery crusade. He was simply shut out of several black church premises. His requests for permission to use church facilities for antislavery lectures were turned down in several places in Pennsylvania, Ohio, Delaware, and Michigan. For example, there were about ninety-six black churches in the suburbs of Pittsburgh and Allegheny, yet blacks in these areas manifested very little antislavery consciousness, due largely to the opposition of the church elders and their refusal to commit church facilities to functions other than purely religious ones.[54] He received mixed reactions in Ohio. Two of the leading black churches in Hanover, the Methodist and the Disciples, accused Delany of "infidelity" because of his anti-slavery lectures and shut him out of their premises. The only exception was the Colored Presbyterian Church, which hosted his meeting.[55] In Chillicothe, he held meetings in private homes, as the leading churches—the African Methodist Episcopal (AME), the Baptist, and the

Methodist—all opposed his mission. He encountered similar opposition in Columbus, New Lisbon, and Springfield. In Cincinnati, the Fifth Street Congregational Church, the Union Baptist Church, and the Harrison Street Baptist Church all gladly hosted his lectures. However, an incident in the Boyinston's Church in Cincinnati illustrates the dilemma of several black churches. An antislavery man, Rev. Boyinston welcomed Delany to his congregation. In spite of a slight illness, Delany delivered a powerful denunciation of slavery and urged blacks to strive for elevation through moral suasion. Due to the tremendous interest the lecture generated, Delany sought and secured approval from the reverend for two additional lectures, to which the trustees of the church objected on the grounds that his earlier lecture was antislavery and too "liberal." This was also true of the Universalist Church and the True Wesleyan Church in Dayton and the African Methodist Episcopal Church in Milton.[56] In Wilmington, Delaware, Delany was warmly received by two "liberal" pastors and churches, Rev. Abram Cole of the Wesley Church and Rev. Smith of the Bethel Church.[57] In Detroit, he had access to the facilities of the Baptist, the Presbyterian, and the Episcopal churches. However, the largest, and most influential colored church, the Methodist, turned him away, the pastor condemning "every manner of moral improvement."[58]

Many black churches opposed moral suasion due to its propagation of materialism and capitalism—values that, in the judgment of the church leaders, unnecessarily interfered with the obligations of the people to God and to the heavenly kingdom. As Delany found out, the heavenly kingdom was much valued and sought after and thus acquired priority over the injustices and inequities of the earthly kingdom.[59] Blacks were encouraged to "seek first the kingdom of God and all else would follow" (that is, to turn their minds and attention away from the earthly injustices and oppressions they experienced and hope for a better world beyond) and to "stand still and see the salvation of God."[60] Thus, instead of a this-worldly disposition that could have transformed blacks into active agents of change and the economic rivals of whites, they turned otherworldly, entrusting their fate to providential determinism.[61] Religion became the opiate of blacks. Consequently, while whites aggressively sought capital and material wealth (to consolidate their dominance), Delany contended, blacks handcuffed themselves to a false and dubious religious consciousness. As he observed:

> The Colored races are highly susceptible to religion; it is a constituent principle of their nature. . . . But unfortunately for them, they carry it too far. They usually stand still—hope in God, and really expect him to do that for them, which it is necessary they should do for themselves. . . . We must know God, that is understand his nature and purposes, in order to serve him; and to serve him well, is but to know him rightly. To depend for assistance upon God, is a duty and right; but to know when, how and what manner to obtain it, is the key to this great bulwark of strength, and depository of aid.[62]

Further underscoring this point, he observed, "There are no people more religious in this country than the colored people, and none so poor and miserable as they. That prosperity and wealth, smile upon the efforts of wicked white men, whom we know to utter the name of God with curses, instead of praises."[63]

In Delany's judgment, therefore, blacks were held down by a false and misguided religious consciousness inspired by the proslavery establishment to lure blacks into a fatalistic disposition that enabled whites to consolidate their dominance while strengthening black poverty and subordination. He offered blacks a more liberating version of Christianity that was compatible with a this-worldly occupation and orientation. Blacks should not only seek the heavenly kingdom but also the earthly. He offered his "political economy" doctrine as a major key to the earthly kingdom. This doctrine taught blacks knowledge of how wealth is created and maintained. In his judgment, blacks needed this knowledge in order to "live in this world."[64] This is the reason why he emphasized practical education, education that would train blacks how to create and retain wealth, how to be productive.[65] For example, in some parts of Ohio and in Harrisburg, Pennsylvania, Delany observed that blacks experienced difficulty holding on permanently to wealth and profits. No sooner had they created wealth than they lost it to whites.[66] Training blacks how to create and hold on permanently to wealth became crucial aspects of his lectures on "political economy" and advocacy of practical education.

There was also a certain functionalist dimension to Delany's conception of society. He defined society as a social institution regulated by certain universal precepts, the most fundamental being, "There is no equality of persons, where there is not an equality of attainments."[67] This dictum represented Delany's iron law of social relations. It imposes on members of society certain obligations deemed indispensable to the flowering of such societal values as freedom, equality, and overall societal development. It also tied equality to attainment (that is, accomplishments measured in productive and material terms). Industry becomes a fundamental engine of societal growth, a growth that is measured in both ideological and material terms. For society to function effectively, therefore, every member must be industrious and contribute equally to overall societal growth.[68] He applied this paradigm to the relationship between blacks and whites and declared that by virtue of living in one country, both were in effect involved in a contractual relationship for mutual progress.[69] He attributed white elevation and dominance to the accumulation of capital and wealth through industry. He found blacks to be miserably deficient in this regard. Not that there were no industrious blacks. There were. But in Delany's estimation, they constituted a minority. The majority seemed more inclined toward menial and degrading occupations, as barbers, maids, house servants, and cooks—completely surrendering to whites' monopoly of such self-enhancing occupations as the mechanical arts, trade, and farming.[70] As he underscored:

> Until colored men, attain to a position above permitting their mothers, sisters, wives, and daughters, to do the drudgery and menial offices of other men's wives and daughters; it is useless, it is nonsense, it is pitiable mockery, to talk about equality and elevation in society. The world is looking upon us, with feelings of commiseration, sorrow, and contempt. We scarcely deserve sympathy, if we peremptorily refuse advice, bearing upon our elevation.[71]

Delany thus admonished blacks to move beyond menial occupations into the mechanical trades, farming, and mercantile and professional businesses. Besides just entering these occupations, he also suggested a sound and solid knowledge of business education, since deficiency in this critical field, in his judgment, had largely been responsible for the failure of most black business enterprises. As he emphasized, "If, as before stated, a knowledge of all the various business enterprises, trades, professions, and sciences, is necessary for the elevation of the white, a knowledge of them also is necessary for the elevation of the colored man; and he cannot be elevated without them."[72] In unambiguous terms, he praised whites for observing their part of the contract through capitalistic and materialistic ventures that had contributed to the development and advancement of society and had earned them a well-deserved elevated status. Blacks, on the other hand, looked to heaven, satisfied with a subordinate posture, and, as a consequence, denied themselves any legitimate claim to equality with whites.[73] As he declared: "White men are producers, we are consumers. They build houses and we rent them. They manufacture clothes and wares and we garnish ourselves with them. They build coaches, vessels, cars, hotels and we deliberately wait until they have got them in readiness, then [we] walk in as though the whole thing was bought by, paid for, and belong to us."[74]

Blacks, therefore, decidedly assumed a parasitic posture in what should otherwise have been a symbiotic relationship. Even on the issue of racial tension and the volatility of the relationship between the two races, he was not convinced that blacks were absolutely blameless. In Cincinnati, for instance, he found whites "in the main . . . kind and courteous," and the principal cause of the tension between the two races was the failure of the "colored themselves [to take] advantage of the opportunities they have of being sociable with them" (that is, whites).[75]

Believing that racism was the result of the degraded condition of blacks, Delany advised blacks to strive hard to improve their condition as a prelude to elevation. Black elevation depended on economic development, education, moral uplift, and thrift. He urged blacks to seek real estate, to enter agriculture and general business, and not to confine themselves to menial occupations. He emphasized the theme of self-reliance and self-exertion. Eyewitnesses to his lectures confirm that Delany repeatedly advanced "self-exertion" as "the mainstream of human development." He especially stressed the need for practical education and implored blacks to train their children in industrial education.[76]

His ultimate vision was to see blacks become a race of producers rather than consumers. Collegiate education was fine, he argued, as long as it was not prioritized over practical or pursued to the extreme, for "too much of learning makes men mad."[77] Wherever he went, Delany set his eyes on three things: the level of economic development and enterprises among blacks, their moral condition, and their education. As already indicated, he found very encouraging situations in several places. Blacks were making efforts and strides in economics and business. But he wanted more, urging them not to relent but to intensify their efforts. The more capitalistic and entrepreneurial blacks became, the better. On balance, he found blacks to be generally behind in the critical area of economic development. In order to catch up with whites and become accepted and fully integrated, therefore, blacks had no choice but to demonstrate adherence to the tenets of his iron law of social relations.

The racial factor was very peripheral and inconspicuous in this early phase of Delany's antislavery career. In fact, blacks in general gave very little consideration to race in their construction of strategies for reform. The preeminence given condition led many blacks to focus attention on economic and material factors. In other words, Delany and leading blacks sought solutions to the problem of black impoverishment and subordination in the prevailing middle-class values of the dominant white society. Hence, during this opening phase of his career, he did not advocate any confrontational, militant, or counterestablishment strategies. His ideas, values, and strategies were deeply rooted in American traditions and values. He was not alone. Whatever Delany said reflected the dominant ideologies of the leading blacks of his time. He was only a vehicle for the articulation and propagation of those ideas. When he joined the *North Star*, Delany saw it as the means for propagating the answer to the question of import, "What shall we [that is, blacks] do to better our condition?" The paper became the means of unraveling the "Mystery" of the black condition. On several occasions in his lectures and tours, he was joined by Henry H. Garnet, Charles L. Remond, Abraham D. Shadd, William Wells Brown, and other notable blacks, all assisting in this task of laying a solid foundation for black integration.

Although Delany condemned slavery and oppression and assumed leadership of the black struggle, he never hesitated to apportion blame to blacks for their disabilities. Though he saw himself, as he did other blacks, as American, entitled to the same rights and privileges as whites, he nevertheless insisted that blacks should be measured against the same standard as whites and held equally accountable should they fail to maintain this standard. He admired, and had strong faith in, mainstream values and held those values up for emulation by blacks.

During this early stage, Delany had not developed that combative, ethnocentric quality that he has intimately been identified with. Though struggling on behalf of blacks, he had yet to assume an uncompromisingly hostile disposition toward whites. He presented blacks simply as disadvantaged Americans who were, unfortunately, equally implicated in the very circumstances of their predicaments and who must perforce embrace white support, and appropriate mainstream values, in order to become elevated. He saw neither himself nor blacks in general as superior in any respect to whites, his strong racial pride notwithstanding. On the contrary, he seemed at times willing to concede white superiority in economic, social, and political affairs, while emphatically denying any claims of physical or genetic superiority over blacks. In essence, he ascribed white superiority to material and circumstantial factors, a situation for which he held blacks partly responsible.

At this early stage, ethnicity functioned as a double-edged sword. On the one hand, Delany exhibited racial pride and dignity and forcefully championed the cause of black freedom, a posture that evoked strong ethnocentric reactions from blacks as exemplified by John Gaines's glowing tributes. Delany, however, did not always see himself as antiestablishment and struck hard at blacks for their apathy and for their ignorance of and alienation from the positive dimensions of mainstream white society. In this first phase of Delany's career, we clearly see the enduring influences of the prevailing universalistic ethos of his times. He reflected the hope, optimism, and faith that his intellectual and ideological mentors and colleagues manifested in the perfectibility of the American order. He shared their belief in the inherent progressive and democratic character of American political traditions and culture as enshrined in the Constitution and the Declaration, and like many of his contemporaries, Delany attributed societal imbalances and dysfunctions to the moral failures of individuals who had corrupted and undermined what was otherwise meant to be a democratic political culture. He found the solution in appeals to the moral conscience of the nation through exposing the evils of slavery and by educating blacks on the best strategies of dealing with the "Mystery" of their predicament through education, industry, economy, character reform, and temperance. As a firm believer in all of these, he assumed the responsibility of a vehicle for propagating the ideas and helping bring about change. His admonitions to blacks to assume a direct role in their elevation through self-help reflected his subscription to early-nineteenth-century faith in individuals as agents of change—a basic philosophical underpinning of the evangelical movement and of the Second Great Awakening. The reform impulses of the era seemed to have convinced blacks of the irrelevance of race, believing that what seemed like racism and racial intolerance were indeed manifestations of negative reactions to deficiencies in the condition of blacks and flaws in their moral character.

While Delany was struggling to uphold a biracial and integrative strategy, however, white power and dominance were being manifested in ways too distasteful and ominous to ignore. The white society he urged blacks to emulate was, in fact, moving in ways that undermined the very rationale for his optimistic and integrative solutions and strategies. It started even before his departure from the *North Star*. Moral suasion failed to revolutionize society. The more blacks attempted to conquer poverty and attain moral elevation, the more they seemed to provoke violent reactions from whites. None was more vulnerable than Delany, whose moral suasionist crusade taught blacks to seek immediate outlets from poverty and degradation and thus threatened the racial and social status quo. It was in the small Ohio village of Marseilles that he and Charles Langston were confronted by a hostile and violent mob as they prepared to host antislavery meetings. They narrowly escaped being tarred and feathered by the angry mob chanting "darkey burlesques," "burn them alive, kill the niggers! They shall never leave this place."[78] Pennsylvania in the 1830s and 1840s witnessed outbursts of antiblack violence aimed specifically at black businesses and institutions. Property and buildings were destroyed. The level and extent of violence led some to declare Philadelphia the "race riot capital of the country, if not the world."[79] The intensity of this violence, in such "free" black havens as New York, Ohio, and Pennsylvania, must have turned many blacks and black institutions away from antislavery to providential determinism. Even the antimoral suasionists were not immune from the violence. A leading opponent of moral suasion in Philadelphia was Rev. Stephen Gloucester, whose "zealous opposition to 'anti-slavery' " was almost legendary.[80] His religious zeal and opposition to moral suasion could not shield him. A founding member of the American and Foreign Anti-Slavery Society, Gloucester had come face-to-face with antiblack violence and had paid severely. He and his congregation lost their church, the Second Colored Presbyterian Church, in the two-day Meyamensing riots of 1842 in Philadelphia.[81] A native Philadelphian, Charles Godfrey Leland acknowledged the prevailing culture of violence when he observed: "whoever shall write a history of Philadelphia from the Thirties to the era of the Fifties will record a popular period of turbulence and outrages so extensive as to now appear almost incredible. These were so great as to cause grave doubts in my mind whether the severest despotism, guided by justice, would not have been preferable to such republican license as then prevailed in the city of Penn."[82]

The legal system offered very little comfort, if any, to blacks. This development resulted in a radical redefinition of the cause and course of the black struggle. Racial and ethnocentric consciousness assumed dominance as blacks realized the depth and pervasiveness of racism. Leading blacks, including Delany, convened in Harrisburg, Pennsylvania, at a state convention in December 1848 to demand political rights, underscoring declining faith in moral suasion.[83] Each delegate was taxed one dollar per annum for the establishment of a political newspaper to be called *Campaigns*, which would be issued every year during elections and the session of the legislature "for the purpose of agitating the great question of enfranchisement and political rights of the colored free men of Pennsylvania."[84] Delany later joined a delegation led by John Vashon and Robert Purvis to the state governor, William M. Johnson. Purvis impressed on the governor the determination of blacks to become, "participants in all the privileges enjoyed by others."[85] On the last day of the convention, the delegates unanimously agreed that blacks suffered discrimination largely because of "complexional intolerance" rather than "conditional basis." Consequently, they deemed it useless for blacks to continue to adhere to the doctrine of "conditional elevation before equality." They had come to the conclusion that no amount of social, economic, and intellectual efforts and achievements would ever win equality for blacks.[86] Black Pennsylvanians thus rejected the basic philosophical rationale of the moral and self-efforts movement of the era, which assumed that prejudices were the result of the degraded conditions of blacks and, consequently, that they would cease in proportion to how blacks improved themselves. The experience of these black Pennsylvanians, and of blacks generally, showed something different. White prejudices deliberately created those degraded conditions as means of justifying black subordination. Significantly, the very same black leaders who spearheaded the movement for moral reform and self-efforts, after years of repeated frustration, realized how incompatible black freedom was with American herrenvolk democracy.[87] From a strategic point of view, the most critical outcome of this convention was the declaration that "complexional intolerance" and not "conditional deficiency" was the root cause of black problems.[88] The delegates declared unequivocally,

> The barriers that deprive us of the rights which you enjoy find no palliative in merit—no consolation in piety—no hope in intellectual and moral pursuits—no reward in industry and enterprise. Our ships may fill every port . . . our commerce float on every sea . . . we may exhaust our midnight lamps in the prosecution of study . . . yet with all these exalted virtues we could not possess the privileges you enjoy—because we are not *white*.[89]

The delegates thus repudiated the doctrine of "conditional elevation before equality." Perhaps no reversal of position was more indicative of the failure of the central ethos of moral suasion than that of William Whipper himself in the last issue of the *National Reformer*, the official journal of the American Moral Reform Society, of which he was editor: "We have been advocates of the doctrine that we must be 'elevated' before we could expect to enjoy the privileges of American citizenship, we now utterly discard it, and ask pardon for our former errors."[90] He now came to the realization that it was not condition but complexion that had deprived blacks of equal treatment. No amount of religious, moral, or intellectual accomplishments and endeavors would positively impact the condition of blacks precisely because of their color. Whipper viewed the earlier emphasis on improving condition before elevation as an acknowledgment of inferiority.[91] Delany shared the frustrations of black Pennsylvanians. The *North Star* project had exposed him to certain realities of the black community. He discovered, contrary to prevailing racist assumptions, that blacks were not generally docile and indolent. He found ample evidence of industry. Many blacks were striving to improve their condition, and they were succeeding. White America, however, refused to take cognizance of this. No matter the achievements of blacks, he concluded, the color of their skin had imprisoned blacks in the dungeon of white society. His personal experience illustrated this phenomenon perfectly. His voice, vision, and strategy threatened the status quo. He advocated fundamental changes in the established order. He urged blacks to outgrow their marginalized status, insisting that the values of the American Dream belonged as much to them as to whites. He commenced his moral suasion crusade with high hopes and enthusiasm but ended in despair.

As American racism crystallized into rigid orthodoxy, even in the face of obvious black economic, social, and moral improvements, Delany's conception of the black struggle also gradually ossified into a race consciousness. When Douglass wrote in the *North Star* of June 29, 1849, that "by a mutual understanding with our esteemed friend and coadjutor, M. R. Delany, the whole responsibility of editing and publishing the *North Star* will devolve upon myself," it was obvious to most observers that something was amiss.[92] Yet neither Delany nor Douglass provided any further clue as to the cause of the split. A biographer of Douglass suggested that the split resulted from Delany's inability to raise sufficient funds for the paper.[93] Though plausible, this does not adequately explain the separation. Throughout 1848, the tone of Douglass's letters to Delany suggested that the *North Star* was going through hard times. In a letter from Rochester dated January 12, 1848, Douglass complained that "subscribers come in slowly and I am doing all I can by lectures and letters to keep our heads above the water. Ohio does not respond in anything like the number which I had a right to expect." "Do all you can for us in Pittsburgh," he urged Delany. Douglass then reported that expenses far outran income and further urged Delany to "send on subscribers and money." A week later, Douglass acknowledged the receipt of $20 from Delany and complained again that subscriptions were still very small, adding, "the work is uphill just now, but I hope there is good time coming."[94] There was, however, nothing unique about this. Black journalism had always been a financially risky business. Both men were aware of this from the start. Consequently, their growing conflicting ideological responses to the America of the late 1840s was more central to the split. As already indicated, Delany had become disillusioned and frustrated by the failure of moral suasion.

Although, equally frustrated and disillusioned, Douglass would not give up on America. He held firmly to his integrationist ideals and intensified his attacks on colonizationists like Henry Clay. In a lengthy article, Douglass categorically rejected colonization and reaffirmed the determination of blacks to stay and fight. As he strongly insisted, "Humble as we are, degraded, imbruted and enslaved as we have been, if Henry Clay or anyone else should propose to remove us, he would have his insolence rebuked, and if he should force us, it would be force against force."[95] For Douglass, there was no going back. Blacks must realize their destiny in America.

Delany felt differently. He elevated ethnicity to the core of his thought in a scathing review of "American Civilization" published in the *North Star*. Inspired largely by negative personal experiences, the article observed a "fixed determination" by whites to undermine and destroy every vestige and semblance of humanity in blacks.[96] He described white Americans, adults and youths, as racists who held blacks in utter disrespect and contempt.[97] It is this alienated Delany, this angry and frustrated person who proceeded in the next decade to advocate emigration and black nationalist ideas, who became the subject of instrumentalist scholarship, to the neglect of almost all other significant aspects of his life. The next phase of his career, the nationalist and emigrationist, lasted for about a decade (1852–1862), during which he wrote and published extensively on the subject of emigration, underscoring the imperative of an independent black nationality abroad. Delany saw no hope in continued struggle for integration in the United States.

Developments in the 1850s reinforced his alienation and pessimism. The Fugitive Slave Law of 1850, the Kansas-Nebraska Act of 1854, and the *Dred Scott* decision of 1857 all convinced him of the existence of a national consensus on black inferiority and subordination and the imminent nationalization of slavery.[98] The Fugitive Slave Law was one of the most pernicious pieces of legislation in the annals of the black experience. It came as part of a package of compromises meant to diffuse the mounting sectional conflict over the admission of new states. It sought to strengthen slavery by facilitating the return of fugitives to their owners.[99] To thousands of free blacks, it spelled doom since it prima facie defined all blacks as potential fugitives. It confronted free blacks with either of two dreaded alternatives—reenslavement or colonization. Paradoxically, the law affected a coup de grâce on nonviolence. Increasingly convinced that safety lay in strength, many free blacks began seriously to consider violent alternatives. In various state conventions, free blacks emphasized their determination to resist both reenslavement and colonization.[100] Delany shared the dissatisfaction of other blacks. At a public meeting in Allegheny County, he vowed to resist the law till death. He reminded the audience that the right to resist tyranny was inherent to the American revolutionary tradition and pledged to resist the tyranny of the Fugitive Slave Law.[101] In fact, the conviction that slavery was sectional and racism national gave way, soon after the passage of the Fugitive Slave Law, to the growing conviction that slavery was moving inadvertently toward becoming a national institution, as evident in the capitulation of the federal government to proslavery interests.[102] The Fugitive Slave Law represented, for Delany, the ultimate indicator of the direction the nation was moving and, most significantly, of the pervasive and endemic character of racism. There was just no hope that whites, united as they seemed on black inferiority, would ever concede black rights and privileges. He voiced this belief strongly in a letter to Frederick Douglass in 1853, reacting to Douglass's solicitation of help from the white abolitionist Harriett Beecher Stowe. In this letter, he unambiguously declared his loss of faith in white liberals and predicted the ultimate nationalization of slavery.[103] As he argued,

> Mrs. Stowe . . . KNOWS NOTHING ABOUT US, . . . neither does any other white person—and consequently, can contrive no successful scheme for our elevation; it must be done by ourselves. . . . I shall not be surprised to see, at no distant day, a solemn convention called by the whites of the

North, to deliberate on the propriety of changing the whole policy to that of slave states. This will be the remedy to prevent dissolution; AND IT WILL COME, MARK THAT! Anything on the part of the American people to SAVE their UNION. Mark me—the non-slaveholding states will BECOME SLAVE STATES.[104]

Douglass, of course, responded, accusing Delany of being overly theoretical and not in touch with the realities of the black struggle, as well as being critical without offering any concrete solution. According to Douglass,

> To scornfully reject all aid from white friends, and denounce them as unworthy of our confidence, looks high and mighty enough on paper; but unless the background filled up with facts demonstrating our independence and self-sustaining power; of what use is such display of self-confidence? Brother Delany has worked long and hard—he has written vigorously, and spoken eloquently to colored people—beseeching them, in the name of liberty, and all the dearest interests of humanity to unite their energies, and to increase their activities in the work of their own elevation; yet where has his voice been heeded? And where is the practical result? Echo answers, where? Is not the field open? Why, then should any man object to the efforts of Mrs. Stowe, or anyone else, who is moved to do anything on our behalf? The assertion that Mrs. Stowe "knows nothing about us" shows that Bro. Delany knows nothing about Mrs. Stowe; for he certainly would not so violate his moral, or common sense if he did. When Brother Delany will submit any plan for benefiting the colored people, or will candidly criticize any plan already submitted, he will be heard with pleasure.[105]

Douglass then pledged, "Whoever will bring a straw's weight of influence to break the chains of our brother bondmen, or whisper one word of encouragement and sympathy to our proscribed race in the North, shall be welcomed by us to that philanthropic field of labor."[106]

By the 1850s, therefore, Delany had moved from an optimistic disposition to one of pessimism, induced by what he discerned as a global white conspiracy against blacks. What was happening in America, in his judgment, was just one aspect of this global conspiracy to keep blacks down permanently.[107] He sought solution in racial unity and the construction of an independent black nationality, powerful enough to combat this global threat.[108] Delany consequently spent the entire decade, 1852–1862, preoccupied with pursuing the realization of this nationality. His anger, frustration, and alienation are all reflected in his speeches and writings.[109] Emphasis on European conspiracy pushed Delany to the racial essentialist position that he advanced in his presidential address to the National Emigration Convention in Cleveland in 1854.[110] This is what many scholars erroneously project as the defining character of his entire nationalist ideology. Yet despite this racially defined and constructed scheme, he was never quite comfortable with or consistent on race. The entire nationalist and Pan-Africanist construct that he developed reflected this ambivalence. This notwithstanding, his anger was loud enough, his alienation clearly visible, his racial essentialist convictions loudly and militantly proclaimed as to distinguish him, even among his fellow emigrationists, as a racially driven and motivated black leader, reinforcing his perception as the quintessence of blackness and prompting Frederick Douglass to proclaim him "the intensest embodiment of African nationality." It is this racially defined and ideological personality that the activists of the 1960s, in search of validation and heroes in the past, embraced and extolled, to the almost total neglect and obliteration of his other personalities and dispositions. This is the most studied and popular phase of his career. It is the basis of the conception of Delany as a militant and uncompromising person. It is what informs definitions and conceptions of his legacy. This emigrationist phase has, however, been subjected to critical analysis in recent scholarship, revealing a much more complex phenomenon than represented in instrumentalist historiography.[111] It is important at this juncture to confront and analyze the next, perhaps most crucial but neglected phase of Delany's career—his second integrationist phase.

FOUR

Second Integrationist Phase
1863–1874

NOTHING IN DELANY'S perception of national politics in the 1850s had prepared him for the sectional conflict. His disillusionment began with the passage of the famous (or infamous) Fugitive Slave Law of 1850 and would deepen as the decade wore on. He denounced America as irredeemably racist and offered blacks a new direction and future in an independent black nationality in Africa. In his estimation, the Fugitive Slave Law itself constituted incontrovertible proof of the depth of racism, and most significantly, it revealed the true character of America as a whites-only nation that would never accept blacks as integral members. "By the provisions of this bill," he declared,

> The colored people of the United States are positively degraded beneath the level of the whites—are made liable at any time, in any place, and under all circumstances, to be arrested—and upon the claim of any white person, without the privilege, even of making a defense, sent into endless bondage. . . . We are slaves in the midst of freedom, waiting patiently, and unconcernedly—indifferently, and stupidly, for masters to come and lay claim to us, trusting to their generosity, whether or not they will own us and carry us into endless bondage.[1]

The Fugitive Slave Law, therefore, epitomized the essence of what Delany characterized as the "national compact"—a kind of contract

that served as the heart of the nation, sustained by a herrenvolk democratic ideal that guaranteed and nurtured the freedom and privileges of
whites, the subordination and exploitation of blacks, and the denial
of blacks' basic and fundamental rights. In other words, the national
compact required that in order for the liberties of one race (white) to be
protected and preserved, those of the other race (black) had to be sacrificed. It required a hegemonic social and political structure in which one
race is superimposed upon the other. According to him, the "basis of the
American Union" mandated the juxtaposition of freedom and slavery.
Indeed, slavery was indispensable to American national survival. Blacks
had to be kept perpetually in bondage. Conceding civil rights to blacks
under these circumstances would, in his judgment, "endanger the
national compact, as slavery was the basis of the Union."[2] He tendered
the Fugitive Slave Law in evidence to anyone who doubted his contentions. The law became, for Delany, the final nail in the coffin of the
integrationist dream. It conferred legality to the national pact—the heart
and soul of the nation, the basis of its survival and longevity. The compact thus made mockery of liberal and abolitionist ideas and schemes.

In essence, regardless of the liberal or abolitionist convictions of
whites, their progressivism ended at the point of intersection with the
national compact, that is, the point at which such values threatened
or jeopardized the compact. This explains his objection to Frederick
Douglass's solicitation of aid from the white abolitionist Harriet Beecher
Stowe, predicting that slavery would eventually become a national institution. Delany denounced white liberals as phony and deceptive. He
had completely given up on America and ridiculed those blacks who
manifested faith in white liberal assistance. "I would not give the counsel of one dozen INTELLIGENT COLORED freemen of the RIGHT
STAMP, for that of all the white and unsuitable colored persons in the
land," he declared.[3] He accused the entire nation of complicity in a conspiracy to subjugate blacks ad infinitum, a conspiracy that was nurtured
by a pervasive culture of white supremacy. He consequently grew disdainful of both the proslavery establishment and white liberals. In a
scathing review, he portrayed America as a society that was sharply
divided along racial lines, with one race, white, dominating and seeking
the perpetual domination of the other, black. Subsequent developments

such as the Kansas-Nebraska Act of 1854 and the *Dred Scott* decision of 1857 strengthened Delany's growing cynicism and distrust of whites. Convinced of the existence of a national consensus to enslave and subordinate blacks, he predicted that slavery would soon become a national institution as it spread its tentacles northward.[4]

The decade of 1852–1862, therefore, marked a turning point in Delany's life. Driven by frustration and alienation over what he saw as a pervasive and endemic culture of racism that had prevented blacks from achieving meaningful freedom and integration, he jettisoned the integrative aspirations and visions that had consumed his attention and passion for an alternative African nationality and identity. Throughout this decade, he articulated and propagated emigrationist, black nationalist, and Pan-Africanist ideas and schemes. In fact, the name "Delany" became synonymous with emigration and acquired the nationalist, Pan-Africanist, and antiestablishment reputation that many have since come to identify as exemplifying "the essential Delany."[5]

In 1852 he published his first major political tract in which he made a strong argument for emigration, contending that blacks would never be accorded their rights and privileges in the United States. He offered a solution in the establishment of an independent black nationality abroad.[6] Emigration was, however, unpopular among blacks. Emigrationists and colonizationists shared a common assumption—that racism was unconquerable. Colonizationists believed that innate inferiority rendered blacks totally unfit for civilized society. Blacks were deemed simply inassimilable into American society. Without realizing it, Delany's advocacy of emigration strongly tied him to the dreaded colonization scheme.

To most blacks, however, racism was neither invincible, nor were blacks innately inferior. As Douglass emphasized, "For blacks to accept emigration is to stab their own cause. Is to concede a point which every black man must die rather than yield—that is, that the prejudice and maladministration toward us are invincible to truths, invincible to combined and virtuous efforts for their overthrow."[7] Emigration came under attack in several black state conventions, attracting sympathy only in very few places. Blacks did not make any distinction between emigration and colonization, and they applied equal force against the two. Even in Delany's home state of Pennsylvania, the dominant mood was for blacks to "remain and fight" in the United States for as long as one black remained in bondage. For instance, in Sandy Lake, Mercer County, Pennsylvania, blacks resolved to "unhesitatingly and with the feelings of the greatest indignation oppose ANY and EVERY scheme of colonization."[8] Perhaps the most vicious attacks against Delany came from the Illinois convention of 1853. The delegates accused him of advocating disunion, a scheme they considered fatal to the hopes and aspirations of blacks.[9] The nationwide opposition to emigration crystallized around Frederick Douglass, who did not believe that race was the essential underpinning of the black experience, as Delany seemed to suggest. If it were, Douglass argued, the slaves would equally have been detested by whites. It was not the slaves whom whites wanted to get rid of but the free blacks. The essential factor then, according to Douglass, was the socioeconomic aspirations of free blacks for self-determination and elevation.[10]

Undeterred by the widespread rejection and condemnation, Delany summoned a National Emigration Convention in Cleveland in August 1854, where he delivered perhaps one of the most stirring emigrationist speeches of the decade, which lasted almost four hours. Titled "Political Destiny of the Colored Race on the American Continent," the speech was a detailed and exhaustive account of the torturous and unrewarding saga of blacks in America, carefully underlining the futility of integration. He closed with the offer of emigration as the only viable option left if blacks were to become elevated and realize their potentialities as human beings.[11]

Delany was appointed chair of a National Board of Commissioners established by the Cleveland convention delegates to promote the emigrationist cause. His focus and interests turned abroad, first to Canada and then to Africa, in search of a more conducive environment for black elevation. He relocated to Chatham, Canada West, in 1855 and for the next two years campaigned vigorously for emigration. One year after the Cleveland convention, Delany's pessimism seemed to have strengthened. In his annual presidential report to the Board of Commissioners, he strongly condemned his integrationist opponents for their myopia in failing to perceive the dangers of white liberalism.[12] He presented a gloomy analysis of the federal and state constitutions, concluding that no fundamental differences existed between so-called free and slave states. They all shared a common feature—racism. He insisted that no state in the entire American nation recognized and protected the rights and privileges of blacks. Emigration remained the only viable option.[13]

There was no indication that the Board undertook any significant steps in the direction of emigration at this time. It expanded its scope, however, with the addition of two auxiliary boards, one for trade and the other for publication. The former was expected to oversee a new North American and West Indian Trading Association. The latter would publish a new journal, the *Afric-American Quarterly Repository*. Neither materialized.[14] Hemmed in and incapacitated by the antiemigrationist tide, members of the National Board sought a more supportive atmosphere abroad. In 1856 the Board moved its headquarters from Pittsburgh to Chatham, Canada West. As a terminus of the Underground Railroad, Chatham had developed a commercially viable and relatively prosperous black community. Although discrimination existed in Canada, the society was more permissive. Delany purchased a plot of land and settled his family. His antislavery reputation had preceded him and made his name a household one among the fugitives in Chatham. He quickly became active in local Kent County provincial politics. But local Kent politics was the least of his priorities. Developments in the United States concerned him much more, and what he saw only reinforced his pessimism.[15] In his second annual report to the Board, he observed a worldwide conspiracy involving Britain and the United States to exploit and subordinate blacks ad infinitum, and he reiterated his call for emigration.[16]

In 1858, accompanied by the West Indian Robert Campbell, Delany traveled to the Niger Valley of West Africa to explore and investigate the logistics and prospects of emigration. Both men spent the next eighteen months in Africa, gathering information on the resources—economic and human—for the projected independent black nationality. For Delany, the journey was both productive and satisfying, strengthening his optimism about the future prospect of the African nationality. It also reinforced his conviction that Africa possessed the resources for the development of a powerful black nation. It was, therefore, with a renewed and invigorated sense of determination that he returned to the United States late in 1860, just as the Civil War was beginning. He publicly proclaimed his intention to relocate permanently to Africa and immediately published his findings, launching a nationwide campaign to highlight the potentialities of the independent nationality and to encourage as many blacks as he could to emigrate with him.[17] He ignored the growing sectional controversies and focused attention on his nationwide lecture tour, highlighting information on the wealth and potentialities of Africa.

Delany's lectures blended in with the growing momentum generated by the colonization movement early in the war. As "liberal" opinion in the North suggested the inevitability of emancipation, colonization schemes of different sorts emerged. Few whites wanted a multiracial society.[18] President Lincoln initially coupled his emancipation plan with some project for colonizing freed blacks in Central America. In fact, Delany's "Political Destiny" was among the documents presented by apologists of colonization in the Thirty-seventh Congress.[19] The Haitian emigration scheme also generated some interest. After years of rejection by blacks, the American Colonization Society sponsored a movement called the African Civilization Society, which included several prominent blacks and professed to be antislavery. Delany condemned the Haitian movement, projecting his own African nationality scheme as more viable and realistic. He called upon black leaders of "highest intelligence" to meet and deliberate on the appropriate action to take in the wake of what he presented as a global Anglo-Saxon conspiracy against blacks.[20]

Curiously, Delany would neither return to Africa nor generate enough support and momentum for emigration among blacks. He soon found himself seduced by the promises of the Civil War and quickly returned to his cherished integrationist aspirations. The nationalist phase of his career is, unfortunately, outside the scope of this study and has, in fact, been exhaustively studied and analyzed by several scholars.[21] However, it is worth noting that it is precisely this particular phase that formed the basis of the instrumentalist construction of Delany that has dominated and shaped scholarly, and popular, conceptions and interpretations of his life and struggle. Yet as vociferous, vocal, and articulate as he propagated emigration, the entire scheme, and its defining Africanist consciousness, inhered a certain fragility and shallowness. This became evident with the outbreak of the Civil War. This war, Delany would later admit, completely upstaged his emigration scheme, compelling the revision and abandonment of his earlier conception of America as irredeemably racist.

The Civil War thus transformed Delany's ideological convictions, pushing him from a position of extreme alienation (emigration) to that of extreme endearment (integration). The war was a turning point, cutting deep into the fabric of his emigration ideology, especially his entire "national compact" theory. The emancipation of blacks, the group upon whose subordination the stability of the compact rested, rendered his monolithic conception of whites problematic. As he acknowledged, "And, in the United States, by the late Civil war, slavery has become extinct, the blacks enfranchised, and the civil and political rights of the whole people acknowledged."[22] In place of the conspiratorial consensus he earlier described, he now envisioned a different American society plagued by internal divisions and conflicts over issues ranging from politics and economics to slavery. Realizing the depth of sectional discord over slavery and its implications for the future of blacks, he jettisoned emigration, projecting a utilitarian conception of the war. Regardless of the postulations of national politicians, for Delany and the majority of blacks, the Civil War was a conflict between two forces—freedom and oppression. His optimism restored, Delany joined the call for active black participation, describing the war as a welcome opportunity for blacks to deal a final crushing blow on slavery.

Lincoln's inaugural address had not given blacks much cause for optimism, since he promised to sustain slavery and the Fugitive Slave Law.[23] Delany, however, viewed Lincoln's policy more positively. In October 1861 he confided in President Mahan of Michigan College that the war had become part of his daily existence and that nothing short of full black participation would satisfy him.[24] He sought and secured an audience with President Lincoln and implored him to adopt emancipation as a war strategy and to authorize the enlistment of blacks into the Union Army. This measure, he assured Lincoln, would effectively cripple the rebellion.[25]

Lincoln was finally compelled by Delany's persistence and power of persuasion, and by the exigencies of the war, to approve the recruitment of blacks. In a letter of recommendation to E. M. Stanton, secretary of war, Lincoln urged him not to fail to have an interview "with this extraordinary and intelligent Blackman."[26] After a series of interviews with Stanton, Delany was commissioned a major of infantry and ordered to proceed to Charleston, South Carolina, and raise his black regiment (Corps D'Afrique) under General Rufus Saxton. To be the first black field major in the Union Army seemed like "a light illuminating, with a strange wild splendor, the hitherto dark pages of his people's history, heralding the glory of the future."[27] Delany urged black Charlestonians, and all blacks, to rally round the American flag, that it was the duty of every black man "to vindicate his manhood by becoming a soldier, and with his own stout arm to battle for the emancipation of his race."[28]

He was first assigned to assist in recruiting the 54th Massachusetts regiment. No sooner had this unit been filled than he was appointed agent to help recruit the heavy artillery in Rhode Island and Connecticut. His successes there earned him services elsewhere. Through the recommendation of a Rhode Island artillery officer, Delany got the greatest contract of all—state contractor for the western and southwestern states and territories. From his headquarters in Chicago, Delany launched a massive successful recruitment drive. Recruitment had become for him, "one of the measures in which the claims of the black man may be effectively recognized without seemingly infringing upon those of others."[29] He assisted in recruiting several other colored regiments, including the Connecticut Volunteers and the 102nd, 103rd, 104th, and 105th United States Colored Troops. His combat capacity was, however, never tested. The war ended before he could engage in active service.[30]

THE CONSERVATIVE REPUBLICAN

The war and subsequent Reconstruction gave blacks access to long-denied rights and privileges. On January 1, 1863, Lincoln issued the Emancipation Proclamation, which suddenly freed slaves in the rebellious states. Blacks hailed and celebrated emancipation with fanfare and thanksgiving.[31] But the struggle was far from over. The Proclamation did not free slaves in the border states, and blacks in the North continued to be discriminated against. In 1865 Congress passed the Thirteenth Amendment, formally abolishing slavery. Subsequent amendments—the Fourteenth and Fifteenth—extended citizenship and the franchise, respectively, to blacks, among many other provisions. On the crucial issue of citizenship, the Fourteenth Amendment states, "That all persons born in the United States and not subject to any foreign power . . . are hereby declared to be citizens of the United States; and such citizens, of every race and color, without regard to any previous condition of slavery or involuntary servitude . . . shall have the same right, in every State and Territory in the United States . . . and to full and equal benefit of all laws and proceedings for the security of person and property, as is enjoyed by white citizens."[32]

These developments persuaded Delany that blacks had become "an integral part and essential element in the body politic of the nation," signaling the end of the suspected national conspiracy.[33] The integration he had aspired and fought for seemed within the realm of possibility. It appeared achieved, even if imperfect. Delany's commissioning into the Union Army symbolized the acceptance and recognition that had long eluded him. Enlarging his own personal experience, Delany saw (or thought he saw) the dawn of a new and progressive age for blacks, obliterating any justification for racial animosity and with great prospects for racial harmony, if undisturbed by radical, premature, and irresponsible political demands.

Delany was undoubtedly aware of the limitations and fragility of the reforms of the Reconstruction era. Blacks had attained neither full integration nor equality with whites. Nonetheless, he discerned something "revolutionary" about the reforms. Almost overnight, the United States was transformed beyond his imagination. Few blacks had anticipated this degree of change. The reforms had significantly opened up immense opportunities for peacefully transforming the society. Delany saw a new age with great prospect for integration and racial harmony. Consequently, he portrayed the reforms as bridges across the racial boundaries. This inspired in him a strong desire for compromise. The stability of these bridges, and the success of integration, however, depended on the willingness of blacks to compromise. Delany consequently advocated unconditional pardon for, and reconciliation with, former slaveholders and ex-rebels, imploring blacks to harmonize with the former slave-holders, insisting that the interests and destinies of the two were inter-twined.[34] He quickly became resentful of the radical policies of the Republicans, contending that for Reconstruction to succeed, these poli-cies had to accommodate, rather than alienate, Southern whites. He repeatedly cautioned blacks against supporting radical policies that alien-ated Southern whites, preferring a policy of appeasement that, in his estimation, would permanently end racism.

Contributing to the ongoing debate over the implications of seces-sion, Delany defined secession as a political, rather than a territorial, act. The Southern states had not seceded territorially, he averred, an interpretation that mandated a moderate and reconciliatory Reconstruc-tion program. President Lincoln himself had once suggested that seces-sion was the actions of individuals and not the states, thus diminishing its political significance.[35] Advocates of this limited perception of seces-sion espoused a moderate Reconstruction program. It was his identi-fication with, and sympathy for, this group that prompted Delany's advocacy of unconditional pardon and amnesty for ex-Confederates. Though he acknowledged the federal government's right to define the terms of Reconstruction, Delany opposed punitive measures, prefer-ring a Reconstruction policy that emphasized compromise and recon-ciliation at the expense of the political objectives and goals of blacks.[36]

Furthermore, Delany's perception of white liberals (whom he once admired) and conservatives (whom he had castigated) underwent a rever-sal. He now came to trust the latter, while distrustful and disdainful of the former. Where other black leaders saw and sensed danger, Delany had cause for optimism. When other blacks advocated radical and res-olute responses to their problems, Delany counseled moderation and compromise. From the beginning of his postbellum career, therefore, Delany's ideas seemed tailor-made for controversy. This was especially true of his response to the political elevation of blacks. Whatever the shortcomings and limitations of the new reforms, in Delany's estima-tion, they represented fundamental stepping stones for future develop-ments. Consequently, he suggested a policy of reconciliation toward the South as the most desirable and effective way to solidify and develop the reforms. He believed that such a policy would appeal favorably to Southern whites. Delany wanted efforts concentrated on creating and nurturing a reconciliatory and compromising climate that would facilitate goodwill and cooperation between blacks and Southern whites. This cooperation would, in his estimation, enable blacks to gain a share of the economic resources and power of the state still under the control of the former slave owners.

Land ownership was, of course, a major source of economic power. From the onset of Reconstruction, therefore, Delany loudly and persistently called on blacks to seek economic power through the acquisition of land. He advocated land redistribution so as to enable blacks to acquire land and become independent farmers. In a fiery speech to a gathering of about 600 blacks and whites on St. Helena Island, South Carolina, he strongly urged blacks to seek land ownership.[37] Many blacks, in fact, acquired land in 1863 when abandoned lands were auctioned for nonpayment of U.S. direct taxes. After his muster from the army, Delany was reassigned as subassistant commissioner of the Bureau of Refugees Freedmen and Abandoned Lands (Freedmen's Bureau) and posted to Hilton Head Island, South Carolina, a position he held from 1865 to the demise of the Bureau in 1868. The Bureau had been established by an act of Congress on March 3, 1865. Its duties included the supervision and management of all abandoned lands and also the dispensation of all issues relating to freedmen and refuges. As a Bureau field agent, Delany defined his primary responsibility as that of enabling freedmen to achieve salutary results from their freedom. He started out uncompromisingly advocating land ownership for blacks. He strongly believed that blacks had earned their freedom in the war and consequently deserved adequate compensation in land grants.[38]

Delany began a series in the *Hilton Head New South* titled, "Prospects of the Freedmen of Hilton Head," in which he advocated land redistribution.[39] He presented philosophical rationalization for economic power under the rubric "political economy," a concept he first introduced early in 1849 in a series in the *North Star*. He gave two complementary definitions. First, he defined it as "[t]he science of the wealth of nations . . . practically the application of industry for the purpose of making money." Second, he simplified it thus, "Knowledge of the wealth of nations, or how to make money." Both definitions underscore the primacy of economic power.[40] Economic power came through industry— the ability to generate and accumulate wealth. He described land acquisition as the quickest and most viable source of economic power and strongly upheld the rights of blacks to the land. "Political economy must stand most prominent as the leading feature of Negro elevation," he insisted.[41] There was, however, little of "politics" in Delany's "political economy." The prime concept was "economy." Land ownership would enable blacks to generate and acquire wealth and ultimately win some measure of economic power and independence. The concept "political economy," therefore, encapsulates his strategy for a viable Reconstruction. It prioritizes economic power.

Delany considered the acquisition of economic power the most crucial of the challenges confronting blacks. In his speech to freedmen in St. Helena Island, he stressed the importance of land and industry, urging freedmen to, "Get up a community and get all the lands you can."[42] He envisioned the emergence of an independent black yeomanry, in pursuit of which he advocated a breakdown of the plantations and large-scale land redistribution. On the issue of land, he touched upon something dear to the hearts of freedmen. Land was one thing that most freedmen eagerly sought, and early Reconstruction policies raised their expectations with the establishment of the Freedmen's Bureau.[43]

Delany's Reconstruction ideology entailed blacks attaining economic power through the pacification and appeasement of the defeated Southerners. He believed that only a policy of reconciliation and compromise would induce, in reciprocity, concessions of economic benefits to blacks. He consequently began advocating unconditional pardon and amnesty for ex-Confederates, who, despite losing the war, remained a formidable economic force that blacks could not afford to alienate. The central question of his "political economy," therefore, was "Will the Negroes be able to obtain land by which to earn a livelihood?"[44] Earning a livelihood, however, entailed two complementary strategies. The first involved a breakdown of the plantations and redistribution of lands. Although at the expense of the old planter class, such a redistribution would benefit not only blacks but also the entire community through increased productivity.[45] "Political economy" became his strategy for effecting redistribution in a manner satisfactory to all parties. As he reasoned, "It is a great fact of political economy that a given amount of means divided among a greater number of persons, makes a wealthier community than the same amount held by a few."[46] The second component was "political conservatism"—the insistence that blacks adopt a less aggressive and less assertive course on matters of political rights and power. He believed that the pain and discomfort that local whites would experience in consequence of land redistribution would be more than compensated for by the adoption of a politically conservative course by blacks. For blacks, this entailed the complete surrendering of political power to whites.

The principle of a domestic "triple alliance" formed another component of Delany's "political economy." This was basically an economic construct aimed at effecting a partnership between Northern capitalists, Southern landowners, and black laborers. He offered this as the triadic foundation for a successful Reconstruction policy, and it emanated from his association of progress with cooperation between the three productive factors, each receiving adequate compensation. The success of the alliance would, he suggested, attract Northern capitalists to the South either to help finance land purchases by blacks or provide Southern planters with the capital to cultivate lands and to be able to hire black laborers in the process. The end result would be a three-way benefit to all. Delany presented this paradigm as the most potent framework for peace and reconciliation, and it became the basis of his Reconstruction policy.[47]

The experience of being accepted and elevated, coupled with the political reforms of the war and early Reconstruction, shaped Delany's renewed sense of optimism. These reforms, he opined, had already effected revolutionary changes in Southern society—slavery was gone, blacks had become citizens and enfranchised. These irreversible changes, in his view, had totally eliminated the need for a racially exclusive policy or program. He warned blacks against identifying with a racially exclusive and vindictive Republican Party program and urged them instead to court the friendship and goodwill of their former-enemies-now-turned-friends, with whom they supposedly shared a destiny.[48]

Although Delany's controversial conservative views derived partly from the changes that followed the war and Reconstruction and partly from his personal accomplishments, which, to him, became a measure of overall black success, there was also a strong element of pragmatism. The vicissitudes of the war and the political reforms of Reconstruction had not significantly undermined former slave owners. They remained economically dominant, albeit within a new economic dispensation. A firm believer in the supremacy of his "political economy" (that is, wealth accumulation), Delany exhorted blacks to pursue measures that would enhance their economic status. If blacks were to be effectively and meaningfully free as well as elevated, he intimated, they had to appease their former enemies and oppressors, who still controlled economic power. Necessity and prudence, therefore, dictated moderation toward, and reconciliation with, Southern whites. Delany was right in underlining the fragile and dependent economic status of blacks. In spite of the war and the political reforms of Reconstruction, many blacks remained dependent on their former slave owners for their livelihoods. In Charleston, a pivotal county, for example, more than 80,000 blacks, the overwhelming majority, depended on local whites (mostly Democrats and former slave masters) for employment.[49]

The success of land redistribution and the prospect for an independent black yeomanry, however, depended on the resolution of the land question. With the establishment of the Freedmen's Bureau, those abandoned lands in the Confederate states that had come under Union control would be assigned to each freedman/refugee at not more than forty acres, and they would be protected in the use of such land for up to three years at an annual rent not exceeding 6 percent of its value.[50] The task before the Bureau was formidable. It had to create a functional relationship between two inherently contradictory aspirations and visions—those of the freedmen for land ownership and independent economic status, against those of the planters and former slave masters for a reliable labor force, that is, a landless black underclass. Blacks did not make any secret of their desire for land as the foundation for consolidating freedom. "Forty acres and a mule" perfectly captured the dominant mood and desires among them. They favored a subdivision of the larger plantations into smaller units among themselves.[51]

The economic aspirations of blacks, however, conflicted with what some describe as the unrepentant chivalry of the average Southern planter/Confederate who was determined, as one critic put it, "to fight over politically the ground [he] had lost in battle."[52] What Southerners demanded, according to one authority, was a black agricultural proletariat, not an independent black yeomanry.[53] During the war, some degree of expropriation of lands took place through confiscatory taxation. Such lands were sold to freedmen at $1.25 per acre. Few freedmen benefited from this, as the bulk of the land went to Northern speculators and investors, who usually offered higher prices and then leased the lands to blacks at exorbitant prices.[54] Large-scale expropriation also took place in the Sea Islands of South Carolina as a result of Sherman's Field Order No. 15.

During General William Sherman's triumphant march through the Carolinas, large numbers of slaves who were seeking liberty swarmed to his column. To settle the fate of these slaves, he issued the field order, which set aside all of the Sea Islands from Charleston south, not already disposed of, and all of the abandoned rice fields along the rivers for a distance of thirty miles inland. Blacks settled here, and each family secured "possessory titles" to more than 40 acres, until Congress should provide a final solution. About 40,000 freedmen settled here under its proviso. By the end of the first summer of operation, the Bureau had about 800,000 acres of land and 5,000 pieces of town property under its control. These were leased to blacks for small rental fees or sold to them at any time within three years for a nominal price.[55]

Unfortunately, Delany's vision of an independent black yeoman would not materialize. Although the Bureau initially served as a framework for experimentation in black land ownership, the entire edifice soon collapsed under the weight of Southern opposition. Before blacks could effectively consolidate their new economic status, President Andrew Johnson, who succeeded Lincoln after Lincoln's assassination, issued his amnesty proclamation granting pardon to ex-Confederates, "with restoration of all rights of property, except as to slaves and except in cases of where legal proceedings have been instituted."[56] Many planters reclaimed their lands. Disposed freedmen were offered the option of contracting to work for the planters.

Overwhelmed with sorrow, many blacks threatened to leave the Sea Islands. Some vowed to resist restoration with violence. Nonetheless, backed by a government order, the Bureau proceeded with restoration. Ex-planters, however, demanded more than just the restoration of their lands. In addition, they wanted a reliable labor force. The task of the Bureau therefore became one of devising a scheme that would bring hitherto hostile forces together in a working relationship. This gave rise to the contract system. Many Southerners perceived the Bureau as an instrument of Republican despotism, attacking and vilifying its agents. In many localities, freedmen viewed Bureau supervised contracts as tailored to suit the interests of the planters. In sum, on both sides, the Bureau acquired the reputation of a negative institution. The situation was, however, different in Hilton Head. In his capacity as a Bureau agent, Delany had jurisdiction over some twenty-one government plantations. His role entailed creating a modus operandi between planters and freedmen that would keep the plantations working under the new dispensation of black freedom.

The Bureau became Delany's medium for realization of the vision enshrined in his "political economy." In the *Hilton Head New South* series, he reaffirmed his call for land redistribution and deconstructed prevailing notions of black indolence by highlighting black contributions to the development of the nation and carefully stressing the innate capacity and propensity of blacks for industry and their compatibility with American values.[57] He emphasized the centrality of blacks to Reconstruction and the development of the South. However, as the old planters regained their economic dominance, he came to the realization that his dream of an independent black yeomanry was just that, a dream. If blacks were to attain economic elevation, therefore, they had no choice but, as he had repeatedly urged, to seek compromise and reconciliation with their erstwhile oppressors. To do this, they needed to pursue a course that obliterated the mutual distrust and animosities of the past. Since blacks had no choice but to rent or lease lands from rich planters or even contract to work for them, Delany offered, as the most effective basis for constructing an economic relationship of mutual trust and dependence, his "triple alliance" system. He proceeded to apply the principle of equality embedded in his alliance to the contract system he devised for freedmen and planters in his jurisdiction. In addition, he also devised means of helping blacks save money through a cooperative system that enabled them to pool their resources together for better management.[58] Despite tremendous odds, he assisted many blacks in securing land at reasonable rates. Through his assistance, these blacks acquired landed property, albeit for a brief duration, since the continuation of restoration soon deprived many of their lands.

By the last year of his agency, there was a drastic reduction in the plantations under Delany's control and in the quantity of land owned by the freedmen under his jurisdiction.[59] This notwithstanding, he was satisfied that his triple alliance had worked. The mutual distrust and suspicion between planters and freedmen disappeared as both trooped to his office for contracts. News of his success reached official circles.[60] This was inevitable given that similar experiments had failed in almost all other Bureau districts. His superiors soon exploited his success. Disturbed over the unpopularity of the Bureau and the strained relationship between planters and freedmen, General Sickle, the assistant commissioner for South Carolina, summoned Delany to headquarters and assigned him to undertake a tour of the entire district on his behalf.[61] He placed troops at Delany's disposal, giving him all the powers of a commander. Delany toured Edisto Island, Port Royal, and the Sea Islands, visiting plantations and organizing meetings with representatives of planters and freedmen. In most places, he discovered that the refusal of freedmen to sign contracts was a major cause of friction. It was not unusual to find contracts drawn up that proclaimed the superiority of the planters. Most contracts, instead of spelling out mutual obligations and protection, simply sought to impose on blacks "discipline" and restrictions reminiscent of slavery. In such places, he simply offered his triple alliance and was readily accepted.[62]

The triple alliance system worked principally because it defined duties, responsibilities, and rights that applied equally to both parties. Planters accepted it because its provisions guaranteed them a dependable labor force. Freedmen complied with it because it guaranteed them a "just" return for their labor and safeguarded them from the hitherto unrestrained exploitation of the planters. It became the practice of the government to send Delany with a detachment of troops to pacify the situation, wherever there was news of insurrection or likely insurrection involving freedmen.[63] His "system" soon restored peace to the Sea Islands. An editorial of the *New South* observed "a continued improvement in the labor question in Hilton Head and neighborhood."[64] Freedmen were willing to work, and hundreds of them, along with planters, usually congregated at Delany's office to have contracts adjusted. The *New South* praised Delany's impartiality in the conduct of his office. "Our whole community is taking heart. One obstacle after another to thorough regeneration is being removed," it commented.[65]

Despite the obstacles against black land acquisition, therefore, his triple alliance succeeded in pacifying the Sea Islands and establishing a workable biracial mechanism. Ironically, his arrival in Hilton Head Island had initially caused a stir among the planters and even among some sympathetic whites. It should be noted, however, that the triple alliance was only triple in name. There were indeed only two principal actors in the alliance—black laborers and planters. The third critical partner—Northern capitalists and investors—was not involved at this time. Delany would later resurrect the triad in the early 1870s and would again not succeed in attracting Northern capital.

It should be noted that the equality implied in Delany's economic construct is rendered problematic by his social and political conservatism. In his overtures to whites, Delany made concessions that many blacks found disturbing and unsettling. Some concessions smacked of self-denigration and acknowledgment of black inferiority. This is unambiguously represented in an address in 1868 in which he advised blacks to accord whites "first choice and first place" and to concede white superiority, declaring, "we are not equal to our white friends in many ways. Not equal in general intelligence."[66] Publicly disavowing the need for social equality, he warned against attempts to enforce social interactions across racial lines, insisting that people should be left free to choose with whom they would associate.[67] In return for these concessions, Delany hoped, blacks would gain the goodwill of local whites, peace, and harmony—all of which he deemed indispensable for mutual progress—and a possible share of the economic power monopolized by whites. From the onset of his Reconstruction career, therefore, Delany condemned what he characterized as slavish adherence of blacks to a Republican Party radicalism that was propelling them along the path of confrontation with local whites and eventual destruction. He portrayed Republicans as selfish politicians who were more interested in advancing narrow political interests, conveniently exploiting black ignorance and gullibility in the process.

With the demise of the Bureau in 1868, the economic framework for Delany's experimentation in racial alliance disappeared. Consequently, he turned to active politics in South Carolina, entering the political arena, a vocal advocate of unconditional pardon and amnesty for former Confederates. Like other black leaders, he joined the Republican Party, regarded by blacks as the party of freedom; but unlike them, he came not as a Radical Republican, determined to pursue the promotion and consolidation of black political rights and power, but as a conservative Republican, opposed to the consolidation of such rights and power precisely because, in his judgment, they jeopardized the chances of compromise with conservatives in the state. He was undoubtedly driven by the conviction that he could translate the success of his economic cooperation into the political arena and effect the same kind of reconciliation and compromise that he had achieved in the Sea Islands. But the extension of his political economy doctrine to the political landscape portended problems, since it was essentially an economic construct that de-emphasized politics. Furthermore, its subordination of politics to economics suggested a politically conservative course, one that diametrically contradicted the prevailing orientation of the black political leadership and its ally, the Republican Party. The stage seemed set for conflict.

In the Sea Islands, Delany had only to contend with freedmen and planters, both of whom were united by the lure of economic fortune. In the political arena, however, he encountered black leaders and the Republican Party, both united by the desire to consolidate as much political power as possible. The aspirations of the black political leadership included political power and resources, which mandated strong ties with, and support for, the Republican Party, which had been responsible for opening up the political landscape to blacks. The extension of Delany's political economy construct to the state political arena, therefore, became problematic almost from the start, because it entered an arena that prioritized precisely what the construct de-emphasized—black political power. From the start, therefore, the political arena seemed too radically political and partisan to sustain the kind of alliance envisaged by Delany's "political economy" and "triple alliance" paradigms. If his scheme were to succeed, Delany had to reshape the political landscape to make it so attractive and conducive as to appeal favorably to conservative whites in control of the economic resources of the state. This would not be easy.

Delany's next major challenge, then, was applying his scheme statewide. For the system to succeed statewide, he believed, blacks must be willing to jettison radical political aspirations. But there were obstacles to his scheme, perhaps the most critical being the paradoxical context of black elevation. This paradox entailed juxtaposing the politics of black political rights and empowerment with the economics of black powerlessness—that is, the conferment of political rights and power on blacks in the context of their economic poverty or, more appropriately, in the context of their reliance upon their erstwhile masters for economic sustenance. Given this reality, Delany considered it imprudent for blacks to become politically adversarial to a class they relied upon for economic sustenance. In his judgment, although Radical Republicanism had the capacity to elevate blacks politically by giving them rights, it could not empower them in the more critical arena of economic power, which, due largely to presidential pardon and the failure of the Freedmen's Bureau to advance the dream of land redistribution, remained firmly under the control of former slave owners, a group that viewed black political power with resentment.

Despite failure to accomplish land redistribution, Delany believed that with cooperation between capitalists and land owners, black labor could still function productively to gain ultimately a credible share of the economic resources. The keys to this cooperation and share were the willingness of blacks to adopt a politically conservative course, on the one hand, and moderate and conciliatory policies on the part of the Republican Party, on the other. Given these prescriptions, Delany grew resentful of the existing scenario in which blacks, who were economically weak and in a state of dependence on local whites for livelihood, prioritized political rights and power, choices that only further alienated them from the very people in position to empower them economically. Faith in the potency of industry and in the possibility of elevation through economic power, therefore, inspired his de-emphasizing political equality and power—a major agenda of the black-Republican Party alliance.

But there was more. His subordination of politics to economics was also the product of an enduring faith in the democratic character of American political culture. Delany believed that America possessed an inherently democratic and progressive political culture, which, left undisturbed, would result in universal freedom and equality. According to him, "Equality of political rights was the genius of the American government, and therefore, like all great principles, will take care of themselves, and must eventually prevail."[68] Since America was inherently democratic, he implored blacks to spend less time agitating for political rights and privileges. His was not an isolated optimism. In the past, blacks demonstrated strong faith in the Constitution and Declaration of Independence and had invoked both in justification of their struggles, earnestly persuaded of the universality of the values enshrined in both documents. The dominant conviction among blacks seemed to blame corrupt and racist politicians for allegedly conspiring to undermine and destroy what was deemed fundamentally a democratic political culture. However, although other black leaders equally perceived the Civil War and Reconstruction as milestones in the evolution and progression of American political culture toward perfection, unlike Delany they prioritized the quest for political empowerment and were prepared to do anything in order to gain and retain political power. Contrary to Delany's postulations, leading black politicians in South Carolina and, in fact, across the nation believed that the attainment, consolidation, and enhancement of political power held the key to economic power. It is clear, therefore, that the pervasive, optimistic, and progressive perception of American political culture did not inspire consensus among blacks. Fundamental differences persisted on the ideological and practical dimensions of Reconstruction. It became obvious that while the economic components of Delany's "political economy" mirrored the aspirations of the black masses, its political values, or more appropriately, its lack of political agenda, alienated the black political leadership and its supporter, the Republican Party.

Consequently, though other black leaders equally expressed enthusiasm and optimism about the new dispensation, they were, however, cautiously guarded in their optimism, given the glaring objections and ill-dispositions of the former slave owners to the political, social, and economic implications of the new realities, especially the emancipation of blacks, and the dreaded prospects for equality suggested by the constitutional amendments, especially the Fourteenth. The outlook in the South was not encouraging, and because they sensed continued threats to their freedom, blacks were determined to strengthen their relationship with the Republican Party as a guarantee of securing their freedom and the accompanying rights and privileges. From the onset of Reconstruction, therefore, Delany found himself advocating ideas and values that contradicted those of other black leaders and the Republican Party.

An in-depth knowledge and understanding of the conflict between Delany and the black-Republican Party political leadership in South Carolina require some background knowledge of the broader political context within which the drama took place. Wilbur J. Cash suggested that defeat in war and the coming of Reconstruction marked the opening of a second frontier in the South. In this frontier, new social directions and organizations had to be developed. But life was perilous on this "rocky and dangerous" frontier.[69] Lacy K. Ford Jr. also described the latent conflict in Southern societies after the war as a struggle between modernizing and traditional habits and values. What made this new frontier all the more "rocky and dangerous" was the problem of how to deal with the newly enfranchised blacks.[70] Under President Johnson's amnesty, many ex-Confederates had taken the oath of loyalty and had been restored to their former positions. The former Confederate states, under Johnson's provisional governments, were directed to summon constitutional conventions to draw up new constitutions. Benjamin F. Perry, provisional governor for South Carolina, set the tone for the new policy that ultimately emerged from the conventions. He opposed the extension of suffrage to blacks because, in his view, they were inferior. Governments were intended for whites only, he insisted.[71] Little wonder then that the constitution that emerged from this convention, made up mostly of ex-Confederates, subordinated blacks to a quasi-form of slavery.[72]

Logically, blacks rejected the South Carolina constitution. Meeting on September 4, 1865, at St. Helena Island, they petitioned the state assembly for suffrage and equal rights. Late in September, some one hundred blacks in Charleston petitioned the state legislature for constitutional changes to remove the disabilities created by the provisional government. They demanded absolute equality and a recognition and acceptance of their rights.[73] Meeting again in November, Charleston blacks offered friendship and peace to white Carolinians, while insisting upon their citizenship rights—"Our past career as law-abiding SUBJECTS, shall be strictly adhered to as law-abiding CITIZENS." As an honorary member, Delany addressed the delegates on the subject of discipline and obedience to the law.[74] But white Carolinians would not listen. Their worldview had no place for black equality in the true sense of it. As a South Carolinian admitted, "Everyone thinks and every child is trained up in the belief, that the Negro is meant for the use of white people, and was brought here, and should stay here for no other purpose."[75]

From the very beginning of Reconstruction, the black political leadership unequivocally declared its prioritization of political rights and power. No sooner had Reconstruction begun than they sent a delegation to President Andrew Johnson. Led by Frederick Douglass and William Whipper, the delegates presented the president with a list of demands that included complete enfranchisement.[76] This was perhaps the earliest indication of the political agenda of the black political leadership. Conscious of the revolutionary implications of their newly won liberties and apprehensive of the future, given the hostile disposition of former slave owners, these blacks sought reassurance from the president on the sanctity of their political rights. But Johnson's response reinforced black apprehension. Not only did he reject their demands, but he also expressed regret that blacks had benefited from the war at the expense of whites. Instead of reassurance, he suggested colonization as a solution and offered to be their "Moses" in leading them toward a new nation elsewhere.[77] Needless to say, the delegates left disappointed but undeterred in their continued rejection of colonization.

The president offered a solution that the majority of blacks had consistently rejected and objected to since its introduction in the early 1800s and most recently resurrected in the early phases of the Civil War.

It is interesting to note that colonization surfaced early in the war and was offered as a possible solution to the problems, challenges, and implications of black emancipation. Its underlying impulse was the conviction that blacks and whites could not coexist on the basis of universal freedom and equality.[78] President Lincoln agonized over this problem as he considered the possibility of emancipation and had, in fact, initially coupled emancipation with colonization. As already suggested, Delany's "Political Destiny" was one of the major corroborating documents presented by the procolonization lobby both within and outside official circles in the early phases of the Civil War.[79] In a letter to the delegates, Delany enjoined them not to be discouraged or disheartened by Johnson's remarks. He reminded them that blacks already had cause for glorification—the war had ended slavery and unleashed the process of emancipation. Affirming the imperative of racial differences, Delany counseled the delegates not to expect too much from the president, reminding them that being white, Johnson should be expected to prioritize, protect, and advance the interests of his race. He urged moderation, imploring the delegates to trust in the ultimate wisdom and power of God.[80]

Confronted by a president who seemed unsympathetic to their political rights, blacks quickly strengthened their relationship with the Republican Party. After all, it was a Republican president, Abraham Lincoln, who had issued the Emancipation Proclamation. It was also a Republican Congress that had passed the Thirteenth, Fourteenth, and Fifteenth Amendments. In the short period from the outbreak of the war to 1871, blacks had been transformed from slaves and quasi-slaves to citizens, with promised access to all the rights and privileges common to all, including the equal protection of the law. At the same time, blacks were aware of Democratic Party opposition and aversion to the new reforms. Southerners, however, viewed the partnership between blacks and the Republican Party with misgivings. First, they characterized Reconstruction as undue interference in the internal affairs of the South. Second, many of them refused to acknowledge and come to terms with the political elevation of blacks. The freedom of blacks and their political elevation were too revolutionary and repulsive to the sensitivities of those who deemed politics the exclusive preserve of the "superior white race" and who were accustomed to treating blacks as slaves and servants. Many blacks suspected, with justification, that Southerners would revert to the status quo antebellum at the slightest opportunity. There was, therefore, little to suggest to them that white Carolinians, or Southern whites generally, had changed and deserved the considerations and concessions Delany advocated. The majority of blacks were determined to hold on to the political concessions they had won. For them, politics became a "countervailing force" (to borrow Foner's concept), and they were most uncomfortable with any policy that seemed to jeopardize it. The stage seemed set for conflict with Delany.

Delany's plea to the black delegates had little impact on the course of events. Johnson remained adamant, and blacks grew increasingly political in their orientations. The year 1866 also witnessed a radical resurgence in Congress. Convinced that the South wanted to resurrect slavery, Radical Republicans quickly assumed control of the course of Reconstruction. They gained control of every Northern state legislature, every statehouse in which there was a contest, and the U.S. Senate and House.[81]

Radicals interpreted this widespread victory as a mandate to throw out presidential policies, thus inaugurating a conflict between Congress and Johnson. Congress declared South Carolina's constitution null and void and refused to admit the state's delegates. It extended the Freedmen's Bureau bill over Johnson's veto. It also passed the Civil Rights Bill and the Fourteenth Amendments in spite of his opposition. While disfranchising many whites for participating in the rebellion, the bill extended universal suffrage and citizenship to blacks.[82] In March 1867 Congress divided the Southern states into five military districts, each under a general who was assigned to supervise new guidelines for Reconstruction. North and South Carolina came under the Second Military District. Congress also authorized a constitutional convention consisting of delegates elected by all male citizens regardless of race, color, or previous condition but "exclusive of those disfranchised by the proposed Fourteenth Amendment."[83] This convention would draw a constitution granting suffrage to all male citizens. Such a constitution must then be ratified by the electorate and approved by Congress. The new legislature must then ratify the Fourteenth Amendment. Only after all these preconditions were satisfied was the state considered reconstructed and its delegates admitted into Congress.[84] Black Carolinians responded enthusiastically. They voted overwhelmingly for the convention and the new constitution. Due to the disfranchisement of whites, the convention had a black majority. The new constitution granted universal suffrage and equal rights. It abolished racial discrimination and ratified the Fourteenth Amendment.[85]

White Carolinians were less enthusiastic. They insisted that the constitution usurped their ancient rights and glories. It had, some lamented, subverted the natural order of things, putting an inferior race above a superior one. Consequently, they declared it illegal and ultra vires.[86] In a determined effort to subvert the ratification and acceptance, they appealed to blacks and to the Senate. Their spokespersons insisted that slavery had had salutary effects on blacks and that, due to innate inferiority, blacks needed continued white guidance and lordship in order to prevent reversion to primitivism.[87] They advised blacks to eschew radical politics and seek immediate, and unconditional reconciliation with their former masters.

Black political power was, many state conservatives argued, at best ephemeral, and they vowed never willingly to make any political concessions to blacks. "The discussion of political subject with the colored is now forced on us," lamented a leading Democrat, "we have no choice. But we will not extend it beyond the limit of actual necessity. We will make no promise or compromise."[88] This "limit of actual necessity" meant some token concessions of civil and political rights to blacks, excluding suffrage. Suffrage, they argued, was not a right but a trust that is conferred according to expediency and in consonance with the political doctrine of the greatest good to the greatest number. Since blacks were deemed inferior, they could not be entrusted with suffrage.[89] In fact, according to leading Democrats, black needs were material, not political.[90] Since Radical Reconstruction had been imposed upon the South, Democrats felt compelled to concede some form of qualified and limited political rights to blacks. This was the "limit of actual necessity." However, there was no sincerity to this concession. Qualified suffrage was simply a device to oust blacks from positions of political responsibilities. A leading Democrat admitted that qualified suffrage would only be granted to the few educated and property-owning blacks. So few, in fact, that not even a shadow of power would accrue to blacks in consequence. In essence, Democrats stuck dogmatically to one conviction—this is a "white man's country" and must remain so.[91]

Democrats were further encouraged in their intransigence by the early demise of Radical Reconstruction in Connecticut and the rising tide of antiradical momentum in Alabama and Mississippi.[92] Reacting to these favorable signs, conservative spokespersons and the press in South Carolina urged whites to unite against blacks. Furthermore, most conservatives sought solace in the aphorism "blood is thicker than water." As one conservative brazenly told blacks, "This is a white man's country. You are deluded if you think those 'friends' [that is, Radical Republicans and carpetbaggers] will stand by you. Blood is thicker than water. They will stand by us."[93] Consequently, the conservatives were always quick to remind blacks of the nationwide demographic preponderance of whites. This reasoning inhered a Manichean conception of the struggle along racial lines, a reality to which blacks, according to conservatives, had been blinded by radical politics. The conflict in South Carolina, according to a conservative, was a microcosm of a national conflict.[94]

South Carolina conservatives, therefore, were determined that the radical government, and its constitution, would not outlive 1870. As the year approached, realizing that few blacks had been intimidated by the violent rhetoric, the Democrats changed tactics. The only effective way to woo blacks away from radical influence, many reasoned, was for the Democrats themselves to assume radical postures. Accordingly, an ex-slaveholder advised his fellow Democrats to insist "inflexibly upon full rights for blacks, proper remuneration for their labor and ample legal protection."[95] Masquerading as a Union Reform Party, the Democrats convened and agreed to recognize the 1868 radical constitution. They also advocated universal amnesty and an end to the political disabilities of whites. Although the State Democratic Convention recognized blacks as part of the body polity, entitled to full and equal protection, it would only grant blacks qualified suffrage based on intelligence and property.

As the *Anti-Slavery Reporter* rightly observed, the platform of the Democrats remained questionable. It demanded the restoration of states rights and the destruction of the very foundation for black elevation and freedom. In fact, if there was any doubt about the conservative nature of the platform, the *Daily Phoenix* dispelled this when, responding to a charge by the *Mercury* that the Democratic Party, by recognizing blacks as members of the body polity, had significantly "repudiated the platform of a white man's government," it insisted that those concessions were necessary to stem the tide of Republican radicalism. "Our suffrage is based upon intelligence and property," it reiterated, and it was meant to keep this a government run by whites.[96]

Thus the tactics of the Democrats clearly demonstrated the utilitarian nature of their liberal pretensions. However much they feigned radicalism, they could not completely disguise their pathological opposition to black elevation. They called for the abolition of the Freedmen's Bureau and all political instrumentalities of black political participation.[97] While campaigning to "breathe air of conservatism into blacks," they also used violence or the threat of it. One Democrat urged blacks to heed quickly the conservative warning or risk being "ground to powder between the upper mill-stone of northern prejudice and the lower mill-stone of southern repudiation."[98] Democrats reminded blacks of the transient nature of their demographic preponderance in South Carolina. They predicted a shift in the demographic tide in favor of whites through increased immigration and natural increases.[99]

It was obvious, as even the conservative press admitted, that the "radical" concessions of the conservatives were smokescreens. Their ultimate objective was to prevent "Africanizing" the state and to restore white supremacy.[100] Perceptive blacks knew that the conservatives presented blacks with clear choices—either surrender and accept some quasi-slavery status or continue to struggle and advocate equal rights. At a Radical Republican convention in 1869, therefore, blacks rededicated themselves to the Republican Party. They urged the Democratic Party to accept and recognize their rights as freedmen and political equals. They pledged never to mortgage their political rights.[101] It is against this backdrop of conflicting configurations between the interests, and political aspirations of blacks and the intransigence of the Democratic/conservative forces in South Carolina that one can adequately examine, understand and appreciate the significance and implications of Delany's political ideas.

Delany entered the political arena concerned that political rights were both problematic and marginal to the immediate needs of blacks. In fact, he considered the exercise and enjoyment of political rights and power by blacks ill-advised given the prevailing climate of racial discord. Furthermore, he characterized the attainment of political power by blacks, devoid of a solid economic foundation, as, at the very best, a superfluous accomplishment. Economic power became the leitmotif of his Reconstruction philosophy. However, his prioritization of economic power conflicted with the political agenda of Radical Reconstruction, an agenda tied closely to the political elevation of blacks.

The political emancipation of blacks constituted the most revolutionary aspect of the postwar reforms, the one change that Delany suspected white Carolinians would have difficulty accepting. Though a welcome development, the political elevation of blacks would, in Delany's judgment, prove destabilizing to the process of national integration, particularly if blacks refused to exercise their political elevation with caution and prudence. On this fact, Delany's evinced foresight. He was quick to realize how objectionable and loathsome Southerners perceived former slaves in their new roles as citizens and political actors. His objective in de-emphasizing politics, therefore, was to prevent blacks from interpreting their newly won political rights as emblems of political power and authority. In his assessment, emancipation and the acquisition of civil and political rights were far-reaching and revolutionary enough. These reforms positioned blacks to begin the gradual process of readiness and qualifying for the eventual exercise of political rights and power and assuming responsibilities as political actors. But first blacks must be oriented and socialized at the lower echelons of government where little or no experience was required.

Delany's problem with blacks exercising political authority at the high levels of the state and federal governments had to do with their lack of experience and preparation. Put bluntly, he thought that blacks were not qualified to assume roles at such levels. He consequently deemed the political emancipation of blacks premature because it conferred political rights and privileges on a class that was not quite ready for such roles and responsibilities. Furthermore, it infused in blacks a false sense of competence and the erroneous consciousness that the mere possession of civil and political rights necessarily qualified them to exercise political power at all levels of government. He made a distinction between the possession of political rights and the exercise of political power, depicting the former as the lesser of two evils.[102] White Carolinians would perforce accommodate the spectacle of blacks *possessing* political rights; however, they would have greater difficulty with blacks *exercising* political authority. The pervasive consciousness among Southern whites was that blacks had no business in politics. Politics, more precisely, political power, was deemed the exclusive preserve of the "superior" white race.[103] By avoiding political power, blacks, in Delany's judgment, would tremendously facilitate reconciliation with whites. Instead of political power, he focused the attention of blacks on measures that would enhance their economic fortunes, precisely because he considered the quest for economic elevation less problematic, since blacks and whites needed each other on the economic terrain.

After officially joining the Republican Party, Delany immediately positioned himself as a moderating counterforce to what he perceived as the "radical/racial" agenda of the mainstream black political leadership, an agenda he credited to the "selfish and destructive" influence of the Republican Party. He accused the party of inaugurating a reign of terror and violence in the South and thus seriously jeopardizing the chances of blacks ever becoming politically, and economically, stable and integrated.[104]

Delany thus accepted and popularized the perception of Radical Republicans as carpetbaggers who came south primarily to dominate and exploit the region. To accomplish this objective, according to popular legend, they deceived, misled, and exploited ignorant and gullible blacks. He dismissed Radical Reconstruction as a dismal failure. It had advanced neither the interests of blacks nor national development but had instead nurtured a culture of violence and ignorance in the South.[105] His anger and frustrations were equally aimed at blacks, presenting a very gloomy portrait of black politicians, whom he characterized as ignorant and corrupt, having assumed political functions and responsibilities for which they were neither ready nor qualified. As he argued, blacks emerged from an experience—slavery—that allowed them few or no duties and obligations, and they occupied few or no responsible positions in society.

Emancipation and political enfranchisement theoretically gave them access to immense responsibilities and roles in society, "hence the necessity of possessing such information and having such qualification as to fit us for the high responsible and arduous duties of the new life into which we have entered."[106]

The unpopularity and rejection of his ideas and schemes led Delany to begin to question the intelligence and capacities of the black political leadership and to seriously doubt the ability of the leaders to gauge the political landscape intelligently and realistically. Deceived and blinded by "political radicalism," these blacks, he argued, failed to perceive how the civil and political rights that had elevated them had actually left them economically shackled to their former masters. Consequently, instead of redefining and readjusting their values and policies in line with post–Civil War reality and acting prudently to advance their interests, they left themselves open to the manipulations of selfish and destructive Northern agents and interest groups.[107]

Delany's views won the hearts of white Carolinians, who applauded his "prudence" and "intelligence." The mood was different, however, within the Republican Party and among other black leaders. Many blacks listened with disbelief, wondering if this was the same Delany of antebellum days, and they began seriously to question his professed commitment to black freedom. It was the Civil War that had transformed Delany's ethnocentric consciousness in ways unimaginable, even to his closest ideological comrades. It almost completely erased the racial/ethnic boundary line that had defined his emigrationist scheme, now inspiring him to campaign for forgiveness, reconciliation, and cooperation between blacks and whites, particularly former slaveholders. What was unique about Delany's volte-face was not so much his revived optimism—many blacks shared the same feeling—but the extremity of his optimism and the often ambivalent scheme and strategies that he proposed, many of which seemed completely to relegate race and ethnicity to the background. In fact, it was Delany who now accused fellow blacks of advocating narrow, ethnocentric, and racial policies.

Delany appeared comfortable with a paternalistic and condescending approach to black political rights and seemed willing to allow whites the freedom to decide when it might be appropriate to concede whatever rights and privileges they deemed blacks deserved, instead of blacks assertively dictating their wants and preferences. For example, in a letter to Rev. Henry H. Garnet, he castigated black leaders for being too assertive and overambitious.[108] He was particularly critical of, and categorically rejected and condemned as premature, the call for a black vice president for the country made by Wendell Phillips at the session of the 1867 State Constitutional Convention in Columbia, South Carolina. He deemed the idea "nonsense" and the product of youthful exuberance. "No wise black would make such premature political demand," he affirmed, urging blacks instead, to "be satisfied to take things like other men, in their natural course and time, prepare themselves in every particular municipal positions, and they may expect to attain to some other in time."[109] He further advised blacks not to seek political offices until they were "*ready*" and "*qualified*." Instead of such high-ranking positions, he suggested local and minor municipal offices.[110]

The following year, at a meeting of the Colored Members of the State Nominating Convention in Charleston, blacks decided to nominate more representatives to run for Congress, and Delany's name came up as a possible candidate. His known opposition to black political power notwithstanding, some delegates held him in high esteem and believed he would make an effective representative. They delegated L. S. Langley to communicate this information to Delany and to request his consent to be nominated as a candidate for Congress for the Second Congressional District, comprising Charleston, Beaufort, Colleton, and Barnwell Counties. In a reply declining the nomination, Delany, who was then a Bureau official, repeated his conviction that it was premature for blacks to seek representation in Congress. He urged "discretion and prudence" as blacks exercised their enfranchised status, depicting congressional representation as premature and too advanced for blacks. Furthermore, he contended that blacks did not need representation at such a high level in order to advance their cause.[111] As he argued,

> It is not necessary for our claims as American citizens, nor important for the accomplishment of that end, that a black man at this period be a representative in the national halls of legislation. This, let me insist with emphasis the nation (the American people generally) are not ready for.

And when they are ready for it, of course, there will be no objection, and consequently no harm done, and should they never become ready, then that will be the end of the whole matter.[112]

In very candid words, Delany declared opposition to black representation at the national level of political power. He was "entirely opposed at this period of political experience of the country, to any person identified with the black race entering any council of the nation as a member."[113]

Delany's conservative approach and objections to black political elevation won the endorsement of the *New York Times*, which ran a lengthy commentary praising his "prudence" and "sensibility."[114] The paper concurred with Delany that blacks were unfit for political power and authority, quoting him profusely. In a veiled criticism of the Fourteenth and Fifteenth Amendments, the paper insinuated that blacks had been prematurely made citizens and rejected any linkages between suffrage and officeholding. It expressed concern that a race (that is, blacks) "that had just been raised to manhood . . . [is being] stimulated to risk all manhood is worth in the scramble for the reward of party.[115] In the words of the paper, "The blacks have been made citizens before they are fit for the responsibilities of electors. It is the very deviltry of demagoguism to flatter them with the chimera that they are fit to take part in governing others."[116] Denying any logical connection between the enfranchisement of blacks and political officeholding, the paper warned, "It is a mistake to suppose there is any logical connection between the right to vote and the right, if it be not an abuse of terms to call it so, to hold office."[117] The fact that blacks possessed the suffrage, it contended, did not automatically qualify them for officeholding. The latter function required intelligence, something, it insisted, blacks lacked.[118] It condemned Wendell Phillips for advocating a black vice president, calling him the "great misleader" and "arch-agitator," among other negative epithets.[119] Furthermore, the *New York Times* admonished blacks to concentrate on character development. Emphatically denying their capacity for political responsibilities, it advised them to be satisfied with local offices "requiring a low grade of capacity." In the ideal state, however, according to the paper, blacks "would be far better and happier out of politics."[120] It further invoked Delany in corroboration of its contention that an elevated position at the national level would not make blacks the social equals of whites. No political reforms can effect social equality, it insisted. The existing and glaring social distinctions between the races, which in the judgment of the paper justified black subordination, are the result of "social distinctions" that sprang from "natural diversities; and are maintained by sympathies of feelings, of tastes and pursuits."[121] Political radicalism can change the political landscape, it contended, but it cannot change "these inborn individualities. It cannot new create human nature."[122]

For the *New York Times*, therefore, invoking Delany, the political emancipation and empowerment of blacks resulted from misdirected radical policies that ignored the prevailing and inherent reality of insurmountable differences between the races—differences that were unbridgeable, given ingrained prejudices. The paper did not foresee the possibility of blacks developing a character that would eventually render them fit for political authority, a fundamental conflict with Delany's position. In a related response, one FIDES, writing for the conservative *Daily Phoenix* (Columbia), also quoted Delany in objecting to black representation at the national level.[123] Contending that the nation was not ready for universal suffrage or black representation in Congress, FIDES praised Delany's "sagacity" and "foresight," quoting profusely from his letter to Langley.[124] FIDES also singled out the "pretended" friends of blacks (that is, Radical Republicans) for severest condemnation, urging blacks to turn instead to Southern whites, their true best friends. Citing what he characterized as the sectional bias of Radical Republicanism in corroboration, FIDES concluded that radicals only empowered blacks in the South. Their "political radicalism," therefore, did not include the empowerment of blacks in the North.[125]

Delany's next attack against political radicalism came early in 1868 at a great ratification meeting in Epping Hall, Charleston, in the presence of all candidates for state offices. Listening attentively to the various speeches, Delany, "as might be expected," heard lots of "ill-timed and extravagant advice."[126] When it was his turn to speak, he emphasized the theme of "moderation of action and sentiments," reminding blacks,

> we are only one sixth of the entire population of the country, that the white people are the ruling element of the nation, *and must take the*

first rank, and would have the first and choice places, though we would get some; that in conceding rights to us, they had no intention of surrendering their own; that whatever we claim for ourselves, we should take care not to interfere with the rights of others. That *we must not in finding room for ourselves undertake to elbow the white people out of their own places* [emphasis added].[127]

At the close of his speech, he heard lots of buzz and murmurs of disapproval, and a "gentleman" and "prominent leader" declared loudly, "that man (that is, Delany) should never be permitted to hold office in this state!"[128] According to Delany, many blacks were encouraged by their radical leaders to denounce him as an agent of the old planter class.[129]

The conviction that progress for blacks would come only in the context of reconciliation with local whites, and not in the friendship of and alliance with Northern Radical Republicans, formed the core of Delany's conservatism. According to him, beneath the seeming age-old conflict and antagonism between blacks and former slave owners lay profound commonalities, shared interests, and aspirations that both could build upon to solidify a relationship for their mutual benefit. Consequently, he refused to see the intransigence, open or clandestine, of former slave owners as problematic or a cause for concern. What disturbed him the most was the intransigence of blacks, backed by what he characterized as vindictive radical policies that only served to antagonize Southern whites and aggravate the racial situation. He was undoubtedly naive in ignoring the seething resentments of Southerners to black elevation and in believing that, with the demise of slavery, blacks had nothing to worry about. He refused to believe that blacks needed the continued presence, friendship, and support of the Radical Republicans, in order to protect and guarantee their newly won rights and freedom.

Delany was undoubtedly a shrewd observer of the political scene who seemed to have anticipated the problematic of Radical Reconstruction. Though slavery had been abolished, racism persisted, and Radical Reconstruction policies, according to critics, seemed geared more toward sustaining a culture of intolerance and confrontation rather than reconciling black and white Carolinians. Furthermore, a critical examination of the political gains of Reconstruction revealed that blacks had attained neither social nor political equality. Although a liberal atmosphere appeared dominant, the nation was far from being fully integrated. Whites remained in political control, and Delany was not convinced that the liberal platform of the Radical Republicans suggested that America had become a color-blind society. In fact, he discovered racial biases in the political programs of the Radical Republicans. The conviction that Radical Reconstruction harbored and reflected a dynamic racial bias strengthened Delany's distrust of Republicans, and he warned blacks of the racial undertone of the alliance they embraced. His commitment to compromise and reconciliation seemed unflinching, and nothing, not even his imminent isolation, would compel a reversal.

Delany characterized black adherence to Radical Republicanism as foolish and misguided. America remained a race-conscious society, and he viewed any alliance with one group of whites (Radical Republicans) against another as ill-advised, especially in a context in which the economic fortunes of blacks remained tied to the apron strings of the other group (former slave owners), the very class that abhorred Radical Republicanism. It should be noted, however, that Delany's advocacy of reconciliation was not necessarily a denial of the race-conscious disposition of Democrats and ex-slave owners whom he favored. He remained conscious of the racist dispositions of Democrats, his optimism notwithstanding. However, given the changes wrought by the war and Reconstruction (the most significant being the attainment of freedom and citizenship by blacks), Delany believed that South Carolina Democrats had no choice but ultimately to accept these changes. This acceptance, however, entailed a painful and gradual process of readjustment, the success of which depended on the willingness of blacks to tread the political landscape with caution. In essence, he believed that the key problem was not so much that blacks had become citizens but what they proceeded to do and how they went about doing it. Put differently, the prospect of white Carolinians accommodating the political elevation of blacks depended, in Delany's estimation, on how painless blacks themselves rendered that experience. Gradualism seemed, for him, the best approach that would render the experience painless.

Yet there is a certain curious paradox in Delany's reasoning. Although critical of black leaders for allying with a party and policy that he deemed driven by a segregationist and racialist philosophy, he advised them nonetheless to identify with the Democrats, another group that did not mask both its racist values and almost pathological resentment of blacks. He thus sensitized blacks on the racial character of one alliance, while ignoring or desensitizing them on the racial reality of the other. Curiously, this paradox itself reflects a certain degree of realism. Delany was not absolutely convinced of the sincerity of the Radical Republicans or of the depth and stability of Radical Reconstruction, hence his discomfort with radical policies that seemed to pit blacks against white Carolinians. He characterized Radical Reconstruction as a self-serving program designed to advance the narrow interests of the radicals. Deep within, he harbored distrust of white liberals and radicals, believing that they would never expunge racism from their consciousness, their liberalism notwithstanding.

There was another pragmatic explanation to Delany's distrust of Radical Reconstruction, particularly his doubting of the reliability and longevity of the Radical Republican program. By the early 1870s, tensions within the Republican Party over Reconstruction had reached irreconcilable proportions, with those opposed to Radical Reconstruction identifying themselves as "Liberal Republicans." Delany suspected that Radical Reconstruction had a shaky foundation and had not attracted sufficient federal support to justify the political assertiveness of the black leadership. In fact, no sooner had these blacks begun to exercise political rights than several of them were kicked out, underscoring the fragility of their new political rights and power. By early 1870s, according to several scholars, Radical Reconstruction existed in name only, as conservative forces bulldozed their paths to power in a number of states, thus undermining, and in many places ending, the very fragile and precarious constitutional rights of blacks.[130]

Within the Republican Party, therefore, Delany launched a spirited internal battle against radicalism, accusing the party of exploiting black ignorance and gullibility to advance a punitive radical agenda. To tame Radical Republicanism, therefore, he began to advocate the appointment to leadership positions of "intelligent and experienced" blacks who, he hoped, would redefine and redirect party policies. He deplored the prevailing practice of confining party leadership to whites and relegating blacks to subordinate roles, regardless of qualification and intelligence. He responded with the slogan, "Black musts have black leaders. We must lead our own people," insisting upon the appointment of more blacks to positions of political responsibility.[131] Some blacks construed his ideas as selfishly motivated, a ploy to secure a position for himself, and refused to endorse it. A few others, however, shared his views and joined in the call for more black representation. The cry of "black leaders for black men" caused quite a stir within the Republican Party, and radicals vowed to fight back "with severity."[132] Although some blacks sympathized with Delany's views, the vast majority rejected them. Recalling his earlier opposition to black political rights and power, many vowed to oppose what to them was his attempt to gain a political office.

Delany's conciliatory and moderate ideas alarmed many and created problems for him within the Republican administration. Most critically, it made other Republicans, blacks and whites, deeply suspicious and resentful of him and therefore determined to isolate him politically. Consequently, from the very beginning of his active political involvement in South Carolina, he was confined to the status of an outsider, denied access to the corridors of political power and authority. There was some validity to the charge that he was after a political office. Late in 1868 (sometime after he left the Bureau), he pleaded unsuccessfully with Republican governor Robert Scott for a job. Early in 1869, he turned to the Republican administration in Washington and solicited again unsuccessfully for the post of first black minister to Liberia. He returned to South Carolina a politically frustrated yet determined man.[133] He would later attribute the repeated oppositions he encountered to the "chicanery of wily politicians."[134] This experience, however, only strengthened his resolve, intensifying his advocacy for more black representation within the Republican administration.

By the early 1870s in South Carolina, Radical Republicans and the state conservatives were locked in conflict. While leading blacks advocated "uncompromisingly radical course" and opposed any movement toward conservatism, the state conservatives responded with a carrot-and-stick approach. Determined to make 1870 "the year of the happy deliverance," they intensified criticisms of the radical administration, adopting a "reform" platform that pledged to uphold and respect the Fourteenth and Fifteenth Amendments, obvious concessions aimed at attracting blacks. This quintessentially "Conservative-Republican" concession developed from a "new departurist" platform, the underlying motivation for which was actually the enfranchisement and political empowerment of ex-Confederates. Democrats nominated an ex-Republican, Judge R. B. Carpenter, for governor, and an ex-Confederate, General M. C. Butler, for lieutenant governor. Though this platform accepted the Fourteenth Amendment and universal suffrage, an article in the Democratic *Carpetbagger Journal* of Charleston revealed that the Democrats were just "playing radicals" for appearance sake. Their ultimate goal was to get rid of blacks.[135] Theirs was a compromise ticket designed to appeal to both ends of the political spectrum. However, despite the pretense at being liberal and reformist, there was a strong opposition to "Negro equality" at the convention, easily illuminating the shallow and utilitarian character of their "liberal" pledges. This kept many blacks at a safe and respectable distance.

Within the Republican Party itself, on the other hand, an internal reform movement had developed. Acknowledging the existence of corruption and other problems within the administration, many Republicans advocated reform and the election of honest men. Few, however, desired a split in the party. Francis L. Cardozo, South Carolina's black secretary of state, denounced the conservative "reform" initiative as fraudulent. White Carolinians had not changed fundamentally, he warned, and there were no grounds for blacks to take their "liberal" and "reformist" pretensions seriously. The platform of the Republican Party, on the other hand, was as radical as it could be—it accepted the Fifteenth Amendment; pledged firm, fearless, and unfaltering support for the Civil Rights Bill; and demanded strict enforcement of its principles as part of the practical assertions of the civil equality of all Americans. It also advocated more lands for freedmen.[136] Leading blacks, therefore, preferred strengthening the Republican Party. Delany's contribution to the reform initiatives created a storm. His persistent advocacy of more black representation within the Republican administration proved unsettling. However, he was not alone in this. Some other prominent blacks, including Rev. Richard Cain and Robert DeLarge, soon added their voices to the call, but Delany seemed to have been the most artic- ulate and forceful. "No people have become great without their own leaders," he declared, reiterating both his call for more black represen- tation, and for universal amnesty for all ex-Confederates.[137]

At a grand rally in Edgefield, Delany's strong advocacy of black repre- sentation elicited equally strong condemnation from other Republicans. Many saw his call for more black representation to mean more "pure blacks," such as himself, and not necessarily inclusive of mulattoes. One critic described Delany's speech as a selfish move to enhance his declared interest in a Senate seat. In other words, they accused him of speaking more to enhance his own chances of getting a job. Rumors had it that Delany, Cain, and DeLarge were contemplating forming a third party.[138] The "third party" rumor disturbed the Republicans, and they were determined to fight it "with severity wherever and whenever we see this movement rear its head, we shall strike our hardest blows."[139] Delany's obsession with peaceful reconciliation with white Carolinians seriously hurt his chances of acceptance by, and assimilation into, the Republican Party fold. Perhaps more important, his advocacy of universal and unconditional amnesty for ex-Confederates and slave owners, even in the face of their continued intransigence and threat to black freedom, alienated many Republicans. His conservative utterances and conces- sions of black inferiority further hurt his chances.

Several key Republicans deemed Delany's advocacy of more "black" representation uncalled for since, by virtue of their demographic pre- ponderance in the state, blacks had always been decisive in electing state officials. His call for more "blacks" was, therefore, interpreted as cleverly conceived to enhance his own chances of securing a position as a "pure black." Few took him seriously, and many saw him as a des- tructive force bent on undermining the Republican Party. At what was described as "[t]he largest assemblage of people ever gathered" in Edge- field, summoned by Republicans to celebrate the Fifteenth Amendment and the Declaration of Independence, Delany attempted to reassure members of his fidelity by reminding them that he had once rejected the overtures of those he termed "palpitrators," who had attempted to lure him away from the Republican fold. They included General

M. C. Butler and other notable candidates of the Union Reform Party, who were also in attendance. He had boldly rejected their overtures, insisting that he already had "a good Church and a good pastor and does not intend to change for a long time yet."[140] Delany thus distanced himself from the "palpitrators" and their "reform" platform, which he had earlier characterized as a devious scheme designed to lure blacks away from the Republican Party. According to him, they had no intention of honoring those liberal promises.[141]

Delany's persistent advocacy of subordinate political roles for blacks undermined his attempts to placate Republicans. His concession of black inferiority was perhaps the most provocative of his ideas. In suggesting that blacks were indeed inferior, Delany called for social differentiation and inequality. At a mass meeting of Republicans held at Liberty Hall in Charleston, he explained what he termed "[t]he basis for the new campaign": "We are not equal to our white friends in many qualities, and we require therefore a principle to depend on. We must be valued for something. We are not equal to the white race in general intelligence, and, we must therefore have an offset to be equal, and let that offset be 'honesty' and 'Justice.' "[142] His notion of "honesty" required that blacks admit inherent deficiency, especially in "general intelligence." Justice, therefore, in accordance with this "honest" assessment of the condition of blacks, mandated social differentiation and inequality. As Delany further declared, "I don't believe in social equality, there is no such thing. If we want to associate with a man, we will do it, and without laws."[143] But "justice" also required that blacks be given representation within the Republican administration commensurate with their intelligence and number. He advocated a "colored lieutenant Governor, and two colored men in the House of Representatives and one in the Senate, and our quota of state and county offices."[144]

At a 4th of July celebration in Charleston, Delany again publicly denied attempting to split the party. "Although we may disagree, I am not at war with you," he informed the gathering.[145] His growing unpopularity notwithstanding, Delany continued to feature in, and attend, Republican campaign rallies and meetings, utilizing every opportunity to reassure Republicans that he meant good. During one such meeting in Summerville in mid-August, a reporter for the *Daily News* observed that Delany's attempt to address the gathering "was met with such a storm of yells, shouts and jeers, accompanied by blasts on the tin horns, drumming on pans, etc, that he was compelled to desist. An effort on the part of a member of the other side met with a like reception, after which the meeting was broken up and the two parties retired in opposite directions."[146] Delany later refuted the report, insisting that he "was listened to with respectful attention by the assembly till I have finished my remarks, when they left, having held their meeting at noon, or a little after, without one word of interruption."[147] At another gathering of Republicans specifically summoned to discuss the "Principle of Republicanism" in Military Hall, Charleston, Delany lamented that the essential principle of Republicanism had been neglected and ignored in the political realm of the state. Recalling the founding of the Republican Party, he advanced the following as the essential doctrine of Republicanism, "Let us know no color, either white or black, but treat a man as a man."[148] He thus reiterated his familiar critique of the racialist character of Radical Republicanism, a tradition that, he argued, had driven a wedge between the races in the state. He urged fellow blacks to remember that "it was the white man who gave us what we now possess and who first brought us here," and he stressed the imperative of upholding Republicanism.[149]

Delany's reassuring speeches may have come too late. When Charleston Republicans assembled in late July 1870 to elect delegates to the state nominating convention, Delany's name was on the ballot for a senatorial race. He had earlier indicated his intension to contest for the U.S. Senate. Opposing Delany's bid, one critic, L. J. Taylor, harshly condemned Delany and DeLarge for advocating more black representation. While a Bureau agent in Beaufort, Delany, Taylor claimed, crushed the aspirations of blacks in nine out of ten cases. "If you want colored men for office, get good men and not those I have spoken of," he emphasized. Another critic, C. C. Bowen, called Delany an enemy of the Republican Party who frustrated the aspirations of blacks in Beaufort. Delany lost the contest. For the 1870 election, the Republicans nominated incumbent governor Robert Scott for a second term and Alonzo Ransier, a mulatto member of the statehouse, as his running mate. Despite internal problems and the intimidation of black voters by the

Ku Klux Klan, the Republican Party won the election by a vote of 85,071 to 51,573 for the conservatives. The newly elected House of Representatives had 22 conservatives and 101 Republicans, 75 of whom were blacks.[150] The election brought no meaningful change in Delany's fortune. In desperation, he again approach Governor Scott for an extremely low-paying job of a jury commissioner for Charleston County, "I am in hope that your excellency will give me this little appointment, as I have never received any remunerative position at the hands of your excellency . . . and this will pay something and thus help to bear expenses," he pleaded in desperation. Scott gave the post to someone else.[151]

Continually frustrated and disappointed in politics, Delany sought relief in business. Early in 1871 he began a land agency and note brokerage business. He had always believed that the rich and unexploited lands of the South held the key to economic prosperity for blacks. Part of the reason he had persistently appealed for peace and reconciliation was to create the peaceful atmosphere that, he felt, would attract Northern capital to the state. His formula for progress, as enshrined in the triple alliance, entailed the marriage of Northern capital to Southern land and black labor. He appealed to Northern capitalists to come to the South and help finance land purchases by blacks. Rich and surplus lands existed in South Carolina, he argued, that freedmen would willingly purchase, if assisted by rich capitalists. Furthermore, there were white landowners with little capital to develop their large lands and, therefore, eager to sell, just as there were landless blacks anxious to acquire lands but without the necessary capital. Delany thus assigned the philanthropic capitalists of the North a central role. Such a development would significantly redistribute wealth for the benefit of all.[152] Behind this ostensible humanitarian appeal, however, lay Delany's personal business interests. The chances of success as a real estate agent and note broker depended on the availability of capital and finance. Such capital, he insisted, must be dispensed "through [special] agencies for this object" (such as his).[153] He fared no better in business.

By mid-1871 Delany had just about had it with "political radicalism." After repeated failures to tame Radical Republicanism, on the Fourteenth of August he wrote a devastating review of Reconstruction. Addressed to

"Hon. Frederick Douglass" and titled "A Political Review," this review underlined the depth of Delany's frustration with, and alienation from, Radical Republicanism. Although meant for Douglass, Delany undoubtedly had a wider audience in mind, for he did not mail the letter to Douglass but instead published it as an open letter in the *Charleston Daily Republican*. It was later reprinted in the *New National Era*.[154] He accused the radicals of a litany of offences, including the promotion of a culture of violence and political victimization in the South and the exploitation of blacks, thereby undermining their prospect for elevation and for racial cooperation. He questioned the Republican Party's professed support for, and commitment to, black political rights. Blacks had been deceived and duped into accepting the rhetoric and propaganda of Radical Republicanism and had consequently turned against their best interests and true friends (white Carolinians), whose goodwill and support they needed if they were to achieve a meaningful degree of economic elevation and, ipso facto, political elevation.[155]

The letter can be divided into three dominant themes—political, social, and ethnological. The first is a castigation of those Delany characterized as outsiders and adventurers from the North (Radical Republicans), who came to the South to exploit the ignorance and gullibility of blacks in order to advance their narrow political agenda. They used a combination of deceit, lies, and cheating to impose themselves on blacks as their leaders, and in the process, they drove a wedge between blacks and local whites and exacerbated racial tension by nurturing a culture of violence. These "adventurers," according to Delany, transformed blacks from "a polite, pleasant, agreeable, kindly common people, ever ready and obliging . . . [into] ill-mannerly, sullen, disagreeable, unkind, disobliging populace, filled with hatred and ready for resentment."[156] These "renegade intruders" changed blacks from a "people proverbial for their politeness" into sullen, cantankerous, and violent people. He then criticized the prevalence of color consciousness among blacks, a disposition he held responsible for the socially divisive distinction between the mulattoes and the pure blacks, attributing it also to the historical experience of racism. He urged blacks to unite or risk "social and political death."[157]

The second part of the letter deals with the racial policies of the federal and state governments. He observed a strong bias in favor of mulattoes.

Although the government no longer discriminated on the basis of race, it continued to discriminate on the basis of color, reflected in its favoritism toward mulattoes to the neglect of pure blacks. Delany found only two exceptions of pure blacks in government employ in Washington, D.C. He attributed the appointment of one James H. Cunningham, a pure black, as postmaster of Manchester, Virginia, to the solicitations of Democrats and as further proof that Democrats were more sympathetic to blacks than were Republicans.[158] The other appointment came after tremendous pressure from a Republican. With these two exceptions, Delany contended that generally, pure blacks were assigned menial jobs. He found such discriminatory practices to be rampant among high-ranking federal cabinet members and in the various state governments, accusing the federal and state governments of deliberately hiring incompetent and corrupt blacks whose failures were then used to further discredit the entire race.

The above discrepancy led to the third theme of the letter, the ethnological, in which he identified "justice, and equal rights to all men" as the core principles of the Republicanism that is at the root of American democracy. This Republicanism, he averred, was designed to "accord to him [that is, the black man] the enjoyment of all the rights and privileges of American citizenship."[159] This principle had been perverted. He called for a return to its original intent by "reorganizing this state based upon intelligence, responsibility and honesty. The discordant element must become harmonized. One class or race must not be permitted to enjoy privileges of which another is debarred."[160] Eliminating ingrained racist consciousness would pave the way for equality of access to political power and resources for blacks on the basis of the principle of proportional representation. Since blacks constituted one-eighth of the nation's population, they were entitled, he reasoned, to representation in proportion to their number in Congress and in executive appointments. He called for an end to discrimination on the basis of race and color. He wanted opportunity opened to all, regardless of race and color. Again, he deplored the poor representation of intelligent blacks in the Republican administration in Washington, accusing the Republicans of perpetuating a culture of ignorance among blacks in order to create a compliant and docile constituency that would uncritically endorse party programs.

This sudden intrusion of race/color consideration casts serious doubts on Delany's professed commitment to a color-blind strategy. Delany offers an explanation for this apparent ambiguity. His intention was to expose the hypocrisy of the Republican administration. While posturing as liberals in favor of black elevation, they retained racist biases and values as reflected in their discriminatory policies against darker-skinned blacks. The ambiguity he exposed in Republican policies was both racial and geographical. He characterized Republican liberalism as sectional rather than national. Though Radical Republicans vigorously encouraged black political power in the South, they did not apply equal vigor to the advancement of black rights in the North, a clear indication that the Republicans were not really interested in black freedom but only in exploiting blacks to further the party's platform of dominating the South.[161] But Delany is not consistent on this issue of social relations. Here he criticizes and deplores the existence of social division among blacks based on complexion and calls for unity.

Yet Delany himself had once, and would later again, acknowledge that social equality could not be enforced or legislated and that individuals should be left free to mix with whomever they felt comfortable. He first made this declaration in reaction to the prevalence of discrimination against blacks, believing that de-emphasizing social equality would make whites less hostile. He objected strongly to any attempts at enforcing social equality that would deny individuals the freedom to choose with whom to associate. Of course, one has to understand the political context in which he made this concession. The first was during his Bureau agency when he was responding to demands by black leaders for political rights and equality. In this early phase of Reconstruction, as already established, Delany advocated amnesty and unconditional pardon for ex-Confederates and campaigned vigorously for reconciliation and compromise between blacks and whites. Social equality was such a sticky and potentially explosive issue that he urged blacks not to contest for it. The second came later during his Independent Republican Movement run for the state office as lieutenant governor on a ticket with ex-Confederates. It is not clear if Delany was trying to appease the racial sensibilities of white Carolinians, many of whom were known racists who had never disguised their opposition to black equality but whose support and goodwill he deemed indispensable to black elevation.

Delany attempted to expose the racism that he felt informed Republican Party policies at the federal level, in spite of the party's defense and furtherance of black interests in the South. If the party was genuinely interested in advancing black interests, such commitments, he suggested, should have been manifested nationwide and not just in the South. He accused the party of straining the relationship between blacks and Southern whites and, in the process, undermining the prospect for a productive Reconstruction program. He did not spare blacks either. They were not all helpless victims of Republican manipulations. He portrayed black politicians as corrupt, ignorant, incompetent, and perpetrators of violence, a liability upon and a disgrace to South Carolina. The overall performance of the black political elite at the state level was not only appalling, in his view, but also constituted an indictment of all black political aspirants.

This letter remains perhaps one of the most negative appraisals of black political performance by a black during Reconstruction. Its significance lay in the fact that it spoke to the concerns and apprehensions of South Carolina Democrats and former slaveholders, echoing and trumpeting their criticisms of black political empowerment. Delany's ideas served as grease for the conservative machine. As South Carolina conservatives cringed under Radical Republican rule, Delany's became the only loud outlet or voice for conservative ideas and interests; the conservatives press, internal and external, gladly embraced, trumpeted, and reproduced his ideas, almost verbatim, to underscore a correspondence, wherever possible, with their own often discredited and rejected values. Delany thus offered South Carolina conservatives an outlet of respectability—something they desperately needed.

These conservative forces were quick to applaud the letter, describing Delany as "a conscientious man, who writes from conviction and well established premises."[162] They co-opted the letter, transforming it into a potent weapon in the arsenal of their warfare against black elevation. The conservative *News and Courier* (Charleston) ran a three-part commentary on the letter, underlining correspondence between Delany's ideas and those of the state conservatives. It tendered the letter in evidence against the political empowerment of blacks, "since our own [evidence] to the same tenor have been systematically ignored," and urged Delany to join the conservatives in the "clearance of this worse than Augean stable he so graphically described."[163] The paper agreed with almost everything Delany said in criticism and condemnation of blacks and Radical Reconstruction. It then quoted Delany to suggest that the intrusion of Northern elements, and not slavery, was responsible for the negative character and disposition of blacks. Had blacks been left alone with their former masters, their character would not have degenerated, the paper argued.[164] It also invoked Delany to advance the view that blacks and the Radical Republicans, and not the Klan, were solely responsible for the violence in the state. Radical Republicans taught blacks the "erroneous view of the duty of the laborer, and false ideas of right and wrong."[165] The *News and Courier*, however, disagreed strongly with Delany on his ethnological critique, contending that "there is now more real sympathy in the South for the Negro than at the North or we think our people are disposed to treat him in his civil capacity with all due consideration, to give him a fair share of the offices suited to his abilities, and to aid him in his efforts to improve his physical condition, but we doubt the expediency on his part of attempting to obtain concessions which are not judicious, or to strive for utopian theories."[166]

It seems curious that while the paper concurred with Delany's social and political ideas, particularly his de-essentializing of black political power and social equality and his contention that blacks and Radical Republicans were responsible for the violence of the era, it disagreed with him on the ethnological dimension, where he argued for racial equality and proportional access to political power. Even this was too much for the paper. It used Delany's own words and concessions to affirm the notion of black inferiority, predicated on Eurocentric depictions of Africa as morally and culturally degenerate and of black Americans, including Delany, as fortunate to have been taken out of Africa to be "civilized" through the school of slavery. But for slavery, it argued, even Delany would not have had the fortune of education and erudition that he demonstrated.[167] This review clearly suggested that Delany's ideas reflected the core of conservatism in South Carolina, for the paper presented Delany's ideas as a representation of much of what South Carolina Democrats and conservatives had articulated but for which they had been derided, condemned, and castigated. Coming from the pen of a black leader of Delany's status gave these conservative ideas added significance and compelling force, and the paper was not wont to let this dimension go unnoticed.

The letter predictably compounded Delany's problems. An ex-slave master could not have written a more virulent attack on blacks. Although his demands included racial equality, paradoxically, the thrust of the letter, and his contradictory and ambiguous positions on race, seriously undermined the grounds for the equality he advocated. Investigations, however, revealed that Postmaster Cunningham got his job at the solicitation of a Republican, the Hon. Charles H. Porter of Richmond, Virginia.[168] More blacks began to question Delany's integrity and professed commitment to black freedom.

The suggestion that blacks and the Republican Party were solely responsible for the violence that engulfed South Carolina during Reconstruction flies in the face of the evidence. In spite of a subdued political stance, the state conservatives persistently opposed Radical Reconstruction through violence, perpetrated largely by the Klan and other white supremacist groups, whose antiblack terrorist activities overwhelmed South Carolina in the 1860s and 1870s. The violence and reign of terror that followed compelled the introduction of federal troops to protect the lives, property, and rights of blacks.[169] Notwithstanding the strength of Delany's concern, the fact that his letter espoused conservative values disturbed blacks.

Needless to say, the letter stunned Frederick Douglass. What kind of image of Delany came through to Douglass? Not a positive one. But for years of acquaintance with Delany and his efforts, Douglass admitted that he would have mistaken Delany for a spokesperson of the old planter class. Other blacks had no doubt that Delany had capitulated to the rank of the enemy and seemed to be undermining the efforts of his own race. Douglass published his reply in the *New National Era*. "Were you not Martin R. Delany," he responded, "I shall have said that the man who wrote this of the colored people of South Carolina has taken his side with the old planters."[170] Although he agreed with much of Delany's observations, Douglass had a few critical areas of disagreement. First, he acknowledged that corruption was a problem in Reconstruction but insisted that the much-maligned carpetbaggers and Republicans deserved commendation. Even the so-called ignorant black leaders that Delany castigated deserved more credit. Douglass blamed the system for their ignorance. Due to this ignorance, blacks were bound to fall victims of manipulation and exploitation. But this would change, he optimistically affirmed. Second, Douglass took exception to Delany's suggestion that blacks were solely responsible for the culture of violence in South Carolina. Blacks did not invent violence but were only responding to it, he insisted. Although he would not condone violence, Douglass maintained that blacks had a right to defend themselves. As he put it, "I shall never ask the colored people to be lambs where the whites insist on being wolves . . . there can be no peace without justice, and hence the sword."[171]

Douglass also disagreed with Delany's negative depiction of the character of blacks in South Carolina. What Delany saw as the offensive and insolent attitudes of blacks was more a reflection of their changed social relations. They were no longer slaves. Furthermore, Douglass equally acknowledged the existence of color distinction among blacks and endorsed Delany's call for unity, but he disagreed with Delany's characterization of government policy as racially biased in favor of color. Douglass found many more appointments of pure blacks in government positions. Finally, he deemed the call for proportional representation absurd and impracticable.

Delany's letter categorically called for unraveling of the black-Republican Party alliance. Douglass seemed the wrong person to whom to address such a suggestion. In fact, only a few days before Delany wrote his letter, Douglass had publicly called for strengthening of the Republican Party with a declaration that underscored his unflinching devotion: "I had better put a pistol to my head and blow my brain out, than allow myself in any way to the destruction of defeat of the Republican Party."[172] By addressing his letter to Douglass, Delany seemed either unaware of Douglass's strong and publicly declared commitment to the Republican Party or was just determined to force a showdown on the issue.

Other blacks were not so temperate in their responses to Delany. A black senator, S. E. Galliard, called Delany a traitor and an enemy of the black race and suggested that the letter was motivated by a vengeful reaction to his failed run for the Senate. He believed that the letter was sent to Douglass, a high-ranking black official in Washington, and made open so as to attract government attention and thus secure appointment for Delany as "representative of the pure black man."[173] Delany, Galliard declared, "ought to be the last man to growl about 'leaders.' " The senator made three other critical observations. First, he recalled Delany's earlier opposition to black political power, suggesting that his review was selfishly driven by his desperate search for a job, especially in the wake of the termination of his Bureau agency. Second, he described Delany's criticism of the social relations among blacks as a sinister ploy designed to foment racial tension, precisely what Delany professed to be against. Third, he characterized Delany's call for "black leaders for black people" as a "diabolical dogma" and another self-serving ploy that Delany, Cain, and a few other disgruntled blacks injected into the election campaign of 1870, which almost resulted in the defeat of the Republican Party in Charleston County.[174]

Delany's choice of South Carolina as the focus of his review and criticism of Reconstruction, and of his scathing indictment of the Republican Party and its policies, is understandable, given the strategic significance of the state, with its preponderance of blacks. If Reconstruction had any chance of success, many felt that it would happen in South Carolina. What Delany perceived as the atrocious performance of radical politicians, the rampant corruption, and the racial tension became for him sufficient justification for wresting the control and course of Reconstruction from the hands of blacks and their radical friends. Unfortunately for him, other blacks saw the situation differently. Two months after his blistering review, black political leaders from Alabama, Arkansas, Florida, Georgia, Louisiana, Maryland, Mississippi, South Carolina, Tennessee, North Carolina, the District of Columbia, and Texas descended upon Columbia, South Carolina, for the opening of the Southern States Convention of Colored Men, aimed at affirming greater appreciation for Radical Reconstruction and strengthening their relationship with the Republican Party.[175]

Although taking place in what had become his home state, Delany understandably boycotted the convention. Despite conservative attacks on and vilification of Radical Reconstruction, the delegates came determined to forge stronger ties with the Republican Party and to provide clear and unambiguous explication of their Republican ideals and convictions. A letter addressed to Robert Brown Elliott of South Carolina from some members of the Third Congressional District in Virginia captured the mood of the delegates. While emphasizing the necessity of strengthening the Republican Party, these members called for a "battle cry" against "Treasonable Democracy" and its most "truculent and dangerous ally—conservatism."[176] In resolution after resolution, the delegates affirmed "unswerving devotion to the great principles of the Republican Party."[177] One resolution introduced by J. T. Walls of Florida expressed the sense of gratitude that blacks felt toward the Republican Party: "Whereas in the struggle in the Southern states between the two great political parties of the country, the colored people have, almost to a man, taken sides with, and given their undivided support to the National Republican Party, believing that to that great party, if to any political source they owe any allegiance, they are most highly indebted."[178]

Other resolutions underscored the imperative of loyalty to the Republican Party based upon its record of accomplishments on behalf of blacks. While acknowledging the prevalence of corruption within the party, the delegates rejected corruption as a sufficient basis for destroying the party. As A. J. Ransier of South Carolina insisted: "That reforms are needed and errors to be corrected I will not deny, but let them be made and the errors all corrected within the Republican Party. . . . I maintain that the Republican Party in every state of the Union has within its bosom sufficient honesty, intelligence and appreciation of principles, to correct those errors without resorting or fleeing to the ranks of the Democratic or any other party that exists."[179] The delegates flatly rejected the conservative "New Departure" movement.[180] F. G. Barbadoes of the District of Columbia described the Republican Party as "that great organization to which the American people are indebted for the preservation of the Union and the Constitutional assertion of equal liberty and equal rights for all."[181]

Although Delany's letter to Douglass was widely circulated and seemed to have provoked a debate on the nature and course of black

Reconstruction, and while it could not have drawn, and categorically did not draw, blacks to Columbia, the overwhelming declaration of support for the Republican Party seemed a direct response to Delany's negative characterization of the party's activities and policies. This notwithstanding, his letter touched on two fundamental issues—corruption and racial tension. Even ardent supporters of the Republican administration acknowledged the prevalence of corruption, and it became a major issue in the ensuing 1872 state gubernatorial election. Several Republicans advocated reform, but unlike Delany, they were opposed to undermining the Republican Party. They did not want a repeat in South Carolina of what happened in Missouri, where a split in the Republican Party resulted in the election of more conservatives/Democrats. Unfortunately, the Republican Party could not escape a split. Although Democrats had withdrawn from statewide tickets, concentrating on municipal contests, the Republicans contested the election against each other.[182] For governor, the Republican Party nominated Franklin J. Moses, the former ill-reputable Speaker of the statehouse, and Richard Gleaves, a wealthy mulatto, for lieutenant governor. Due to his tarnished reputation, Moses's nomination disturbed reform-minded Republicans who bolted and, with the support of the state conservatives, nominated Reuben Tomlinson, described as "a scrupulously honest and highly capable," as their candidate for governor.[183] Consistent with his anti-radical and anticorruption crusade, Delany allied with the bolters. Curiously, the regular Republicans felt uncomfortable with Delany in the opposition camp. With the concurrence of Moses, Cain pleaded with Delany to reconsider his decision. He assured Delany that Moses had been misrepresented and that he would, if elected, deal with corruption. Perhaps most compelling, Cain informed Delany that Moses had agreed to reward him with a job if elected.[184]

Delany accepted Cain's overtures and became a loyal Moses campaign speaker. To restore confidence in the state finances, Delany traveled to New York, the nerve center of South Carolina finance, to reassure South Carolina bondholders, and potential bondholders, that Moses would not repudiate any of the state's debt and that his election would restore credibility to the state. He published two letters in the *New York Times* vouching for Moses's character and inviting potential investors to the state. In the first letter, he assured his readers that Moses was determined to honor the state's financial obligations and indebtedness. "He would not have received the nomination . . . had he not been in favor of every legal and legitimate measure tending to promote the credit, interests and integrity of the state," Delany wrote.[185] In the second letter, he pledged that South Carolina would not repudiate its debts. The new government would, as a matter of priority, restore the credit of the state. As he vouched, "The state is full of resources, her population industrious and producing, her staples abundant and valuable and her revenue equal to the demands of her liabilities. A change in the administration of her government will prove this."[186]

Moses defeated Tomlinson in an election marred by fraud. The cause célèbre was the election of one John J. Patterson ("honest John") to the U.S. Senate. "Honest John" bribed potential opponents, and his "agents" canvassed the state purchasing votes. Delany later testified before a Senate investigating committee that he witnessed an agent of "honest John" offer a cash reward to Robert B. Elliott, the black congressman, in return for his withdrawal from the contest.[187] Electoral fraud, however, was child's play compared to the corruption that the new administration unleashed. The diary of Josephus Woodruff, clerk of the Republican Printing Company, is replete with accounts of how key Republicans, black and white, abused their official positions and plundered the treasury.[188] While corruption engulfed the state, Delany had to contend with a broken promise. No offer of appointment came from Moses. He had, in fact, supported and campaigned for Moses on the promise of reward. The year 1873 was particularly difficult for Delany, and making a living became increasingly problematic.

Since the demise of the Bureau, Delany had been literally unemployed. With pressing family problems, his situation became desperate. He turned to a "personal friend," General H. G. Worthington, the collector of Customs in Charleston, who consoled him with the position of "duty inspector" under federal patronage. Though timely, the job did not significantly alter Delany's desperate condition.[189] A disappointed Cain sent a passionate plea to Governor Moses, reminding him how "impolitic" and "dangerous" it was to break faith with friends. He implored Moses to place Delany in a position that would enable him "render the state some service while making a living for his wife and children."[190] Cain pleaded further, "I have felt much concern about my friend Delany and my pledges to him before he consented to abandon his opposition to your nomination. . . . Delany's condition is a needy one. He has staked all on your word, for heaven's sake do not cast him away . . . you know doubtless what it is to be without money, without friends, without position, with pressing necessities."[191] There was no response from the governor. Moses did not listen, and thus again Delany had his hopes dashed. Moses, in fact, lived up to his reputation. According to one authority, he bore, externally at least, many of the earmarks of the ideal Southern gentleman—"a shrewd, unscrupulous scoundrel, untrue to his friends and unfaithful in his public trust and devoid of fine moral instincts."[192] Cain's letter illuminates Delany's desperate financial condition and his alienation from the Republican administration. The lack of a governmental position or reward undoubtedly exacerbated Delany's growing alienation from the political leadership of the state Republican Party. If he was angry and alienated, Delany did not publicly display it. Instead, he rode the moral high horse, his voice growing increasingly louder, as he nitpicked at what he perceived as the endemic corruption of the Republican state administration and advocated both a firm stand against corruption and a more conciliatory policy vis-à-vis the state conservatives.

Feeling much more goaded in his antiradical crusade, Delany wrote a letter to Jonathan T. Wright, the black associate justice of the state supreme court, reaffirming his earlier call for compromise with white Carolinians. He recalled how his persistent pleas for moderation toward, universal amnesty for, and reconciliation with ex-planters had been ridiculed and ignored. He warned that black political power in the state was not destined to last forever and that already whites were making moves to offset black preponderance through increased white immigration. He again blamed radicals for exploiting, misdirecting, and miseducating blacks and also for instilling in them a false sense of security. Whites, he argued, had no desire to empower blacks politically. He warned of the ephemeral nature of black political power, which had depended on demographic preponderance, a situation now threatened by the rapid increase in white immigration into the state. He predicted that in five years or less, blacks would be in the minority. Given this reality, blacks needed to be enlightened on what proper political policies to adopt toward local whites. He suggested a system that guaranteed minority representation to whites, one that accommodated their interests and needs. This would allow whites representation and participation in proportion to their number so that in future they, too, would reciprocate when eventually they assumed demographic and, ipso facto, political dominance. Expounding on his earlier theme, Delany reiterated that black political power was premature. The nation was not ready. Radicalism had misled blacks into believing otherwise.[193]

As always, Delany's letter won national recognition and support from the *New York Times*, which commended his sincerity and intelligence, describing him as "a sincere and intelligent friend of his race."[194] It referred to the advocacy of minority representation as prudence, since black political power in South Carolina was short-lived. According to the paper,

> Negro supremacy in South Carolina has not been an unmixed blessing, and when whites obtain the numerical superiority, as they shortly will from immigration, they are not likely to be any more liberal in their policy than blacks have been. Unless the blacks now permit the whites their proportionate participation in affairs, they are certainly in their turn to be entirely excluded, and the relations of the two races will thus be always disturbed.[195]

Convinced that white Carolinians would eventually regain power, Delany impressed on black political leaders the prudence of caution and compromise. The letter to Judge Wright, like the earlier one addressed to Douglass, echoed strong conservative values. Minority representation had featured in the resolutions of the state Conservative Taxpayers Convention of 1871 in Columbia. South Carolina conservatives and ex-Confederates had persistently advocated minority representation since the reforms of the Civil Rights Act and the Fourteenth and Fifteenth Amendments. This sudden strengthening of the majority status of blacks seriously threatened the political fortunes of the state conservatives. At the Taxpayers Convention, delegates unanimously called for more minority representation. Daniel Chamberlain, who would later become a Republican state governor, was among the most vocal advocate of minority representation. The conservatives wanted more representation in order to counteract what they perceived as "radical excesses." Whatever the motivation, calls for minority representation bore grievous implications for the consolidation of black freedom. The more political power conservatives attained, the greater their chances of subverting the course of Radical Reconstruction and black freedom.[196]

Delany and the state conservatives thus espoused similar values, albeit for different ends. While Delany's goal was ostensibly to harmonize the two races and enhance the political fortunes of blacks, the state conservatives sought minority representation precisely to gain a platform upon which to overturn Radical Reconstruction and dislodge blacks from politics. Delany's advocacy of minority representation rested on his firm conviction of the ephemeral nature of black political power in the state. He strongly believed in the now famous "population bogey" that the state conservatives propagated since the inception of Radical Reconstruction. According to this, the demographic preponderance of blacks was only short-lived. Black population would remain static, while that of whites would increase through immigration and natural processes. This gloomy prediction was designed to frighten blacks into surrendering political rights.[197]

The *New York Times* praised Delany and hoped other blacks would join him in his antiradical and anticorruption crusade. But most other blacks felt differently and did not believe that concessions to white Carolinians would guarantee black acceptance and elevation. Francis L. Cardozo spoke for many when he observed that men who believed that slavery was divine and fought a bloody war for it "could not in so short a time have entirely changed their opinion."[198] Addressing a gathering in 1870, black congressman Robert Brown Elliott referred to developments in Tennessee, where Democrats had taken over control of the state legislature and had proceeded to enact laws designed to restore the status quo antebellum. Despite the problems of Radical Reconstruction in South Carolina, most blacks embraced it with a deep sense of gratitude and were not convinced that corruption justified its demolition. Moreover, the Republican government had not been totally unmindful of corruption and had in fact instituted some measures designed specifically to alleviate the problem.[199]

This conflicting perception notwithstanding, Delany remained a loyal Republican, albeit with strong reservations about the future of the party. The "corruption and excesses" of the administration remained a troubling problem. His greatest regret, perhaps, was to have supported Governor Moses in the preceding election. The governor, some suggested, seemed to thrive on black ignorance and gullibility and appointed only, "Negroes of the lowest class," those he fondly and condescendingly called "good political niggers."[200] In Delany's judgment, Moses was not an aberration. He exemplified Radical Republicanism at its very worst.

The prevalence of corruption reinforced Delany's determination to assume a politically active position within the Republican administration. Paradoxically, in spite of his earlier opposition to black political power, he finally came to the conclusion that the type of change he favored was attainable only from a position of political leadership. By 1874 his conviction about the counterproductive and destructive influence of Radical Republicanism seemed strengthened. By identifying with this force, blacks, he argued, were equally responsible for the corruption and inefficiency that were the hallmarks of Republican administration in the state. Something had to be done.

The election of 1874 provided an opportunity. At the state nominating convention in Columbia, Delany ran for lieutenant governor but lost to a fellow black, Richard Gleaves, by a margin that underscored his unpopularity—ninety-seven votes to eleven. The delegates nominated Daniel H. Chamberlain, former state attorney, for governor, over Judge John T. Green, a conservative and ex-Confederate officer. This convention was indeed a battleground between conservatives/independents bent of overthrowing Radical Reconstruction and radicals determined to prevent it.[201]

THE INDEPENDENT REPUBLICAN

About three weeks after the Republican nominating convention, Delany and a few others bolted and launched the Independent Republican Movement (IRM) in Charleston to challenge the regular Republicans in the forthcoming election. They nominated Judge John T. Green for governor and Delany for lieutenant governor.[202] The acceptance of a ticket with a white Carolinian, and an ex-Confederate, symbolized Delany's postwar vision of reconciliation with ex-Confederates and Southern whites.

Made up mostly of moderate Republicans and supported by the state conservatives such as D. D. Lesesne, Charleston mayor G. I. Cunningham, ex-governor William Aiken, Senator S. E. Galliard, and General Kershaw, to identify a few, the IRM platform promised reform and honest government. It was undoubtedly conceived to appeal to conservative whites. It succeeded. The Green-Delany ticket stirred the hitherto alienated and politically docile state conservatives, who hailed it as a vehicle for the deconstruction of Radical Reconstruction. The last time the conservatives had attempted to capture state politics was in 1870. At that time, masquerading as the Union Reform Party, they pledged reform and accepted the Fourteenth and Fifteenth Amendments. However, internal squabbling, especially over the political rights of blacks, exposed both the fragility and "political" nature of their conservative liberalism. Perceptive blacks voted overwhelmingly for the Republican Party, which won that election. After the 1870 defeat, the conservatives quietly abandoned statewide elections to rival factions of the Republican Party, contesting only local and municipal elections until the emergence of the IRM.[203]

The momentum generated by the IRM awakened even diehard conservatives from political slumber. They hailed Delany's candidacy. However, what Delany and other blacks in the IRM failed, or refused, to recognize was the insincerity of the conservatives. They did not support the movement out of a conviction that blacks deserved equal rights and opportunities. In fact, as the conservative press conceded, the move by the conservatives did not signal an abandonment of principle. It was instead necessitated by expediency and "neither represented any want of Democratic principle, nor disloyalty to the highest type of Democratic opinion."[204]

Delany's campaign speeches as an IRM candidate were riddled with distortions, and he seemed to have been afflicted by an acute case of historical amnesia. It began even before his official nomination as a candidate. In an address to a gathering of IRM members in Charleston early in October 1874, Delany stated,

> The people of South Carolina have but one common interest and they should act with a view to serve that common interest. . . . What is most desired is that the whites and the blacks in this state should know and understand their duties towards each other, so as to act together and work for their mutual and will and prosperity . . . blacks have at least learned that they were dependent upon the whites just as the whites were dependent upon them, and that it is in their interest to work with, rather than against whites.[205]

He concluded by impressing upon his audience the fact that "each man, black and white, represented a portion of the twofold basis of the land—labor and capital. The black man and the white man must work in cooperation together, and by this mutual cooperation would be worked out the *redemption* of the state, and prosperity and happiness for the whole people" (emphasis added).[206] During the subsequent IRM nominating convention, Delany reviewed the history of Reconstruction in the state, condemning radicals for leading blacks along the path of confrontation and corruption. He urged a "new departure" that took blacks away from what he described as the "old double-dyed corrupt wing of the Republican party."[207] He called for both the adoption of a conservative platform and the nomination of honest men as means of attracting conservative interests and as the best combination guaranteed to defeat the radicals.[208]

Delany's speech called for cooperation and union of blacks and whites for mutual advancement. But he was careful to reassure whites, perhaps conscious of their racial sensitivity, that such union or cooperation was purely economic—labor and capital—and did not necessarily suggest social equality. Delany had never lost sight of the prevailing disposition among local whites against social equality, his enthusiasm for racial cooperation notwithstanding. Hence, he de-emphasized social equality, contending that "social equality must regulate itself." Nobody should be forced into socializing with others along racial lines against their wishes and disposition. Social equality should not be enforced.

He reassured his listeners that blacks would not insist on social equality unless and until whites were comfortable with it. In the meantime, individuals should be left free to choose whom to mix with socially.[209]

It is imperative to understand the basis of Delany's de-essentializing of social equality. White Carolinians—in fact, white Southerners generally, especially the former planter class—remained nervously apprehensive of the social implications of black freedom. Would the political empowerment and freedom of blacks mean the declaration of social equality between races that was hitherto deemed unequal? Would this compel sharing of social amenities on an equal basis? These are a few of the critical questions at the heart of conservative resistance to black freedom and political elevation.[210] When the Green-Delany ticket was formally nominated and approved, Delany was introduced as "the honest exemplar of the honest colored men of South Carolina."[211] In his acceptance speech, Delany pledged to work to advance racial harmony. According to him, "I shall know no party than that which shall have for its object the interest of the whole people, black and white, of the state of South Carolina."[212] He also promised to turn blacks away from the misdirection and miseducation of a radicalism that had alienated them from local whites. Blacks had more to lose in a racial conflict, he insisted. However, in promoting racial harmony, Delany promised not to "lower my standard of manhood in regard to the claims of my race one single step. I do not intend to recede from the rights that have been given us by the beneficence of a just Congress of the nation one single hairs breadth, but I do intend, in demanding all this, to demand the same equal rights and justice for every citizen, black and white, of the state of South Carolina."[213] It is significant here to note Delany's espousal of an interracial ethos designed to effect racial harmony by de-emphasizing race. It is remarkable, considering that blacks came out of slavery less than a decade earlier, that Delany is already talking about color-blind policies.

At another ratification meeting, Delany again insisted that Radical Reconstruction had not benefited blacks. Instead, it had fomented racial divisions and tension. In this speech, he made a definitive declaration of his vision and preference for the future of the state—blacks uniting and cooperating with representatives of the old system in South

Carolina. He wanted cooperation between blacks and "some of the first white men in South Carolina, men who had held high offices of trust *under the old state government*" (emphasis added).[214] Obviously, this is a reference to the pre–Civil War government. While condemning Radical Republicanism for conferring no benefits on blacks, he credited Democrats with black freedom. Furthermore, his analysis of the history of antislavery showed Democrats contributing more to the Underground Railroad and the cause of black freedom.[215]

It is not clear specifically what Democrats, and what freedom, Delany had in mind. It is conceivable that he used the term "Democrats" loosely and synonymous with "democracy" and "Jeffersonian democracy." It is perhaps only in this context that Delany's association of "Democrats" with "freedom" might make any sense. However, if by "Democrats" he meant those who had historically been associated with the Democratic Party, those who defended slavery and fought for secession, the very same group that blacks in general associated with slavery, then his analogy constitutes nothing short of historical amnesia of epic proportion. Furthermore, he declared his determination to teach blacks truths about Reconstruction and would not be "deterred, even by the thirty indictments that I understand are to be brought up against me by some lying scoundrel. Let these swindling adventurers come with their indictments."[216] For the first time Delany gave hint of a possible retaliation and victimization.

He described the lies and excesses of Radical Republicanism as designed to keep blacks permanently down and exploited, and he urged blacks to open their eyes and recognize that "politics are intended for the benefits of the people."[217] Delany thus reiterated a theme he had earlier emphasized—the utilitarian character of politics. It is precisely on the basis of this utilitarian factor that he judged the Republican Party a failure. He called for a "new political relations between the races."[218] Emphatically, Delany implored blacks to abandon their traditional ally, the Republican Party, for the Democratic Party. This is the only relationship that, according to him, guaranteed, "certain success and triumph in our efforts to redeem the state."[219] It is remarkable here to note his introduction of the theme of redemption, a theme that would become particularly essential to the conservative ideology and platform in the near future. He enjoined blacks and whites to unite in a common struggle to redeem the state from the radicals, who, according to him, had not only exploited blacks and defrauded the state but also had misrepresented Democrats as enemies of black freedom. Recommending a dismantling of the Republican Party, he adjudged Radical Reconstruction a failure, having driven much-needed investment from the state.[220]

In a rare display of courage, he declared, "for a long time I have been alone in the Party (Republican), and denounced for my views. . . . I am no longer scared of being called a Democrat."[221] At another IRM gathering in Greenville, Delany informed blacks that their interests and those of whites were one and that prosperity for both races depended on peace and goodwill.[222] General Kershaw, A leading IRM member, strongly endorsed Delany's remarks, contending that they expressed his own sentiments.[223] It is noteworthy that this was the same General Kershaw who, as orator of the day during the Monument Day celebration in Sumter in 1868, reportedly "brought tears from many" as he recalled, among others, the sacrifices of the sons of Sumter in the Civil War, the evil and destructive consequence of the emancipation of slaves, and the subjection of the South to the despoliation and subjugation of blacks, carpetbaggers, and scalawags.[224] The two again spoke at another rally in Chester a few days later, during which Delany acquitted himself "so completely alongside of the first gentlemen of South Carolina," receiving commendation for his patriotism and statesmanship from the conservatives.[225]

The state conservatives endorsed the IRM overwhelmingly. In fact, the ticket attracted the "strongest straight-out Democrats."[226] Delany promised to promote the mutual welfare of the two races. He again blamed the rising racial tensions on Radical Republicanism and called for a new departure, involving a "union of some of the first men of South Carolina who held high office of trust under the old state government [pre–Civil War] and me Martin R. Delany, a John Brown abolitionist."[227] Amid thunderous applause and oblivious to the contradiction in his speech (that is, advocacy of union between representatives of the old order in South Carolina and a "John Brown" associate), the conservatives sang "Bonnie Blue Flag" (the Confederate anthem).[228] Only the mind of a Delany could have conceived of this contradiction, and it was clear that neither he nor his audience recognized it—this particular audience was composed of people who definitely jubilated on that bright December morning of 1859 when John Brown died on the scaffold after an ill-fated attempt to overthrow slavery. They unanimously embraced Delany. The IRM provided the opportunity, as one conservative put it, "to kill the snake of radicalism."[229] Unfortunately for the IRM, blacks stood solidly behind the Radical Republicans, who won the election. However, the total votes cast in 1874 was 149,221, the largest since 1868, clearly reflecting increased white participation.[230] It should also be noted that had the Independent Republicans won, one unintended consequence of their victory, certainly of revolutionary and monumental proportions, would have been the first black governor in the United States. Martin Delany, a black man, would have become governor of South Carolina, "largely through the vote of the white people," because Judge Green died shortly after the election.[231]

Delany's action underscored the depth of his alienation. His willingness to share a political platform with Judge Green, a native Carolinian and an ex-Confederate, and other high-ranking ex-Confederates and conservatives symbolized the new direction in his thought. His call for a "new departure" and union with representatives of the old order revealed that direction. Nothing in his actions, however, made sense to other blacks. To yearn for the old order and to publicly embrace representatives of that order seemed to many blacks the ultimate act of betrayal.

Delany's "new departure," was however, a child of the age. Some conservatives had also called for a new departure. These "realists" Democrats, as they have been tagged, favored compromise with Reconstruction and cooperation with "liberal" Republicans. They propagated a democratic liberal ideology that won the heart of Delany and convinced him that Democrats had changed and were willing to accommodate blacks, if only blacks abandoned radicalism. Delany embraced the "realists," while ignoring the other far more potent and influential group of orthodox Democrats who remained indomitably opposed to the "new departure." More significantly, he failed to comprehend the dynamic and complex character of conservative liberalism. The conservative new departurists were also states rightists who vehemently opposed federal control of Reconstruction. They preferred to see Southerners in complete control, a preference that bore ominous signs for the future of blacks. While endorsing a "new departure," several conservatives openly espoused black subordination. As Eric Foner surmised, "even among its advocates, the new departure smacked less of a genuine accommodation to the democratic revolution embodied in Reconstruction . . . indeed, there was always something grudging about Democrats' embrace of black civil and political rights . . . publicly, Democratic leaders spoke of a new era in Southern politics; privately, many hoped to undo the 'evil' of black suffrage as early . . . as possible."[232] In fact, the baneful effect of the "new departure" was evident to perceptive blacks in South Carolina, who consequently maintained a respectable distance from it. They heard of developments in Tennessee, Georgia, Missouri, and Virginia where conservatives masqueraded as liberal, new departurists to successfully overturn Radical Reconstruction and displace black politicians.[233]

The victory of the Radical Republicans in 1874 was, however, a Pyrrhic one. Although unsuccessful in its bid to unseat the radicals, the IRM did achieve some measure of success. In fourteen of the state's thirty-two counties, conservatives swept local offices. They also elected about two-fifths of their members to the state legislature. For the first time since 1867, the legislature now had a white majority of three.[234] This accomplishment notwithstanding, the IRM fizzled out quickly, leaving conservatives and liberal Republicans without a politically viable organizational base. For Martin Delany, the demise of the IRM seemed auspicious a time to actively pursue a truly "new departure."

FIVE

Third Integrationist Phase
1875–1877

EARLY IN 1875, like the biblical prodigal son, Delany returned to the Republican Party fold. There seemed to be no other option left if he wanted to remain politically active. Although the conservatives achieved some measure of success at the local levels in the recently concluded elections in South Carolina, Radical Republicans retained control of the state government. His dramatic return was by no means an admission of guilt but an extraordinary display of courage and conviction. Delany took his antiradical crusade right back to where it started. Rather than succumb and surrender in the face of overwhelming opposition and political despair, he surged forward and confronted the radicals. The last election drove home one significant lesson that probably influenced his decision to return to the Republican Party. The overwhelming support blacks gave to the Republicans confirmed their dislike for the conservative alternative. Delany's return, however, did not signal acknowledgment, de facto or otherwise, that his ideas were misguided or that he had done anything wrong. In fact, he had not reconciled himself to the policies of the radicals; nor had he so soon forgotten their persistent opposition to his political aspirations. In his judgment, therefore, the return was more appropriately an act of taking the fight right back to where it belonged. Neither were the radicals inclined easily to forget and forgive Delany's negative and destructive utterances and reviews. As he himself recognized, the Independent Republican Movement (IRM) represented his "crowning act of infamy never to be forgotten and sworn to be punished."[1] From the beginning, therefore, the relationship involved strange bedfellows in which neither side felt comfortable with the other. None, however, felt more uncomfortable than Delany himself. He perceived the radicals as conspirators bent on destroying him. Rightly or wrongly, this perception was central to his aggressive responses. Neither the certainty nor uncertainty of radical conspiracy, however, could deter him from the path of aggressive opposition to radicalism.

Early in 1875, he traveled to New York at the invitation of those he described as "most distinguished gentlemen for position and wealth," to address a gathering at Irvin Hall.[2] As already indicated, New York was the nerve center of South Carolina finance. It was where the majority of the state investors, bondholders, and potential bondholders were concentrated. Delany lectured on what he termed "truths" about the South. As always, he charged "radicals" and "selfish politicians" with misleading blacks and fomenting racial tensions in the South. Blacks would have become a great political force, he lamented, but for the misdirection and miseducation of radicals, and selfish politicians. Radical rule, he argued, had sown the seeds of discord in the South.[3] Underlining the degenerative impact of Radical Reconstruction, Delany declared, "The colored people before the war were the best social and domestic element of its class that any country was ever blessed with. Properly directed, when they attained their freedom, they would have formed a political element of which the country might be proud."[4] Regrettably, this did not happen. Blacks, he bemoaned, "turned to the new comers, who took advantage of their ignorance to mislead them. They taught them that whatever was contrary to the interests of their old masters was right. He said knowingly that the class of men who undertook to lead the colored men in general had no interest in either the black or white race of the South."[5] For the first time since the war, Delany carried his antiradical crusade to the North. Northern public opinion had always played a crucial role in developments within Southern states. Southern politicians, irrespective of party affiliations, had always cherished a favorable image in the North. Delany's speech therefore significantly undermined Radical Republicanism in the North. His speech occurred precisely at a time when the Democratic resurgence gathered momentum, not just within

South Carolina but nationwide. Reported widely, the speech created further problems for him in South Carolina. It brought the long-expected conspiracy closer.

His trip to New York occurred also at a very critical time. A turning point in the history of Reconstruction, 1874 marked the beginning of a nationwide conservative slant. The election that year witnessed the resurgence of conservatives in several Southern states, and according to one authority, Northerners not only increasingly began to sympathize with Southern values but also began to question the rationale for Radical Reconstruction.[6] Also within the Republican Party, a liberal and moderate wing became increasingly critical of Radical Reconstruction. Delany's address thus blended with this resurging conservative momentum and provided even stronger justification for jettisoning Radical Reconstruction. To Northerners, his address represented firsthand information from someone familiar with the "excesses of radicalism" in a pivotal Southern state. Reported widely, his speech further infuriated radicals back in South Carolina. Passing by the Charleston city hall shortly after his return, Delany alleged that he overheard someone complain that he (Delany) had gone far enough and "must be put down."[7] Soon thereafter, the state solicitor also allegedly vowed to put Delany in the penitentiary at the earliest opportunity.[8]

Undeterred, Delany intensified his antiradical crusade. Three significant factors sustained him in this preoccupation. First, there was his rugged determination to destroy radical power and the almost religious conviction of his righteousness. The second and perhaps most important reason was the belief that he had the moral and psychological support of the "men of worth" in the state, that is, native whites. Although politically weakened, the fact remained that they controlled the economic power of the state. Third, the election of 1874 witnessed dramatic comebacks by conservatives within the state and nationwide. With such victories, the handwriting seemed clear—the days of radicalism appeared numbered.

The prospect or imminence of radical censure and victimization could not deter Delany. Preparatory to the 1875 municipal election in Charleston, some blacks sought his opinion on the desirability of fielding a black candidate for mayor. He objected strongly on the ground that such a measure was "impolitic" and would damage the reputation and commercial prosperity of the city. He deemed the performance of black politicians at the state level disgraceful, a serious indictment of all blacks, and, therefore, strong ground for the rejection of all aspiring black politicians. Black suffrage had ruined the state, leaving Charleston as, "the only part . . . that gives us credit abroad," he declared.[9] In his judgment, Charleston was like a pristine and shinning city upon a hill, unpolluted by the corruption of black politicians. He strongly advised Charlestonians to maintain their tradition of white mayors.[10]

Applied statewide, Delany's contention constituted grounds for dismantling black political power, a task to which he seemed doggedly committed. He began a weekly, the *Charleston Independent*, which he dedicated to the fight against corruption and radicalism.[11] The title *"Independent"* mirrored his growing alienation from the Republican Party. In the ensuing municipal election in Charleston, he campaigned vigorously for the white mayoral candidate, G. I. Cunningham, a moderate Republican who had also won the endorsement of the conservatives. He used his paper to attack and discredit Republican candidates. Cunningham won the mayoral race, while many radical candidates went down to defeat. In the aftermath of this election, according to Delany, radicals swore to inflict on him "the severest penalty known to the criminal law, even death, if it was legally possible."[12] If Delany was gunning for a showdown with the radicals, he could not have chosen a more potent and effective terrain, for Charleston was indeed a pivotal county.

Politics not only creates strange bedfellows but also oftentimes exhibits irrational and intriguing decisions. One such was Governor Chamberlain's choice of Delany as trial justice for Ward Three of the city of Charleston.[13] The job of trial justice entailed the enforcement of the common laws of property, public order, and domestic peace. In his office on Anson Street, according to Ullman, Delany judged a large number of assault cases and "seemed to prefer any alternative to imprisonment for those he found guilty." Few offenders went to jail. In most cases he imposed fines or placed the offender(s) on peace bonds.[14]

What prompted Chamberlain to take a decision so obviously unpopular with fellow Radical Republicans? The answer is not far-fetched. He had been elected on a platform that promised reform. Strange as it seems, Delany's appointment was in consonance with the governor's campaign pledges. Chamberlain's commitment to reform compelled him to sacrifice party loyalty and appoint men to offices regardless of their past or present political affiliations. He replaced many corrupt radical officials with honest ones, mostly Democrats and conservatives. He also refused to commission two Republican circuit judges elected by the radical legislature (ex-governor Franklin J. Moses and William Whipper).[15] However, if Chamberlain was willing to sacrifice party loyalty for reform, other radicals were not. As Delany well understood, his offenses had gone beyond pardon. The radicals could not so easily have forgotten or forgiven Delany's subversive activities. His appointment to an official position, therefore, provided them with a *causa belli*. Not long after Delany took office, one Rev. Alonzo W. Webster and three blacks filed a suit against him for breach of trust and grand larceny, inaugurating perhaps the most significant crisis of his entire public life.[16]

This crisis originated back in 1871 when Delany functioned briefly as a real estate agent and note broker. As agent for one Mrs. Richardson, he was entrusted with the sum of $200 belonging to the John's Island Wesleyan Church, of which the deceased father of his client was a trustee. He invested the money in county claims and expected full payment. His claims were, however, refused, even as other claims were honored. In consequence, Delany could not refund the church's money. As the claims began to depreciate, he applied for an injunction and entered judgment for $1,131. This included sums he held in trust for other clients. For the first time, a judgment against the county was obtained for $12,000, and an appropriation of some $60,000 was made to pay up county claims. Even though Delany's suit was second on the list, his claims were again not honored. Another county appropriation provided little relief for Delany. Still the county did not honor his claims. Frustrated, he sought to transfer the judgment to the trustees of the church, but they refused.[17] The issue remained unresolved until 1876, when it was resurrected on the heels of his antiradical campaigns of 1874 and 1875. Logically, Delany suspected political motivation.

Delany conceived of the lawsuit as a deep-seated and statewide radical conspiracy that was stage managed to punish him for his "disloyalty."

According to him, radicals and avowed enemies of Mayor Cunningham constituted the entire twelve-man jury—five blacks, seven whites. Witness after witness, he reported, declared one falsehood after another, all in a bid to secure his conviction. The prosecuting attorney allegedly commenced his proceedings by declaring the occasion the happiest of his fourteen years in the legal profession and then proceeded to shower abuses, sneers, jibes, and mockery on Delany. "Then placing himself squarely before me," Delany reported, "with extended arms, fingers almost touching my nose and with full vehemence, shouted 'you tell a damned lie! It is a damned infernal lie!! You are a damned infernal liar!!!' "[18] Delany portrayed the entire trial as a charade and a travesty of justice. "A more shameful perversion of the truth never was perpetrated in a court of justice," he lamented.[19] The trial dragged on for almost a year. As the jury retired for a verdict, Delany claimed he overheard one of them whisper to a lawyer, "He [Delany], is good for the penitentiary!"[20] They returned in less than ten minutes with a guilty verdict. He was sentenced to twelve months in the penitentiary. His counsel quickly appealed the conviction. Pending the decision on the appeal, Delany was set free but relieved of the trial justice post.[21]

Delany was undoubtedly a troubled man. Since joining the abolition movement in the 1830s, never had he felt so depressed and almost completely helpless. The grand larceny crisis bore grievous implications for his future political career. It not only undermined and threatened all that he had accomplished in almost fifty years of antislavery activities, but it also endangered his political future. The response of several Republican papers branding him a "thief" and "hypocrite" was most devastating. Although conservative papers would rally to his aid, Delany felt that untold damage had already been done.

Delany vehemently denied any fraudulent intentions. Was he guilty of misappropriating the funds? The truth may never be known. One can only speculate. There was no doubt that at the time he was entrusted with the funds, Delany was desperately in need. After repeated frustrations and failures in his political aspirations, he had turned to business and had unsuccessfully appealed to Northern capitalists. The funds therefore came in handy, and the temptation was there to reinvest it with a view to making personal profits. Delany, it seemed, never intended permanently to appropriate the funds, but the county's refusal to honor his claims left him vulnerable. The state conservative press, as always, came to his defense. It contended that he was being persecuted for his political views; because of this, the paper called for "unusual consideration" for him in this "undeserved trouble."[22] Condemning those who applauded and celebrated Delany's conviction, the *Charleston News and Courier* came to his defense, vouching for his character and suggesting, as Delany had, that the entire episode was politically motivated. According to the paper,

> We have been for a long time conversant with the facts of the transaction in question, which have been published in this paper; and the issues of the trial does not alter our conviction that the accused is honest, that he attempted no fraud, and that recent action had its origin in political differences and was prosecuted with partisan zeal. The whole record of Col. Delany, from the beginning of the Reconstruction process, has been creditable to him and diametrically opposed to that of his political enemies. He has never failed to urge moderation on the part of his race, an alliance with whites, and an utter repudiation of worthless adventurers and low demagogues. He has been a stumbling block in the way of Ringleaders, and they wish to be rid of him.[23]

By 1876 Delany felt embattled and alienated from the black leadership and its ally, the Republican Party, in South Carolina. His persistent opposition to political rights unnerved many blacks. His entry into Republican politics and calls for more black representation only created more problems for him. Many felt he could not, and should not, be trusted with any political post. At heart, Delany was a conservative who felt uncomfortable with radical policies largely because he sincerely believed that blacks had a better chance of advancement through cooperation with local whites. It was the Civil War that had changed his perceptions and visions, completely obliterating race from his consciousness. To some observers, Delany seemed selfish. To others, he was a betrayer of his race, someone not to be trusted. There emerged an equally determined opposition to his role in South Carolina. This would hurt him badly, as he soon found himself desperately in financial stress and without the means of even caring for his family. He could not secure a steady job. Alienated from the black political leadership, feeling victimized and marginalized, Delany once again turned to the one person he hoped could offer positive suggestions on how to deal with and overcome this tortuous moment of existential reality.

On February 28, 1876, he wrote a second letter to "Hon. Frederick Douglass." In his times of stress, need, and isolation, Delany turned to the one person who commanded national attention and respect and who was among the leaders in the vanguard of the national black struggle. Aside from their long relationship, Douglass had already distinguished himself as a black leader of national repute. He had led the black delegation to President Johnson in 1866 to discuss the suffrage issue and by the mid-1870s was a force to be reckoned with among Republican officials in Washington. Appropriately titled "Trial and Conviction," this was a lengthy letter to which Delany attached twelve supporting documents illustrating his crises and problems with radicalism in South Carolina.[24] He somehow believed that Douglass could intervene to reverse what he saw as a dangerous path along which blacks in South Carolina were being led by Radical Republicanism. It was this conviction that informed his earlier letter and scathing review of Reconstruction. That letter did not seem to have changed the situation much. Instead of mellowing, the radicals seemed to have intensified their activities. The grand larceny trial itself was evidence of the troubling persistence of Radical Republicanism. He felt that left unchecked, these radical political excesses would eventually provoke the wrath of the entire nation against blacks. Delany intimated that the pursuit of racial animosity would only hurt blacks, since in the event of a racial war, whites, regardless of ideological or party affiliations (Republican or Democrat) or geographical locations (South, North, or West) would unite solidly against blacks.[25] In other words, regardless of the Republican Party's professed commitment to black interests, it would eventually seek its racial affinity in times of critical racial confrontation. The combined force of the nation's whites arrayed against blacks would result in nothing short of the extermination of the black race.

Delany portrayed his persecution as just the beginning of a conspiracy that, left unchecked, would eventually result in the exacerbation of racial tension within the South, a situation that could only result in destructive consequences for blacks.[26] To forestall this, he sought the intervention of Frederick Douglass. He defined his objective as primarily to present to the entire nation "the true character of so-called radicalism, as it exists in the state of South Carolina, and the alarming extent to which it has gone, in subverting the rights and liberties of the people, especially those who oppose them whether white or black, as exhibited in my own case."[27] He cataloged how black interests were subverted and misdirected by those he identified as foreign interests and adventurers. He also recounted his years of struggle against "irrational" and often "pre-mature" political demands by blacks, demands instigated, he insisted, by a false sense of security induced by Radical Republicanism. He gave instances of how his calls for moderation and compromise were ridiculed and ignored and how radicals hatched a conspiracy to humiliate and punish him. The letter closed with a grim prediction of racial conflagration, and the eventual annihilation of blacks, in the event that nothing was done to stem the threatening tide of radicalism in South Carolina.[28]

It is significant to note Delany's endearing depiction of the "peculiar institution" (slavery) as much more liberal in its responses to criticisms than the era of freedom (Reconstruction). As he explained,

> In the worst times of ANTE BELLUM days, during the existence of an institution that was national and recognized by the constitution, defended by the North and South, supported by the Supreme Court and Treasury, Army and Navy of the country, you and I could write, speak of, and oppose the policies and parties which supported it, boldly and fearlessly. But since the overthrow of that institution and the power of those who supported it, we dare not oppose the infamies of radical rule under these adventurers and new masters of the whole people, without fear of the loss of liberty, by ignominious convictions, through conspiracy and perjury.[29]

Although Delany meant this letter for publication as a pamphlet, for reasons unknown, it was never published. However, he preserved it in its manuscript form. Given the timing of the letter, he undoubtedly meant it as a warning and a call for a redirection of black political orientation and affiliations, in the context of the approaching state and national elections. It was meant to expose what he termed the true character of political radicalism and the damage it had done in South Carolina. As in the first letter of five years earlier, Delany minced no words in his castigation and rebuke of Radical Republicanism and, in his estimation, the destructive path along which it was leading blacks. Of the twelve supporting documents, the first ten cataloged what he described as "Offenses" that the radicals had charged him with since the advent of Reconstruction, culminating in the grand larceny case and his conviction. The offenses included:

1. His advocacy of caution and gradualism, especially regarding black political empowerment.
2. His scathing indictment of political corruption, particularly his contention that blacks and their Radical Republican allies were responsible for corruption and other political ills, undermining the success of Reconstruction.
3. His call for unconditional pardon for and reconciliation with ex-rebels.
4. His persistent opposition to radical policies of the Republicans at both the municipal and state levels.
5. His calls for concessions to white minority interests and political superiority.
6. His flirtation with the state conservatives in the IRM of 1874.[30]

The above offenses, according to him, so enraged the radicals that they not only frustrated his political aspirations but actively sought every opportunity to humiliate and punish him. The grand larceny case was just the beginning of a devious and far-reaching plan by the radicals to get even and possibly annihilate him physically. His victimization was just the beginning.

As he gloomily concluded,

Now let them succeed and go on in this last scheme of prosecution of theirs to hold the reigns of power, and keep their feet on the people of the South, by using our race as the political instrument of their oppression, let them continue to promote strife between the races, the eyes of the whole North and West being already turned in this direction, and their minds made up, and the first occasion for the murmur of a conflict of races, and the whole country will rise up and rush to arms with such force and power. . . . Extermination will be their theme, their watch-word, "every Negro in the grave!"[31]

Such extermination meant that blacks would "only be remembered among the things of the past!"[32] This letter is also significant in that Delany, in his own words, leaves us in no doubt as to where he belonged on the ideological spectrum. Like the first letter, this is as much a criticism and condemnation of Radical Reconstruction as it is a call for the abandonment and unraveling of the black-Republican Party alliance. There is no indication that Douglass replied to this letter. Delany's catalog of individual and collective recriminations of Radical Republicans (blacks and whites) did not seem to have swayed Douglass or any significant segment of the mainstream black political leadership. On the contrary, the evidence indicates a strengthening of the support for Republicans. In fact, less than two months after he received the letter, Douglass delivered an address at the unveiling of the Freedmen's Monument in memory of Abraham Lincoln in Lincoln Park, Washington, D.C., in which he clearly dissociated himself from Delany's pessimistic and gloomy analysis and predictions. "That we are here in peace today is a compliment and a credit to American civilization and a prophecy of still greater national enlightenment and progress in the future," he informed the audience.[33] Furthermore, underlining the imperative of gratitude and optimism, he averred,

> I refer to the past, not in malice, for this is no day for malice, but simply to place more distinctly in front the gratifying and glorious change which has come both to our white fellow-citizens and to ourselves, and to congratulate all upon the contrast between now and then—between the new dispensation of freedom and its thousand blessings to both races, and the old dispensation of slavery with its ten thousand evils to both races, white and black.[34]

In the horizon before him, Douglass saw no cause for anything other than optimism and hope for progressive changes. Delany's letter was

written on February 28, 1876; the mainstream black leadership convened in Nashville, Tennessee, on April 7 to reaffirm dedication to,
and support for, the national Republican administration.

There were no significant interventions to save Delany from what he
perceived as radical conspiracy. Judging by the tone of "Trial and Conviction," Delany felt abandoned to be victimized by the radicals, alone,
against their avenging wrath. The grand larceny conviction appeared to
seal his fate. He seemed overwhelmed and helpless. It was indeed a
field day for radicals with axes to grind with Delany. Not long after his
sentencing, one Rev. N. N. Hunter wrote an intimidating letter to
Delany, urging him to refund certain money he allegedly owed some
John's Island residents or risk further lawsuits.[35] Delany fired back,
refuting the allegations. Another representative, R. S. Tharin, immediately wrote Governor Chamberlain expressing disappointment at not
being appointed a trial justice in the first place instead of Delany. Antici-
pating Delany's removal, Tharin reaffirmed his continued interest in
the position.[36]

Help soon came from unexpected quarters. Early in April 1876, in a
stunning about-face, C. C. Bowen, the radical who had earlier opposed
Delany's bid for the Senate, appealed to Governor Chamberlain to pardon Delany, indicating that Delany had not only pledged to refund the
money but had actually deposited the sum with him for transfer to the
church.[37] In truth, Delany had only given a signed authorization (not
cash) to "friends" who had volunteered to assist in raising the money.
Two weeks later, Judge J. B. Reed of the First Circuit Court also petitioned
the governor, advising that "in view of the former good character of
Delany, and a doubt that may be reasonably entertained as to whether
he acted with fraudulent intent, the imprisonment be remitted and he be
pardoned on condition that he agreed to refund the money."[38] Two other
petitioners wrote pleadingly to Chamberlain, indicating that the money
had in fact been refunded to the trustees of the church and requesting
a pardon for Delany. According to these petitioners, "M. R. Delany is
dear to us, whatever may be his faults, and if we had the money we
would willingly pay, yes a hundred times over, rather than seeing him
going to the penitentiary." Explaining further, the petitioners wrote,
"M. R. Delany, Governor, happened to be one of the few of our Race of

whom, we are proud to claim, we have waited long to hear of you on the letter of C. C. Bowen, we trust that you will soon relieve us of our painful anxiety by an early reply, being satisfied that its issues is sufficient to justify you in granting the pardon prayed for by your petitioners, and believing and hoping it will come."[39]

Chamberlain suspended action on these requests pending information from Delany that he had refunded the sum. When nothing came, his secretary, R. Jones, wrote a letter to Delany inquiring "why he did not enable [the governor] to act on his pardon by furnishing . . . evidence that the money had been paid."[40] Delany expressed shock and disappointment at the action of "friends" to whom he had entrusted the matter. They had reneged on their promise to help raise the sum. He revealed that he had actually raised the money in the past and had entrusted it to "friends" who promised to transfer it to the church, but they had misappropriated the funds instead. He promised to attend to the matter himself.[41]

This letter is significant in certain other respects. First, there is the unmistakable tone of disappointment with some class of friends. Second, there is unambiguous acknowledgment of Delany's desperate economic condition. Third, and perhaps most significantly, there is the hint of a possible change of party—"I shall proceed immediately among *my friends of another party* as I have not the means within myself to raise the money," Delany informed Chamberlain (emphasis added).[42] Although Delany did not identify these "friends of another party," it seems plausible to infer that he had Democrats in mind. The money was eventually refunded, even though the source remains a mystery. However, there is no concrete evidence to suggest that the Democrats bailed Delany out of his financial quagmire, even though circumstantial evidence seems to suggest that they did. In other words, there is no evidence that the Democrats helped Delany financially, even though his letter implied he was turning in their direction for help. It is, however, tempting to view his subsequent turn to the Democratic Party as representing a quid pro quo.

Chamberlain finally granted the pardon on the August 29 "after the Sheriff of Charleston County, having certified to me that the said money has been placed in the hands of the Trustees of the said Church."[43]

Early in September, Delany wrote to Chamberlain and thanked him for "great and beneficent favor." He pledged to support the governor's renomination bid and promised to discuss the matter with General Elliott, chair of the State Republican Executive Committee, whom he described as a personal friend, "even though we differ on political matters."[44] It is significant to note here Delany's acknowledgment of political disagreement with a leading member of the black Republican political elite in the state. To work effectively for Chamberlain's renomination, however, required immediate consultation with Elliot at his home, "to show him the importance of putting you in nomination, which I think he will adhere to," Delany suggested. He would have to travel a considerable distance to confer with Elliot, and this required funds that Delany lacked. As he lamented, "I regret that I am so circumscribed in consequence of my position, *that I cannot command means as I should, and as the respectful colored men do generally*" (emphasis added).[45] Consequently, Delany requested from the governor "a thousand mile R.R. Ticket" to facilitate his travels.[46]

This pledge of support notwithstanding, the letter powerfully expressed his deepening feelings of frustration and dissatisfaction. He felt disadvantaged because he could not command means like other respectable blacks. He felt wronged. Shortly thereafter, he publicly declared for the Democratic Party. There was, however, nothing arbitrary to this development. It should have been anticipated. He had unsuccessfully appealed to Frederick Douglass and indirectly to the federal government for help. He had been left alone, single-handedly, to confront what he perceived as radical witch-hunting. He felt unjustly victimized. In his estimation, the success of the radicals in the grand larceny trial portended intensification of racial tension, and he desperately sought means of averting the impending cataclysm. Since he had failed to tame radicalism from within, he would now attempt, once again, to destroy it from without.

THE DEMOCRAT

Crises play significant roles in human motivations. Not only do they provide a basis for flashbacks into, and reflections on, the past but also for determining future courses of action. For Delany, the ordeal of the grand larceny trial reinforced his suspicion of and deepened his alienation from the radicals. The pardon could not completely obliterate the ugly fact that he had lost his job and seen his reputation tarnished. Delany, therefore, emerged from the crisis more determined than ever to combat Radical Republicanism. He became convinced that the basis for survival within the Republican Party was nonexistent. Survival had, in fact, been his key preoccupation since the end of the Bureau job. However, if in the past he had thought only in terms of economic survival, the trial convinced him that now his physical survival was even more at stake. Although he had recently pledged to remain faithful to the Republican Party and assist in the renomination of Chamberlain, it was not to be. Unlike 1874, however, developments by 1876 seemed in favor of Delany's move. Federal complacency had rendered ineffective almost all the civil and political rights blacks had won since the war. In the face of this complacency, antiblack violence had reasserted itself to an alarming degree. Also, the resurgence of Democratic sympathies in the North seemed to herald better fortunes for conservatives in the approaching election.

It should be noted, however, that Delany's move, as dramatic as it appeared, was symptomatic of a developing trend, albeit a minority one, within the black struggle that was associated with calls for a "new departure." Delany had himself anticipated this in several of his campaign speeches for the IRM ticket in 1874, where he repeatedly hinted at the need for a "new departure."[47] He apparently still harbored faith in the potency of a new departure. Despite his growing unpopularity, his ideological disposition mirrored both the dilemma black leaders confronted nationwide and the changing nature of black political consciousness.

On February 28, 1876, black delegates from North Carolina, Virginia, Arkansas, Massachusetts, Pennsylvania, and Rhode Island assembled in Washington, D.C., to launch the National Independent Political Union (NIPU). Disillusioned with Radical Republicanism, the organizers accused the Republican Party of misleading and exploiting blacks. Their immediate goal was to effect a speedy normalization of relationship between blacks, Southern whites, and the Democratic Party. The delegates condemned the Republican Party, accusing it of inflaming racial tension in the South. They also accused the party of discrimination against intelligent blacks in dispensing patronage, contending that the Republican Party had only used blacks to further its own narrow political interests.[48]

Conspicuously absent at this convention were notable black leaders like Douglass and Henry Garnet. There was also no indication that South Carolina was represented. The reason for this is obvious. Although disappointed by the Republican Party's policies, leading blacks in South Carolina, including such national leaders as Douglass and Garnet, would not support a movement whose objectives included the destruction of the party. It is noteworthy that Delany also was conspicuously absent. This is more so since the movement represented precisely those sentiments and ideals that he had consistently and persistently espoused since the end of the war. However, the fact is that the movement occurred at an inauspicious time, since the grand larceny problem had not been resolved, and for Delany, this was a struggle for survival and not a time to indulge in any national crusade.

The significance of the NIPU was that it represented, in microcosm, a tradition of black leadership, albeit a minority, whose ideas formed a significant component of the black liberation thought. This tradition accepted and welcomed the liberal rhetoric of the Democrats, insisting that the Democrats had changed and were sincere in their promises and therefore deserved consideration. Despite his absence at the meeting, Delany received glowing tributes from the delegates, who voted unanimously to appoint him as the NIPU's president for all the states south of North Carolina. Rev. Garland H. White of Halifax, North Carolina, a leading member of the convention, communicated the decision to him. Although sympathetic to the NIPU's platform, Delany did not immediately embrace the movement. His appointment coincided with the ordeal of the grand larceny trial. However, soon after joining the Democratic Party, he wrote to Rev. White accepting the NIPU position and exhorting intensified efforts at reconciliation with Democrats.[49] He envisioned the NIPU evolving into a nationwide political movement that would draw blacks away from what he characterized as the misdirection of Radical Republicanism, toward reconciliation with Southern whites.

Delany had never ceased to believe in the importance and efficacy of racial harmony as the strategy for a successful Reconstruction.

Therefore, he welcomed the NIPU because he perceived the movement as having the potentiality of healing the animosity between blacks and local whites, a condition that had prevented the peaceful and orderly development of both races and the entire region. He would embrace any scheme or movement that had the potential of reconciling blacks and whites, for in such reconciliation lay the key to mutual development. As he explained it, "Of the two races, the greater part of one, the African or our race, belongs to the South, who comprising the agricultural element, are the producers of the rich and important staples of this section of the country. We, then, produce the labor, and the white race the capital; we are the laborers and they are the capitalists. Capital and labor must go together, and without harmony and mutual association they cannot be available."[50] Here we hear strong echoes of his triple alliance paradigm.

Nationwide, blacks remained skeptical of the Democratic Party. Despite its resurgence and liberal-reformist pretensions, blacks remained unconvinced of the party's sincerity and pledged continued loyalty to the Republicans. Perhaps in response to the NIPU, leading blacks, including Garnet and Douglass, summoned a National Colored Convention in Nashville on April 7, 1876. At this convention, two Alabama delegates sponsored a resolution recommending a "new departure," and the immediate severance of all ties with the Republican Party. It failed. Instead, the delegates reaffirmed strong support for the Republican Party and likened support for the Democrats to "supporting the devil against God."[51] To underline this pledge, Douglass, along with prominent black congressmen, ex-congressmen, and political leaders, attended the Republican Party National Convention two months later in Cincinnati.[52]

Although its platform of reconciliation was defeated in Nashville, the conservative black leadership tradition remained a vital force and an attractive alternative to many. Within South Carolina, there was no doubt that some blacks favored a policy of reconciliation, and Delany became the most outspoken and visible member of this group. His choice as president of the NIPU for states south of North Carolina seemed logical, since no other black person had so forcefully advocated reconciliation as Delany. In accepting the nomination, he affirmed his conception of the movement and its objectives—the protection of the interests of blacks, de-emphasizing old party lines, and the reconciliation of blacks and whites in the South along lines that would promote mutual economic benefits.[53] There is no indication that the NIPU crystallized into a strong national political force. Its ideals, however, survived and thrived in the actions and policies of its chosen leader in South Carolina.

By 1876 Delany had come to perceive himself as the quintessence of black survival and his ideas as the best prospect for progress for race relations in the state, a perception and conviction that strengthened his dogged opposition to the mainstream black political leadership, even on critical issues and at times when racial unity seemed appropriate. The "liberal" professions of the Democratic Party had not resulted in any fundamental change in the climate of hate and resentment blacks experienced. In South Carolina, antiblack violence, perpetuated by the Democratic Party and its sympathizers, the Klan, and other white supremacist groups, only further alienated blacks, compelling the leadership to summon a convention in Columbia on July 20 and 21, 1876.[54] There were addresses by concerned blacks, including Rev. Richard Cain, Robert Elliott, and William Whipper, all of whom condemned the rising antiblack violence that had become daily occurrences, reaching perhaps its most violent scale at Hamburg, in Edgefield County, on July 8, when several blacks were murdered in cold blood. In an address to the United States, the delegates strongly deplored the massacre at Hamburg, calling it an assault on black political rights and a threat to their physical survival, and they urged the federal government to enforce the law in South Carolina. In an appeal to the government, they wrote, "We appeal to you, in the name of Justice and Humanity, in the name of Peace and Order, in the name of Christianity and the cause of Civilization, to vindicate the honor of the American name, by insisting that the humblest citizen of this Republic shall be made secure in his constitutional guarantee of security for his life, his liberty and his property."[55] Delany was conspicuously absent, even though he had yet to declare for the Democrats. However, in a short note to the *News and Courier*, he completely dissociated himself from the convention and its resolutions. "They are not my sentiments in many parts and I cannot permit myself to be placed in a false position," he concluded.[56] The conservatives equally condemned the convention, describing it as uncalled for and accusing the delegates of attempting to inflame racial tension.[57] In almost every move by black leaders, Delany saw radical sinister conspiracy that demanded strong opposition, and he did not miss opportunities to voice his disagreement with the mainstream black leadership. For him, the antiradical crusade was a personal challenge. If allowed to succeed, he continued, the radical conspirators would not only destroy him personally but also the entire foundation for peace and progress.

The NIPU was itself a response to a national fait accompli—the nationwide rise in pro-Democratic sentiments and the corresponding decline in the fortunes of the Republican Party. In 1874 Democrats had won the national House of Representatives. Most of the Democratic congressmen were Southerners and ex-Confederates. Also by 1876, almost all the Southern states had been redeemed, with the exceptions of South Carolina, Florida, and Louisiana. Even Republican newspapers in the North began expressing pro-Southern sentiments. A special correspondent for the *News and Courier* observed that Republican sympathy for Southern blacks had begun to decline in the North as far back as 1870.[58] As Joel Williamson observed, many native Carolinians soon convinced themselves, and subsequent generations, that Republicanism meant "corruption" and that black Republicanism meant "corruption compounded." Northerners soon accepted the Southern argument and found in it "a certain measure of relief from a sense of guilt for their apostasy. The results were unique: the men who had lost the war in South Carolina, had won the peace."[59] These developments strengthened the Democratic resurgence in South Carolina. The party regrouped; as part of its efforts to woo blacks, it incorporated some liberal promises into its 1876 platform, including recognition and acceptance of the Thirteenth, Fourteenth, and Fifteenth Amendments and all the rights and privileges that blacks had won in the aftermath of the war.[60] This liberal posturing won the hearts of some black Carolinians, most prominently, Delany.

By declaring for the Democratic Party, therefore, and campaigning vigorously for it in 1876, Delany allied himself with forces that, in the judgment of many, ultimately destroyed Radical Reconstruction and, with it, black political rights and freedom. In his letter to Rev. White, cited above, Delany described his vision for a new solid South, rid of all traces of racial animosity, blacks and whites holding hands and working to further their mutual interests. As he informed White, If the objective of the movement is "to unite in one common interest, industrial and political, in each state, both races in the South, regardless of the two old political parties in either section of the country, then am I with you always, even to the end."[61]

Delany's acceptance of the NIPU nomination clearly marked his break with the Republican Party. His declaration for the Democratic Party and his campaign speeches mirrored the dream and ideals of the NIPU. He became a regular and popular campaign speaker for the Democratic Party. His campaign speeches ran counter to the values and ideals that leading blacks, nationwide and within South Carolina, supported and defended. At a meeting of the Colored Democratic Club of the Fourth Ward in Charleston, he urged blacks "to shake hands with their native white people, whose interests were identical with theirs . . . the two races . . . are inseparably connected," reminding blacks that without racial harmony, coexistence was impossible.[62] He ended his speech praising the Democrats and their gubernatorial candidate, Wade Hampton, describing them as sincere in their promises to respect and recognize black rights. They had promised to accept and respect the constitutional amendments and to protect blacks in the exercise of these rights, and they could, and should, be trusted.[63]

Delany did not lose any opportunity to inform blacks that the Democrats had changed and should be given the benefit of doubt, since Republican rule had resulted in no benefits whatsoever to blacks. Repeating a theme in his earlier letter "A Political Review," he insisted that blacks had been prematurely elevated and empowered, and he blamed this on the "evil advice of bad and designing men."[64] At a campaign rally in Charleston, he cataloged the mistakes and errors of Radical Reconstruction, especially in relation to blacks. As he averred, blacks had been "raised to the highest pinnacle of man's ambition without being adequately educated up to the point."[65] If Radical Republicans were genuinely interested in the elevation of blacks, according to Delany, they would first have "educated them and fitted them to fulfill the duties of citizenship."[66] But this was not done. Instead, disregarding inexperience and ignorance, they simply appointed illiterate and gullible blacks to positions of authority, who, in turn, exhibited their poverty of intellect through their corrupt and inefficient activities. Radical

Reconstruction thus thrived on black ignorance and inefficiency. He urged blacks to abandon this relationship for a positive and promising one with the Democrats.

As in his earlier IRM campaign, Delany's historical rendition of the abolitionist movement and the eventual demise of slavery associated "Democrats" such as Thomas Jefferson and Martin Van Buren with abolition, lamenting that blacks had "been misled into the belief that Democracy meant slavery."[67] He characterized Hampton and the Democrats as "The first men to restore the principle of pure Jeffersonian Democracy in South Carolina," men of character and intelligence who could be trusted to keep their words.[68] Justifying why he abandoned the Republican Party, Delany declared that his intelligence and "due regards for his race" led him to the conclusion that the "safety and prosperity" of blacks lay only "in the direction of good relations with the white people."[69] He strongly condemned Radical Republicanism, identifying Republicans with years of misrule and corruption and urging blacks to embrace the Democrats. As always, Delany's speeches elicited endorsement and praises from the state conservative press. The conservative press, needless to say, applauded Delany's every moves and utterances. The *Columbia Daily Register* applauded his actions and called upon other blacks to emulate him, contending that "by all odds, [Delany] was the most original, correct and forceful thinker among the Negroes in this country." It admonished blacks to heed "Martin R. Delany, who has put forth the words of truth and soberness, and indicated by precept and example how you may best secure your rights and interests, and all the blessings of peace and prosperity."[70]

The centennial anniversary of the nation's independence, 1876 was most crucial to Democrats in South Carolina. It reminded them of what many characterized as their "enslavement" to Northern and black radicalism. They pledged to mark the anniversary with the redemption of the state, an objective that required not just a revived and rejuvenated party but also an ideology that was capable of cutting through the solid wall of black-Republican Party alliance. Consequently, at the State Democratic Convention in August 1876, although orthodox Democrats (ultraconservatives) triumphed over fusionists (moderates who favored a new departure), the party's platform incorporated liberal ideas and values, including pledges to recognize and defend the civil and political rights of blacks.[71]

The liberalism of the platform was, however, a political scheme designed to appeal to black voters and woo them away from the Republican Party, and the prevalence of reactionary ideas at the convention cast a shadow of doubt on the credibility of the party's liberalism. Perceptive blacks simply refused to be swayed. Not Delany. His preoccupation with the excesses of radicalism sheltered from his purview the glaring limitations and contradictions of Democratic liberalism. He became a leading spokesman of the Democrats and campaigned vigorously for their gubernatorial candidate. His speeches were elaborations of themes that had featured in the earlier IRM campaign—the negative and destructive legacies of Radical Reconstruction, the desirability of reconciliation between blacks and white Carolinians, and the need for blacks to embrace Democratic liberalism. He blamed the black-Republican Party alliance for undermining law and order and rendering the state corrupt and inefficient. He deemed Radical Reconstruction a failure, affirming confidence in the revived Democratic Party. Presenting the "liberal" platform of the party as evidence, he advocated the immediate abandonment of the Republican Party, insisting that the Democrats had changed and deserved a chance. In another stunning affliction of historical amnesia, Delany identified Democrats as the architects of black freedom. The thrust of his campaign speeches was to try to persuade blacks to abandon the Republican Party for the Democratic.[72]

Delany's decision to join the Democratic Party was, therefore, diametrically opposed to the ideological disposition of the mainstream black leadership. Despite the conflict in aspirations between the black political elite and the masses, they shared a common hope, and confidence, in the redemptive capacity of the Republican Party. The Democratic Party had not only oppressed blacks in the past but also had given clear indications of restoring such a policy should it regain power. Furthermore, blacks had been socialized through experience to identify Democrats with slavery. The party's proslavery reputation had indeed left indelible imprints in black consciousnesses. Reacting to the party's liberalism, one black declared, "Dey say dem will do dis and dat. I aint ax no man what he will do. I ax him what him hab done."[73] Delany's intimation above that blacks were misled into associating Democrats with slavery is therefore problematic. The true identity, party, and political affiliation of the proslavery group was never in doubt. There was no mystery to the proslavery identity and consciousness of the Democrats. And there was no mystery to their violent inclinations and actions. The reality that confronted blacks most vividly was Democratic violence, outrages, and insincerity. For Delany to attempt to sell such a platform to his fellow blacks was most intriguing. There was no indication that he regarded Democratic violence as wrongful and reprehensible. Yet several studies underscore the preeminence of external violence, rather than internal decadence and corruption, as the ultimate cause of the collapse of Reconstruction.[74]

If the Democrats were genuinely concerned about corruption and reforms, Delany's campaign would have seemed less offensive to blacks. Put differently, if the state Republican administration had been as bad (from the point of view of blacks) as the conservatives suggested, blacks would have been more sympathetic to conservative overtures. But Radical Republicanism was working. The government had instituted some reforms and promised others. Black Republicans were also conducting themselves relatively and remarkably well. As W. E. B. Du Bois aptly emphasized, South Carolina conservatives never wanted reforms, even in the narrower sense. They were attacking not corruption but black political rights. Orville Vernon Burton reached precisely the same conclusion in his study of Edgefield County. According to him, Reconstruction succeeded in Edgefield. Edgefield black Republicans were men of impeccable character. Reconstruction ended not because it could not work but because it was working well.[75] Consequently, when on October 14, 1876, Delany appeared at a joint Republican-Democratic rally, many blacks reacted angrily. Most other Democrats addressed the rally with a minimum of interference, but when Delany mounted the rostrum, "the crowd became frantic and the drums of the militia were beaten, the women cursing and pointing accusing fingers at him." He was eventually "howled down" and prevented from speaking. He narrowly escaped death at another rally in Cainhoy, Berkley County, during which the black militia fired at colored Democrats.[76]

Blacks felt deeply betrayed and angered by Delany's contributions to the conservative resurgence in the state. The IRM dealt a crushing blow to the political strength of the Republican Party and, by extension, to black political power. Delany himself estimated that the IRM reduced the radical majority from 40,000 to 10,000.[77] Before the radicals could fully recover from this blow, he struck another, this time in Charleston, where he launched a powerful and effective antiradical campaign that resulted in the defeat of several radicals in the municipal election of 1875.[78] The crowning act of betrayal was his final capitulation to the Democratic Party in 1876.

Theodore Draper has described Delany's switch to the Democratic Party as the "duality of all dualities," the ultimate ambivalence.[79] But many scholars, particularly those of radical-nationalist persuasion, have difficulty dealing with this crucial ambivalence of Delany's career. As already suggested elsewhere in this study, the standard approach thus far has been to offer rationalizations that oftentimes are designed to mask the ideological implications and problematic of the switch. Nonetheless, Draper is right in underscoring the centrality of this paradox. Delany's move was as intriguing as it was inconsistent with the reputation he had built in the past—the Delany of mid-nineteenth-century emigrationism and nationalism. However, it is necessary to understand and assess Delany on his own terms. He never perceived his actions as inconsistent or as a betrayal of his race. On the contrary, they were consistent with his utilitarian conception of politics. He saw no justification for blacks to remain loyal to an organization or party that, in his judgment, had not given them any concrete material gains but had instead exploited and undermined their chances of elevation. This was his conviction. Despite the anti-American underpinnings of his emigrationist schemes and the Africanist consciousness undergirding them, he never completely gave up on America. Even in his most extreme state of alienation from America, he was deeply American in consciousness.

As much as Delany loved America, however, he would not accept to live under the prevailing condition of discrimination and subordination. In a letter to the white abolitionist William Lloyd Garrison, he clearly laid down conditions that would restore his hope and optimism. In a review of Delany's emigrationist book, *The Condition, Elevation, Emigration and Destiny of the Colored People of the United States* (1852), Garrison had accused him of encouraging caste consciousness, a charge to which he strongly objected. "I am not in favor of caste, nor of the separation of the brotherhood of mankind, and would as willingly live among white men as black, if I had an EQUAL POSSESSION AND ENJOYMENT of the privileges," he reiterated, "but shall never be reconciled to live among them, subservient to their will, existing by mere SUFFEREANCE, as we, the colored people, in this country."[80] If Delany had equal exercise of rights and privileges, he would happily live in the United States. His support for emigration, therefore, was inspired by lack of acceptance and integration. Several years earlier, in a lecture to students of Wilberforce University in Wilberforce, Ohio, Delany was equally forthright in defining his goal and the compromise he was willing to make. His goal was for blacks to "constitute an essential part of the ruling element of the country in which they live."[81] He wanted full integration for blacks. However, realizing that the attainment of perfect integration, that is, absolute equality, seemed pregnant with explosive and violent consequences, he quickly underscored his willingness to compromise, to accept some concessions, however inadequate or imperfect. Although he wanted blacks to become part of the "ruling element" of the country, he was not troubled "whether this element be founded on a true or false, just or unjust basis."[82] In other words, he was willing to accommodate some degree of imperfection (not clearly explained) in the nature and composition of this "ruling element." The precise nature of his accommodation would become clear later as he began to concede social, and even racial, inequality.

In Delany's estimation, the Civil War had fundamentally altered race relations, transforming blacks from passive objects into constituents and an "essential element" of the nation. He himself had never anticipated such a revolutionary transformation. Although whites remained the ruling element, significant steps had been taken toward eventually integrating blacks, and he was willing to accept the existing reforms, however imperfect or fragile they might seem, and extend the olive branch to white Southerners. Such friendly disposition, flexibility, and pragmatism were, in his judgment, much more productive than what he perceived as a doctrinaire (all-or-nothing), rigidly ideological posture that foreclosed possibilities of interracial cooperation and mutual progress.

Although the number of blacks who shared Delany's viewpoints and heeded his call to join the Democratic Party has not been accurately ascertained, it is certain that they constituted a minority, for the majority of blacks remained faithful to the Republican Party. The election of 1876 was bitterly contested in South Carolina. Violence and intimidation were used to prevent blacks from effectively participating. Each party accused the other of malpractices and corruption. When the dust settled, the Democrats were declared victorious in South Carolina, under the terms of an epochal Compromise of 1877.[83] In compensation to the Democrats for accepting a Republican administration in Washington, the federal government pledged to withdraw federal troops from the South. The "victory" of the Democrats, and the removal of troops, marked the end of Reconstruction. It remained to be seen if Delany's optimism would be vindicated—if indeed, the Democrats had changed.

SIX

Final Years
1878–1885

THE VICTORY OF the Democrats provided an opportunity to test the depth of their commitment to the "liberal" promises they made during the campaign. Would Delany's optimism be vindicated, or would the Democrats renege on their promises? But first, the victory called for celebration. To South Carolina Democrats, the return to political power heralded the dawn of a "progressive age." According to the *News and Courier*, thanks to the rapid developments in railroads, white Carolinians celebrated this "new age" with mass vacation trips to the plains of the state and to Georgia.[1] The gaieties of the period, according to an eyewitness, rivaled those of antebellum days. Democrats traveled and held picnics, parties, and balls in celebration of the demise of Reconstruction.[2] It soon became obvious that blacks were not expected to reap any lasting benefits from the conservative victory and from the prospects of their new "progressive age."

Governor Hampton, however, did try to fulfill his campaign pledges. Delany was one of prominent blacks he appointed to office, restoring him to his trial justice post in Charleston. He also appointed several Republicans to office. In a message to the General Assembly, he urged its members to remain faithful to the campaign promises. In his inaugural speech, Hampton reiterated the need for interracial harmony and for the recognition and protection of all the civil and political rights of blacks. At the Aiken Schuetzenfast in April 1878, recalling the campaign two years earlier, Hampton affirmed, "I spoke as a Carolinian to a Carolinian, white and black. . . . I appealed to you that it was better to fail in struggling to do right than to succeed in doing wrong." He then reaffirmed his earlier pledge to treat blacks impartially.[3]

Hampton's policies, however, did not fundamentally challenge the basic "tenet that white minority would always rule the black majority."[4] Black appointments were confined to minor local offices. Hampton was no believer in racial equality, his moderate posturing notwithstanding. Like most Democrats, the radical dispositions of blacks disturbed him. But unlike them, he regarded minor concessions to black aspirations an effective means of eroding the force of black radicalism. However, even these limited and ineffective concessions disturbed ultraconservatives. They had consented to a liberal platform merely for campaign and public relations purposes, and they never intended to respect and protect the constitutional rights of blacks. Hampton's "liberal" speeches and conciliatory policy toward blacks and Republicans alienated die-hard conservatives. His public denunciation of partisan politics alarmed many. "I am no party man," he once declared publicly, much to the chagrin of the Democrats.[5] Such a declaration threatened the very core of the conservatism that underpinned Democratic Party restoration in South Carolina.

The ultraconservatives were particularly apprehensive of a possible alliance between Hampton and the Republicans. They accused him of threatening white supremacy.[6] In a letter to Martin Witherspoon Gary, a leading ultraconservative, one J. H. Hudson wrote, "Theorists may twist and distort the matter at will, but the real issue in this, and other Southern states, involves white supremacy and civilization."[7] A strong anti-Hampton, and antiblack, force soon crystallized around Gary and General Mathew Butler. They accused Hampton of extreme "conservatism and niggerism," of being soft on Republican officeholders, and of threatening white supremacy and civilization.[8]

In the face of this intraparty opposition, however, Hampton found support in an unusual place, among Republicans. On June 18, 1877, a Republican, Alfred William of Beaufort, wrote to Hampton urging him not to succumb to the pressures of his party but to push ahead vigorously with his liberal policy. "The opposition within your party, can do you no harm," he told Hampton, "it only adds strength from among your former opponents, and a just recognition of their rights . . . will create for you a support that no power in the state can overthrow."[9] At the August 8, 1878, Republican State Convention in Columbia, there was a considerable support for endorsing Hampton for governor. In the end, however, the conservative forces would prove too formidable.[10]

It should be noted that despite the reactionary turn of events, the immediate postelection period was, albeit fleetingly, a joyous occasion for conservative blacks. A period of "thanksgiving" began for those who found patronage positions in government. Those in private businesses openly displayed their Democratic Party affiliation as a badge of honor. In fact, it was a time to be a black Democrat and proud of it. Black Democrats proudly and boldly displayed their party affiliation. According to one source, it was not uncommon to see displayed in front of black businesses signs that read "patronize so and so, the only Colored Democrat barber, [or shoemaker, butcher, and so forth], in town."[11] A few years earlier, this would have been abominable.

However, this honeymoon between black conservatives and the Democratic Party proved ephemeral. White Carolinians, it turned out, were not unduly concerned about what political affiliations blacks professed. They were more troubled by black aspirations for positions of responsibility, regardless of party affiliation. According to one observer, "The whites regard the Negro as an inferior animal, admirably adapted to work and to wait, and look on him 'in his proper place,' with a curious mixture of amusement, contempt and affection. *It is when he aspires to participate in politics or otherwise claim privileges that their hatred becomes intense*" (emphasis added).[12] Democrats, or "redeemers," as they called themselves, especially the ultrawing that had seized control of the government from the "liberal" wing, established a regime of terror that turned the entire state into a hell for blacks. Delany himself would soon feel the ax of the "redeemers." They proceeded to renege on their campaign pledges to recognize and respect the civil and political rights of blacks and to protect them in the exercise of those rights. By 1878 blacks generally came under siege from a renewed onslaught by hard-line Democrats, who seemed determined to restore some quasi-form of servitude.[13]

Officeholding and political responsibilities, white Carolinians consistently argued, belonged appropriately to whites. For blacks to hold offices constituted a violation and disruption of the social equilibrium. Thus began a relentless determination to purge the state of every vestige of black political power. For blacks in general, and especially for Delany and the many black Democrats, the situation was both physically and physiologically unsettling. The avenging wrath of the conservatives made no distinction between black radicals and conservatives. They unleashed violence against and began intimidating blacks in their bid to "purify" a civilization they felt had been contaminated by ten years of radical rule. They initiated policies that undermined the civil, political, and economic rights of blacks. Socialized to regard blacks as subhuman and inferior, fit only for a place at the bottom of society, the "redeemers" quickly turned their axes on blacks, particularly officeholders, inaugurating a reign of terror and intimidation reminiscent of antebellum days.

The reversal of fortunes that occasioned the return of the "redeemers" was quick and immediate for blacks. For blacks in South Carolina, and indeed in the entire South, the future looked gloomy. At every turn, they confronted political marginalization, economic deprivation, misery, and social ostracism within a pervasive culture of violence designed to stifle any attempts at, or ambitious drives toward, self-improvement. Frustrated and alienated, South Carolina blacks sought escape and succor in colonization. The colonization option began to appeal favorably to an increasing number of black leaders, who now turned to the American Colonization Society for help. In fact, what became the black exodus movement began as early as January 1877, when leading blacks began soliciting assistance from the Colonization Society. Richard Cain was among the earliest to approach the Society. In January 1877 he wrote a letter to William Coppinger in which he reported that "the colored people of South Carolina are tired of the constant struggle for life and liberty with such results as the 'Mississippi Plan' and prefer going where no such obstacles are in their way of enjoying their liberty."[14] In early February he sent a follow-up letter in which he observed that "the political change in the South has worked wonders in the minds of the colored people, and they feel no safety, should the democracy take control of these states."[15] The *News and Courier* also attested to the surge of emigration sentiments among blacks. "It is hardly impossible not to go into a small shop kept exclusively by black men, without hearing 'the land of the molasses tree' [that is, Africa] spoken of in terms of the wildest infatuation," it reported.[16] In Delany's own judgment, the colonization movement developed because of the apprehensions by blacks about their subordinate position in a society they had once ruled for ten years.[17]

The growing sentiment in favor of colonization was, however, not confined to South Carolina. What blacks in South Carolina experienced in the aftermath of the Compromise of 1877 was replicated in other "redeemed" Southern states. Confronted by grinding poverty, shrinking hopes, and sealed doors, blacks in Georgia, Florida, North Carolina, Alabama, and Louisiana also seriously considered emigration. This was the beginning of the exodus movement that took many to Kansas and Oklahoma. Delany, who was still a trial justice, kept aloof from the movement. However, the pervasive antiblack culture and sentiments that had turned many blacks in the direction of colonization would soon catch up with South Carolina's most prominent black Democrat. The response of the "redeemers" to Delany perfectly illustrates the treacherous and perfidious character of their liberal posturing.

Barely one year in office, there was a recommendation to Governor Hampton to relieve Delany of his trial justice post on the grounds that he was "unfit for the office."[18] This was followed almost immediately by a petition signed by some "citizens of Charleston" demanding Delany's removal from office because "the office is conducted by the said M. R. Delany in a manner discreditable to the present administration of the State of South Carolina and repugnant to the feelings of both races in this community."[19] It seems ironic that a person who had staked his career on advancing interracial harmony and had campaigned vigorously for a party that had pledged to advance racial harmony should, so soon after helping to achieve a modus operandi that he thought would facilitate that harmony, be found "discreditable" to that goal. In a letter to Hampton, Delany asked to be given the opportunity to defend himself.[20] A group of Charleston city and county citizens almost immediately followed Delany's letter with a counterpetition to the governor recommending his retention. Underscoring the political character of Delany's predicament, they wrote: "We know that Maj. M. R. Delany is a man of coolness, deliberateness and broad experience, which enabled him to differ widely with many persons of his own race and party, and especially with the extravagant and ultra men."[21] He never quite got the chance to defend himself.

As an astute observer of the political landscape in South Carolina, Delany must have realized that, given the momentum and surge of "redemption," it was a matter of time before he, too, was removed. The obvious and dreadful truth dawned on him. He had gambled and failed. To Delany, and to black Democrats generally, Charleston, and indeed the entire state of South Carolina, must have felt like a world turned upside down. His dream of a reconstructed South Carolina, based on racial harmony and economic cooperation between white capital and black labor, vanished as he watched whites, robed in Confederate gray, overturn the Reconstruction gains of blacks. In 1878 Hampton was elected to the U.S. Senate. It has been suggested that he had become too "liberal" for the Democrats, and the election was meant to distance him from the orbit of South Carolina politics. The election of Hampton to the Senate paved the way for dismantling and dislodging the few Republicans and blacks he had put in office. Delany lost the trial justice post almost immediately.

The disappointment and shock of the "redeemers" reactions turned Delany in two directions, one intellectual, the other, a throwback to the emigrationist platform of the 1850s. First, he felt compelled to respond to the racist "scientific" ethnological postulations of the age. Second, he formally immersed himself in the black exodus movement that sought its "progressive age" in Africa. Both reflect the ambivalent nature of his thought in the closing years of his life, an ambivalence that coupled alienation from the racist environment with strong integrationist and universalistic aspirations.

As several studies establish, the second half of the nineteenth century, particularly the latter part of it, witnessed an outpouring of "scientific" and "ethnological" theories and postulations about black inferiority.[22] This "scholarship" had both domestic and global thrusts and implications. By the last two decades of the nineteenth century, European imperialists were radically redefining their relationship with Africa, moving gradually toward abandonment of their hitherto low-keyed posture along the African coast to one of intrusion into, and full occupation of, the African interior. In the United States, the period saw the flowering of Jim Crow culture, that is, legalized discrimination. Both episodes were strongly backed by "scientific" and "ethnological" theories that "affirmed" African/black inferiority.

Delany responded to this "ethnological" racism by proposing a counterethnological theory designed to erode the "black inferiority" and racial separatist thrust of mainstream science and ethnology. He published his response in 1879 under the title, *Principia of Ethnology: The Origin of Races and Color.*[23] Not surprisingly, this book has been characterized as militant and separatist, infused with doses of Afrocentric ideas, another of Delany's anti-American and anti-European books. A most recent example is Robert Levine's study in which he describes *Principia* as a book that essentializes race and "a radical critique of miscegenation as a blasphemous act that depletes the purity of the races and has harmful effects for the progress of humanity in general."[24] Levine further characterizes the book as encapsulating Delany's "utopian vision . . . of racial purity achieved by black emigration to Africa."[25] In her own analysis, Mia Bay describes *Principia* as a refinement of Delany's "case against the white race." In this book, Bay contends, Delany made "what may well be the most unambiguous argument for the existence of permanent distinction between the races by any nineteenth-century African-American."[26]

The interpretation of *Principia* that Levine and Bay advance is consistent with the instrumentalist construction of Delany. Unfortunately, as interesting and plausible as it sounds, this interpretation highlights only a segment of the book, albeit critical, to the neglect of what I consider a far more critical utilitarian dimension. The critical inquiry should revolve around Delany's motivation for writing and publishing *Principia.* Why the book? The answer to this question will illuminate the critical utilitarian underpinning.

As already established, with the demise of Reconstruction, there was a sudden reversal of fortunes for blacks. Everywhere blacks turned, they were greeted with violence and rejection. This situation turned many in the direction of immigration and separatist solutions. White "intellectuals" and scientists mobilized their intellectual arsenal against blacks, providing ideological justification for black subordination and reinforcing white supremacy and the growing disinclination to accommodate blacks. There was a distinct and unmistakable phobia over the likelihood that black freedom and integration would result in massive miscegenation. This concern only fueled the ambers of hate and antiblack violence. Delany's challenge, therefore, as he clearly stated in the opening segment of the book, was to address a key question, the answer to which, he hoped, would unravel the fear over miscegenation and, ipso facto, demonstrate the fallacy of the racist intellectual tradition. The question was simply, Was miscegenation harmful and dangerous?

Delany began with a frontal attack on the evolutionary theory, adopting instead the Creationist alternative. He insisted that all humans were of one heritage and shared a common identity. He decided to confront, head-on, some of the scientific and intellectual postulations of the day, especially those that reinforced the pervasive antiblack culture, particularly the science of ethnology. The intellectual and scientific postulations, theories, and findings all seemed to question and diminish the role of Africans and Diaspora blacks in, and their relevance to, world civilization. Delany seemed well qualified to engage this debate on the status and place of blacks in American and world civilization. He was well read and had already published on related topics. But, thus far, his writings had not specifically addressed the scientific aspects. Fortunately, even in this field, Delany seemed well qualified. A contemporary described him as someone with "a good head and intelligent face—just the kind of a head which a phrenologist would tell you a man ought to have who makes natural observations and accumulates scientific facts."[27] Paradoxically, although by 1879 when he published *Principia* Delany was also resurrecting his old African dream, the book was not aimed at restoring the racial boundary that had defined his emigration movement in the 1850s. In fact, by the late 1870s and early 1880s racial distinctiveness had become peripheral to Delany's consciousness and agenda. He had developed a higher and nobler objective—to de-racialize human consciousness and debunk racialist and ethnocentric theories. To accomplish this, he proposed in *Principia*, a divine rationalization for the phenomenon of complexional differences.

First, he propounded a monolithic theory of human origin. He traced all races—yellow, black, and white—to one Adamite origin, through Noah and his offspring.[28] According to Delany, "the two extremes of color, from the negative white—(including every possible variety of tint)—up to the blackest are all produced by the same material and essential properties of color."[29] The three sons of Noah—Shem, Ham, and Japheth—were of different complexions, yellow, black, and white, respectively. This complexional variation, he insisted, was not due to any genetic deficiency but resulted from the varying degrees of rouge in each. It was of high concentration in Shem, even higher in Ham (concentrated rouge), and lighter in Japheth. Despite the differences, all three lived as one family for years and would have remained so but for the need to fulfill a divine plan. God had a purpose for everything. Complexional variation, in Delany's judgment, was not an accident of history but part of God's conscious design for the destiny of humankind. God's plan was to "multiply and replenish" the earth with different peoples. To accomplish this, he induced disunity and conflicts of interest into the human family. As each developed a distinct language from the others, their interests diverged, and the complexional factor, hitherto inconsequential, assumed significance, resulting in separation.[30]

Ham went to Africa, Shem to Asia, and Japheth to Europe. Ham, the African, was the earliest to develop and attain a high level of civilization in Egypt and Ethiopia. Long before the other two settled to any meaningful preoccupation, Africans had excelled in literature, architecture, philosophy, astronomy, mathematics, and writing.[31] Delany emphasized the Negroid origin and nature of this magnificent culture and civilization. The accomplishments of these dark-skinned people were soon stolen and copied by others, especially the Europeans. Africans became victims of the greed and cupidity of external forces—the Assyrians, Persians, Macedonians, Arabs, Turks, Romans, and Greeks. These forces wreaked destruction on Africa, pilfered its artistic and cultural artifacts, and transferred much of them to Europe. In the closing section of the book, Delany reassured Africans and blacks everywhere of the imminence of redemption and regeneration. Blacks would soon regain their lost glories, largely through their own efforts and the assistance of God.[32]

It is remarkable that, disturbed by the rising tide of racism and ethno-centrism in the closing years of his life, Delany invoked Whipperian universalism. The leading "scientists" and "intellectuals" of the time justified the mistreatment of blacks on the ground of genetic inferiority. Delany fired back with a universalistic theory that genetically tied the so-called superior white race to blacks in one origin. Complexional differences, therefore, had nothing to do with genetic quality or composition. It was God's means of actualizing a divine purpose. It is also interesting to note Delany's attribution of black decadence and backwardness not to any genetic deficiencies but to historical circumstances.

Principia thus espoused an integrative theory. Enshrined in the complexities of the book is a cultural pluralistic paradigm. Delany assured blacks and whites that it is possible to cohabit without necessarily submerging or losing one's racial or cultural identity in the process. His sense of pride in black identity remained as strong as ever. In the closing section of the book, he acknowledged the reality of miscegenation, a disturbing phenomenon to racists.[33] Again, he assured everyone that miscegenation would not adversely impact cultural/racial identity. It would never result in the permanent corruption or destruction of any one race or culture, as many feared, since, according to him, God wished to maintain the three distinct races in their originality. While this contention is consistent with Delany's consciousness of pride in his "unadulterated blackness," it certainly contradicts the universalistic and integrative thrust of the book. If it were God's intension to keep the races in their purity, would this not constitute divine legitimation of segregation? Would miscegenation, if encouraged, not result in the corruption of the purity of the races?

Delany saw no inconsistency in his reasoning. He described miscegenation as the start of a "resolvent process" that would ultimately lead back to originality.[34] As he explained the process, "A cross only produces one of a mixed race, and a continual cross from a half-blood on either side will run into the pure original race, either black or white."[35] It is not certain if Delany is here justifying interracial marriages. What seems obvious, however, is his attempt to demonstrate to and convince racial purists on both sides that miscegenation was not a negative and destructive process. It was not a fixed and permanent state but a process that would lead inevitably to a purified state of the preponderant race. And he provided divine rationalization: "If indeed it were true, that what is implied by miscegenation could take place the destruction of all or any of the three original races by the formation of a new race to take the place of either or all—then, indeed, would the work of God be set at naught, his designs and purpose thwarted, and his wisdom confounded by the crafty schemes of poor, mortal, feeble man."[36]

When crossed, according to Delany, the sterling races can reproduce themselves into their originality. The process itself begins with the production of an "abnormal race" (that is, mulatto). For example, if any two of the sterling races should reproduce, the offspring is an "abnormal race." However, this is not the end but the beginning of a resolvent process that would lead back to the reproduction of the pure race. If the offspring of a mulatto marries either of the sterling races—black or white—their offspring is a quadroon. If the quadroon marries on the same side and this process continues up to the fourth generation, the result would be an octoroon (black or white), and this is the pure state.[37] According to Delany, each stage in the resolvent process yields abnormality until the fourth and final stage, which is a reproduction of the original. The resolvent process itself, it should be underlined, must be racially exclusive in order for it to result in the original state. That is, if the beginning of the resolvent process is between an abnormal race and black, then all subsequent stages must be within the black race in order to yield a corresponding originality. Miscegenation is therefore only abnormal, and by implication, culturally dangerous, first, if terminated at the early stages, and second, if the resolvent process is not racially exclusive.

Delany developed a complex and intriguing paradigm on race relations. Embedded within it is his life-long pride in and consciousness of racial purity—qualities that most critics agree he epitomized. But there are also two other critical elements. First, there was the aging Delany who was obsessed with the imminence of a racial conflagration and determined to prevent it. Second, there was his growing concern over the upsurge of racism and the widening gap between the races. Delany thus assumed the responsibility of effecting racial unity and harmony. His goal was to convince everyone across the racial boundary, a boundary that he had once defended, of the artificiality of racial divisions, of a universal brotherhood and sisterhood of humankind, and of the need, it seems, to pursue miscegenation, once started, to its "sterling" conclusion. But there is the other side of *Principia*, the aspect that unequivocally asserts the superiority of African/black culture and civilization over all others. This is very consistent with the intellectual Delany. He expressed great admiration for African traditions and values. His vigorous defense of African civilization has often been misrepresented as the essential or substantive defining character of his being.

Given Delany's disappointment and his eventual adoption of colonization, it seems logical to assume that ideologically he would revert completely to his pre–Civil War (1850s) racialist mind-set. This disposition might have inspired *Principia* and thus justify identifying the book, theoretically, with his militant nationalist and separatist historiography. Although plausible, this interpretation reflects only one dimension of the book. Delany's disillusionment induced him to respond to and deconstruct the prevailing intellectual tradition that justified racism and black subordination. He sought to debunk the racist intellectual tradition and stake a claim for the integration of blacks into mainstream America. His espousal of monogenesis was meant to underscore the superficiality and irrationality of the prevailing segregationist culture. In other words, his Creationist theory challenged nascent claims of white superiority. In fact, by his own analysis, if any one group deserved to claim cultural superiority, it was the African. A critical question worth considering at this juncture is why Delany would challenge and deconstruct the structures of white supremacy if his ultimate goal was racial separation. This does not make sense. There was no doubt that when he wrote and published *Principia* in the late 1870s his motivation was driven more by universalistic and integrationist goals than by separatist aspirations.

In *Principia*, therefore, Delany offered an "ethnological" theory designed to facilitate black integration. He sought to contain the growing phobia over miscegenation and reassure whites that they had nothing to fear. Through his theory of one creation, he affirmed human commonality and shared identity. Since miscegenation was so dreaded as to provoke violence against blacks, Delany proposed a "liberal" interpretation meant to convince society that interracial union did not necessarily portend contamination of anyone's original purity. The resolvent process rendered miscegenation a dynamic process that eventually re-creates originality. As he described it,

> That it may be indelibly fixed on every mind, we place on record the fact, that the races as such, especially white and black, are indestructible; that miscegenation as popularly understood—the running out of two races, or several, into a new race—cannot take place. A cross only produces one of a mixed race, and a continual cross from a half blood on either side will run into the pure race, either white or black; the fourth cross on one side from the half-blood perfecting a whole blood.[38]

This was his intellectual response to the separatist tradition of the time. But Delany was also perceptive and practical enough to realize that no amount of intellectual counterpoints on his part, or by any other black leader, would effectively undermine Jim Crow. The proliferation of Jim Crow culture, therefore, reinforced the growing appeal of colonization among black leaders. Many turned toward Liberia in Africa.

Barely two years after the 1876 election, blacks in Charleston organized the Liberia Exodus Joint Stock Steamship Company and shortly thereafter, through the sale of stocks, purchased a ship, the *Azor*. Their plan was for the ship to take migrants to Liberia and return bringing back African commodities that would then be traded for money. This transatlantic trading system was meant to accomplish two objectives— first, the migration and resettlement of blacks in Liberia, and second, the civilization of indigenous Africans through the introduction of Western ideas and Christianity by the migrants. Unfortunately, this grand plan of the Liberian exodus movement confronted immense financial hurdles that almost crippled the movement. As already established, Delany did not immediately join the movement. He was skeptical of the abilities of the organizers and leaders, the ranks of which, according to him, were composed mostly of "inexperienced and unbusiness trained men."[39] His concern proved right. It was not until the movement ran into a serious financial hole and teetering on the brink of bankruptcy that Delany was prevailed upon to head a special financial committee set up to explore ways of turning the financial situation around. He joined the movement sometime in June 1878, while still a trial justice, and appealed to the Colonization Society for help.[40]

On July 8, 1878, in a last-ditch effort to resurrect his emigration dream, Delany wrote a detailed and passionate plea to H. R. Latrobe, president of the American Colonization Society, requesting assistance to bail the Liberia Exodus Company out of the financial difficulties that threatened to derail the emigration movement.[41] In this letter, Delany clearly acknowledged that emigration was the only viable option left for blacks, given the turn of events in South Carolina. One can only imagine how he must have felt acknowledging to Latrobe that on issues pertaining to advancing the interests of blacks, "[a]mong the whites here we have no friends."[42] The significance of this letter lies in the fact that it mirrored Delany's renewed faith in emigration. This renewed faith was no doubt inspired by the loss of the trial justice post after the election of Hampton to the U.S. Senate.

Perhaps most critically, from his own perspective, Delany seemed to have realized the awkward position the failed promises of "redemption" had put him, given what he had once acknowledged as the irredeemable and unpardonable nature of offenses stemming from his antiradical crusade. With "redemption," therefore, he found himself between a rock and a hard place. Betrayed and haunted by "redeemers" and white supremacists, unlike other prominent blacks who secured patronage appointments from the Republican administration in Washington, Delany could not confidently turn to the administration for succor. In fact, by the early 1880s several leading blacks, including Frederick Douglass, Henry Garnet, and a few South Carolina black Republicans displaced by the "redeemers," including Robert Brown Elliott, former chair of the State Executive Committee, and Francis Cardozo, former secretary of state, sought and received favors from the Republican administration. But Delany would continue to remain isolated and kept at arm's length. It was difficult convincing the Republicans that he deserved a chance. Hadn't he actively and aggressively sought the demise of Republican rule in South Carolina? Delany must have realized that his antiradical crusade would not so easily be forgotten and forgiven.

Two years later, he wrote a similar letter to William Coppinger of the Colonization Society in a desperate last-ditch attempt to secure a government appointment.[43] He informed Coppinger that his intention in the 1850s was to return permanently to Africa, but for the outbreak of the Civil War. Now, in the aftermath of the demise of Reconstruction, he was determined to realize that dream. He described Africa as "the field of my destined labor."[44] In this detailed latter, Delany laid bare, in unambiguous terms, his catalog of woes and frustrating experiences of political victimization in the hands of ideological opponents. From the tone of the letter, it is clear that Delany deemed his political career in South Carolina a financial disaster, for he was constantly dogged by unemployment, unable to hold on permanently to any positions, as political opponents sought every opportunity to victimize him for his ideas. As he described his experience, "as I could not be a corrupt politician, you see that I found no favor with those in influence and authority. Hence, I made no money since I have been South."[45] He attributed his repeated failed attempts to gain a government appointment to "the chicanery of wily politicians," and he pleaded with Coppinger to help secure a position in Washington. This would provide him with the income with which to eventually finance his emigration. Specifically, he asked to be appointed superintendent of Freedman's Hospital in Washington.

Since Coppinger and other "friends" in the Colonization Society were to intercede with the Republican administration in Washington on his behalf, Delany thought it helpful to remind everyone of his past sacrifices and patriotism, even as they seemed to remember his antiradical crusade. He seemed confident that his past patriotic services and sacrifices for the nation, especially during the Civil War, would mitigate the lingering memories of his flirtation with the Democrats. He ended this letter thus: "I have thus brought these matters in connection with myself before you—as an old friend, that you may see how studiously and completely I have been ignored by my 'friends' after all my services faithfully performed under the government, in the Army, during four years and ten months."[46]

In a follow-up letter four months later, Delany enclosed his army records and informed Coppinger that he would be in Washington in

February and again pleaded with him to assist in soliciting other Colonization friends for the position of doorkeeper of the Senate.[47] Citing the recent appointment of Frederick Douglass as marshal of the District of Columbia to buttress his case, Delany declared, "I should like to obtain in the first place (and I think the integrity of the country can afford it as well as they could to make my friend Frederick Douglass Marshall of the District of Columbia) the office of Door Keeper of the U.S. Senate. This is my first solicitation."[48]

As already indicated, aside from Douglass, the Republican administration in Washington had appointed a few other prominent blacks to positions of authority. This made Delany optimistic that perhaps finally he, too, would find a place. It was not meant to be. The Republicans could not so soon have forgotten and forgiven his antiradical activities in South Carolina. It seems rather curious that Delany expected patronage from the same Republicans he had spent the past decade and half demonizing. It is not clear if Coppinger, Latrobe, and other "friends" in the Colonization Society interceded on Delany's behalf. What is clear, however, is that he was never offered any position. Delany must have felt despondent and abandoned. Help, however, came from a young protégé and admirer, the newspaper editor John Bruce, who helped Delany secure a job as campaign orator for Congressman John F. Dezendorf, a white Republican who was running for reelection in a predominantly black district in Virginia. Delany addressed rallies in Norfolk.[49] But this "Delany" was a shadow of the vibrant and erudite Delany of the 1840s and 1850s. That voice, once described as "capable of causing a whole troop of African Tigers to stand and tremble," had lost its force.[50] Barely audible, feeble, and unable to cope with the rigors of campaign, Delany was compelled to withdraw. It was clear that Delany's fighting days were numbered. However, the need for economic sustenance kept him on the job trail. He spent the greater part of 1883 traveling between Washington, D.C., Wilberforce, New York, and Boston. No steady job came.

Although the last few years of his life were hard and desperate ones, nothing could extinguish the flame of emigration burning inside Delany. In January 1883, at a gathering in Washington, D.C., to celebrate the twentieth anniversary of the Emancipation Proclamation, in the presence of Frederick Douglass and other black luminaries, Delany toasted to his future in Africa. Unfortunately, his African dream remained in the realm of his imagination, a cherished but distant and elusive dream. Weak, feeble, and exhausted, Delany's fighting days seemed definitely over. The past struggles and recent betrayal seemed to have taken their toll. According to Dorothy Sterling, he "lived for two more joyless years," during which the Supreme Court nullified the Civil Rights Act of 1875.[51] In 1884, for the first time since the war, a Democratic administration assumed power in Washington. These developments must have accelerated Delany's physical and, in the opinion of some, mental deterioration. With everything seemingly to his disfavor and disadvantage, Delany returned to his wife and children in Wilberforce. This was not a happy homecoming. His physical and mental deterioration did not escape notice. In its January 7, 1885, issue, the *Xenia Gazette* reported,

Major Martin R. Delany, a quite noted colored gentleman, is at his home at Wilberforce, O., and in a rather pitiable condition—being, considerable of the time, in a very feeble condition of mind. The gentleman is now an old man and in his prime was a very brilliant one. Many think him to have exceeded Frederick Douglass, in intellect, in his palmiest days. He has been the guest of rulers and potentates of high degree, has taken leading part in politics and is the author of several valuable books. . . . His old friends at Wilberforce are pained at his present condition, which may . . . be demonstrated as a mental and physical wreck.[52]

Martin Delany died on the January 24, 1885. Indeed, a sad ending to an illustrious life.

CONCLUSION

THE CRISES OF Delany's postbellum career clearly reveal a personality different from the militant and radical personality of the relatively brief nationalist epoch (1852–1862), a phase that has unfortunately served as the defining focus and essence of Delany in historical and popular studies. Buried beneath the weight of instrumentalist weltanschauung, the "Delany" of the earlier moral suasionist epoch and that of the later conservative postbellum era simply languished in historical obscurity. The highlighting and exaltation of the emigrationist phase of Delany's career have resulted in overamplification of the nationalist and Pan-Africanist dimensions of his life and struggle to the neglect of other, more critical phases that provide counterpoints and balance and enable an informed understanding of the complexities and paradoxes of his personality and career.

More than three decades after it was made, the call to move black American historiography beyond instrumentalism has yet to affect Delany. Over the last two decades, several micro- and macrobiographical studies have surfaced, built upon commentaries on, and amplifications of, his militant nationalism. Several of these studies fall more appropriately under the rubric of "popular history" and are premised on the conviction that such genre remain relevant, and critically needed, in the struggles for political, economic, and cultural survival in which black Americans are supposedly engaged. The dominance of instrumentalism continues to dictate a very narrow, skewed, and utilitarian conception of Delany. There is, therefore, a need to transcend this limitation and come to grips with the complexities of his life. Acknowledging the complexities neither undermines his image and reputation nor negates his historical relevance. On the contrary, it finally locates Delany within the broader traditions of black leadership orientation generally, revealing that he was not an aberration but that his paradoxes reflected a personality trait that was pervasive among black leaders in the nineteenth century.

The glaring and frequent flip-flops of his career were indeed reflective of the pragmatic responses that black leaders had to make, given the conditions and limitations of their times and struggles. What made Delany's much more conspicuous was due to a combination of timing, context, and the contents of his conservatism. Precisely at a time, and in the context of a struggle, when other black leaders felt the imperative of racial solidarity against what was perceived as a potent threat to the freedom, rights, and privileges of the black race, Delany threw every caution overboard in an enthusiastic embrace of that particularly dreaded threat. Put differently, his conservatism led him to break ranks with other black leaders at a critical moment in history, when the consideration for racial unity was deemed supremely important. In the judgment of his contemporaries, Delany's actions constituted a betrayal of monumental proportions, "sworn to be punished, with death, if possible," as Delany himself would later claim.[1]

Confronting these "unruly" aspects of Delany's career, therefore, enables us to gain a more accurate gauge and understanding of his life and struggle. More important, we gain greater appreciation for him. Regardless of the unpopularity of his decisions and choices, there was no doubt that he had the utmost interests of blacks in mind. He was undoubtedly motivated by the supreme need to elevate his race. Although his choices and decisions might contradict those of mainstream black leaders, there was no doubt that Delany was driven by considerations for the welfare and advancement of blacks. Consequently, his strategy should not be confused with the ends he sought. His career demonstrated versatility and an amazing propensity to adjust to changing circumstances.

No doctrinaire activist, Delany was much more pragmatic than has been acknowledged. At a critical moment in the Reconstruction era, when leading blacks manifested strong ideological convictions and a determination to uphold and defend orthodox party lines, Delany stubbornly invoked political realism and pragmatism. He sought to harmonize the choices and agenda of the black political leadership with what he perceived as practical and realistic alternatives. In this respect, he laid the foundation for renowned future "pragmatist"—Booker T. Washington. The tragedy of Martin Delany was that neither side really appreciated his complexity. His fellow blacks misunderstood him and saw him as a misguided and opportunistic traitor. On the other hand, white Carolinians, whom he embraced with enthusiasm and faith, disappointed him. They used him, it seemed. Victor Ullman was right in one thing—Delany was indeed too complex to be identified with either "the good guys or the bad guys."[2] Curiously, Ullman who seemed to understand Delany's complexity, himself failed to illuminate and deconstruct this complexity in his book. Other scholars have simply ignored the complexity, while isolating, for exaltation, the one personality that suited the instrumentalist demands of their historiography. Unfortunately, this personality is only a skeletal representation of Delany.

The years (1872–1875) between his two seminal letters "A Political Review" and "Trial and Conviction" were indeed troubling and tasking ones for Delany. They were years of agonizing political alienation, and economic impoverishment. The first letter, "A Political Review," alienated many blacks and the Republican Party. As this study demonstrates, this letter was the culmination of years of growing distrust, alienation, and misgivings between Delany and the Radical Republican administration that began with the onset of Reconstruction. Although his conservative ideas, concessions, and scathing criticisms of Radical Republicanism endeared Delany to conservatives in South Carolina, they created serious problems for him among Republicans, blacks and whites. While radicals initially ignored his antiradical harangue, the publication of "A Political Review" brought the boiling animosity to the surface, especially given the appropriation of Delany's ideas, and their amplification, by the conservative media. Delany would feel victimized and uncomfortable yet undaunted in his persistent advocacy of conservative policies. Since the Republican administration had become infamous for corruption and inefficiency, Delany's ideas soon became the focus of reform movements and values. His voice reinforced the growing condemnation of Radical Republican corruption and inefficiency. He was even harder on blacks. He had nothing but disdain for black political leaders, depicting them as ignorant nonentities who blindly took orders from "renegade intruders."

Delany's castigation of black leaders only energized the conservatives, emboldening them in their efforts to discredit and dismantle Radical Reconstruction. It is, therefore, not surprising that blacks reacted angrily. Senator S. E. Galliard and many others pushed vigorously for the political marginalization of Delany. This would eventually happen. Whether by design or not, Delany had difficulty getting anyone in the Republican administrations at both the state and federal levels to offer him a job. He soon learned how difficult it is to be a conservative critic in a state run by Radical Republicans without an independent source of income. There is no doubt that from the start of his active political career Delany had sought to become an insider, to position himself strategically within the Republican administration and be able to influence and shape party policies along more conciliatory lines. This did not happen. His virulent attacks on Radical Reconstruction and the political elevation of blacks only further strengthened the resolve of the radicals to isolate him.

In order to assess Delany fairly, it important to first understand his opposition to black political elevation from his own vantage point. It should be acknowledged up front that he never denied the necessity for civil and political rights for blacks. His writings clearly suggest that he recognized the importance of those rights. As he once declared, "It must be understood that no people can be free who do not themselves constitute an essential part of the ruling element of the country in which they live." Furthermore, as he once argued, "To place the black race in possession of equal rights, and enfranchise it with all the claims of citizenship, it was only necessary to remove all legal disabilities, and repeal all unjust provisions against it, and make the black man stood in the United States a citizen by nature, with claims and rights as inviolable as the proudest."

He reiterated this critical importance of black political emancipation in a letter to President Andrew Johnson in July 1868. "What becomes necessary, then," he informed the president, "to secure and perpetuate the integrity of the union, is simply the enfranchisement and recognition of the political equality of the power that saved the nation from destruction in a time of imminent peril—a recognition of the political equality of the blacks with the whites in all of their relations as American citizens." Thus Delany did not completely oppose black political rights. In fact, he strongly argued that through their patriotism and sacrifices in the Civil War, blacks had earned entitlement to those rights. His concern, however, was with how blacks generally began to translate this possession of political rights into the exercise of political power—in essence, thrusting themselves into roles and responsibilities they had not been adequately prepared or qualified for by the experience of slavery. In his judgment, the newly emancipated black political leadership needed political education on the "elementary lessons in national polity" before it could safely and efficiently handle such responsibilities, and he considered himself qualified to provide such instruction. He offered his tract "On National Polity."[3] It should be understood that Delany's affirmation of political equality, in his letter to President Johnson and in some of his early writings, should not be taken literally. The equality implied referred essentially to emancipation and enfranchisement, which eliminated previous obstacles to, and limitations on, black elevation, and not necessarily absolute equality in all areas of life. For Delany, the acquisition of civil and political rights did not necessarily translate into absolute racial equality in all fields. He concluded that it was impossible to transform overnight a relationship that, for almost 300 years, was defined by inequality and subordination.

Delany was, therefore, willing to accept some imperfections in the system. The new order did not have to be completely just and fair. It was sufficient for Delany that blacks had become "essential part of the ruling element" by virtue of the possession of civil and political rights, which meant potential access to political power. Consequently, he was not troubled "[w]hether the element be founded on a true or false, a just or unjust basis."[4] These would eventually be overcome. In this regard, his perception of the political landscape allowed him to accommodate its shortcomings and imperfections and be willing to compromise.

Other blacks were not quite so willing to ignore these imperfections (particularly, the fact that the ruling element was still predominantly white and that blacks were still vulnerable and could ill-afford to ignore the latent resentment of the former slave masters) or diminish their significance and implications. While Delany may have recognized the imperative of political elevation, he seriously circumscribed its scope and dimensions and thus its significance. His admonitions to blacks amounted to advocacy of self-imposed limitations and boundaries of political space, beyond which they were deemed incapable of effectively functioning. They rejected his ideas and formulations, and, angered by his persistence and determination, they reciprocated by politically marginalizing him and frustrating his every move at self-elevation.

That Delany's condition became desperate is clearly corroborated by Rev. Cain's passionate plea to Governor Moses requesting a position for Delany to enable him at least to feed his family. But Delany's attacks and criticism had done so much damage to Radical Republican fortunes in the state that there was very little sympathy left, if any, for his condition, however miserable. Yet Delany did not set out deliberately to hurt his race. His major problem with Radical Reconstruction was that it seemed so heavily focused on assisting and encouraging blacks to exercise political roles and responsibilities that they had not been adequately prepared for and to assume a troublesome visibility that was bound to enrage Southern whites. Regardless of how repulsive his ideas may have seemed to radicals, they were conceived primarily for the advancement of blacks. Delany suggested concessions of political rights as the moral factor to convince whites of the peaceful and reconciliatory intentions of blacks. This, in his estimation, would unlock the doors to the far more critical economic power. His suggestion that blacks should seek lower-level positions and gradually move up the ladder as they became *ready* and *qualified* for higher positions reflected his enduring faith in moral suasion. As this study has shown, the roots of moral suasion lay deeply buried in the sands of the early black abolitionist crusade of the 1830s and reflected the faith of black Americans in the Protestant work ethic. The optimistic projection of industry as the key to success and elevation is inherent to the concept of the American Dream, a dream that promises prosperity and elevation to anyone willing and able to pursue it through industry and perseverance.

Realizing the American Dream through moral suasion became the defining and motivating ideology of black abolitionism and of the Negro Convention movement of the first half of the nineteenth century. That moral suasion had taken a firm grip of black consciousness is evident in the fact that even after it became officially discredited as a guiding principle, moral suasionist ideals of hard work, perseverance, education, and character reform continued to shape the black struggle. In fact, Delany's acknowledgment of black inferiority was predicated upon his belief that the manifestation of "good character" by blacks offered the moral equivalence of, and balance to, deficiency in black intelligence. Since blacks appeared inferior in intelligence, cultivating "good character" became the redeeming consideration upon which to build a strong case for elevation.

Given the conservative and conciliatory trajectories of Delany's ideas, it therefore should not have surprised anyone that he eventually found himself in the camp of the Democratic Party. Consequently, the "duality of all dualities" should have been anticipated. It was a reluctant decision taken after years of failed attempts to reorient the Republican Party. The apostasy, in fact, resulted from two interlocking considerations. First, there was Delany's enduring faith in "political economy," an ideology that prescribed a subordinate role for, and conservative course in, politics. Delany's "political economy" paradigm rejected political dogmatism in favor of flexibility and compromise. It balanced the interests of blacks on a triad, upon which also depended the overall success of Reconstruction—Northern capital, Southern land, and black labor.

Delany's "political economy" was a very complex phenomenon. It defined both utilitarian and existential considerations for political affiliation. Party support and loyalty depended on the nature and degree of material rewards and benefits that accrued to members and also on the relative strength of the party. He thus adduced a utilitarian conception of politics. A political organization/party could justify its members' unswerving loyalty only if it extended some benefits to them. But benefits alone would not guarantee such loyalty, unless the party also maintained a favorable image in the community. In other words, the correlation of forces in the society must be in its favor. If the odds were against it, "run fast out of it," he advised.[5] Or, as he once declared at a 4th of July gathering in Charleston, underscoring the utilitarian underpinning of the black-Republican Party connection, "I want you to stick to them [Radical Republicans] until you find the odds too heavy against them, then get away as fast as you can."[6] To command the unwavering loyalty of its members, therefore, a political party, according to Delany, should not only provide material rewards but also be in position to protect its members. On both grounds, he judged the Republican Party a failure, and consequently it did not deserve the commitment and loyalty of blacks.

In addition, as Delany repeatedly argued, the Civil War and Reconstruction had failed to effect fundamental changes in the economic fortunes of blacks. In spite of the political gains, blacks remained economically dependent on the alienated class of ex-Confederates and planters. He was right. And it was precisely this reality of economic dependence that enabled the Democrats to apply economic blackmail and intimidation against black voters in the 1876 election. For instance, in Charleston, where the majority of blacks "work for and live upon whites," the Democrats adopted what a Newberry woman called the "pocket argument." Some called it the "preference policy."[7] Whatever the name, it meant one thing—discriminatory policy in the employment of blacks. To secure employment or rent land, blacks had to show certificate of membership in a Democratic club. Thousands of black Republicans suddenly faced economic ruin or joining the Democratic Party as options, and hundreds finally began to take the humiliating steps toward the party.[8] Those who resisted lost their jobs. Hundreds of compliant blacks had liens on their crops released, lands rented to them free, supplies provided free, and money given to them lavishly by vote-seeking Democrats.[9] In addition to economic blackmail, the Democrats, led by their candidate for governor, Wade Hampton, emphasized the liberal promises of their platform. During his campaign, Hampton informed his audience that if elected, the Democratic Party would not renege on its promise to recognize and protect the rights and privileges of blacks. He promised to observe, protect, and defend the rights of all citizens irrespective of race or previous condition.

A major flaw in Delany's reasoning, however, was its lopsidedness. Although he correctly gauged the economic situation, his political values unfortunately betrayed naïveté toward, and a misunderstanding of, the dynamics of the Democratic resurgence. It seemed overly optimistic to suggest that whites would readily share economic power if blacks surrendered political rights and power. Delany was undoubtedly astute and perceptive enough to identify some negative features of Radical Reconstruction that other black leaders ignored. He seemed, however, oblivious to something perhaps much more insidious that other black leaders recognized—the perfidious character of Democratic liberalism.

Few critics have given much attention to unraveling the mystery of the central paradox of Delany's career—his support for the Democratic Party in 1876. Victor Ullman and Nell Painter imply that the Democrats duped Delany into taking their professed liberalism seriously. They used Delany in 1876 and dumped him soon after.[10] This is too simplistic an explanation that avoids coming to grips with, or belittles, the ideological shifts—deemed conservative and reactionary by contemporaries—by putting the blame on the Democrats. Delany's support for the Democrats was not inspired solely by their adoption of a liberal platform. His move began long before the Democrats gave any indication of playing the liberal card. He approached Reconstruction with very strong convictions about the new dispensation and what roles blacks should play.

His "political economy," in all three conservative phases, was designed as an integrative construct meant to harmonize blacks with mainstream American values. In the first phase, it was meant to instill in blacks the values of industry and perseverance as means to elevation and integration, values that would equally appeal favorably to whites and bridge the racial gap. In the second and third phases, it was offered as a framework with which to harmonize the two races. Its emphasis on harmony and reconciliation anticipated the broader sectional rapprochement espoused and nurtured by the New South ideology and movement, with, however, one fundamental difference. The New South ideology developed upon a dual alliance between the North and South and never considered blacks as partners. Blacks were instead sacrificed to consecrate the dual alliance. Although Delany developed this framework for a unity across sectional and racial boundaries, the ultimate success of this unity, depended on the existence, a priori, of a subunity that was sectional based, namely between blacks and Southern whites. There was, however, a problem. Though Delany presented the triadic alliance as an economic union of equals, the social and political conservatism it embodied suggested accommodation to segregation and even concession to claims of white superiority.

Delany's "political economy" mandated reconciliation with Democrats. His advocacy of "amnesty" and "unconditional pardon" for erstwhile rebels emanated from deeply felt convictions. While other blacks looked to the North and to the Republican Party for support and assistance, Delany turned southward. The "intelligence," "maturity," and "political wisdom" that he found deficient in the black leadership, he found in abundance, and with admiration, among representatives of the old order in South Carolina. He was more interested in initiating and effecting change than in defending and upholding party or racial orthodoxy. The new postwar reality called for readjustment, one that de-emphasized old party values and dogmas, especially those that tended to impede the prospects for change. The need for pragmatism and flexibility seemed pervasive in the post-Civil War era. Indeed, times seemed to have changed, and political realities were forcing erstwhile enemies together. As a correspondent for the *New York Times* explained it, "Parties are now getting mixed in the South. Other questions than those raised by the war are now making their way into politics . . . which do not leave the old party line clear. . . . Republicans are found acting with Democrats and vice-versa." Delany wanted blacks to embrace this pragmatic culture and abandon what he perceived as their ideological and dogmatic attachment to the Republican Party. When he failed to convince the black political leadership within the Republican Party and felt that Republican radicalism obstructed change and endangered peace, he longed for an alternative. Democratic liberalism was consequently more of a catalyst than the explanation for his dramatic switch in 1876.

Delany's fights against Radical Republicanism reveal, more than anything else, his conservative and pragmatic nature—qualities that negate the "nationalist" and "uncompromisingly militant" images created and popularized by modern scholars. Delany defined his functions in postbellum America as essentially conservative—to preserve law and order and advance interracial harmony. His Freedmen's Bureau position allowed him to pursue these objectives. Vincent Harding's lamentation over Delany's failure to advance black land ownership is, therefore, misplaced. He was appointed a Bureau agent to support and sustain, not undermine, government policy. Though personally in favor of land ownership by blacks, once in office Delany's task was to implement the limited agenda of the Bureau, which precluded massive land redistribution. He was therefore left to mediate and work out some compromise between freedmen and landowners in his district in Hilton Head. Cooperation between capital (whites) and labor (blacks) became the centerpiece of his scheme for a successful Reconstruction.

Delany transcended many and often conflicting ideological boundaries—constantly moving back and forth between conservative, moderate, and radical postures. He was not a doctrinaire activist. He was very flexible. The choices he made and the values he espoused were dictated by his assessment of the situation and by what he felt was in the best interest of blacks. Therefore, what was consistent about Delany was his pragmatism, not his ideology. His ideas included a variety of conservative values—faith in the economically self-made individual, disdain for radical politics, subordination of politics to economics, accommodation, adaptation to white paternalism, advocacy of gradualism, preference for industrial over liberal education, and the notion that white Southerners (former slave owners) were the best friends of blacks. Why have these aspects of Delany's career been consistently de-emphasized? Precisely because they represent negative monumental markers considered inconsistent with the demands of the instrumentalist genre. Put differently, they underscore a personality that is contradictory to, and one that could potentially subvert, the social revolutionary focus of the black struggle. Paradoxically, however, these are precisely the same conservative values that Booker T. Washington later espoused and popularized, which earned him the scorn of his contemporaries and an enduring reputation as a conservative and even a reactionary.

Modern critics have often read too much of race or racial essentialist ideas into their interpretations of Delany. There has been a tendency to overemphasize his supposedly racial/black essentialist disposition without acknowledging the inherent and glaring complexities and ambivalence. In Mia Bay's most recent amplification of this perspective, Delany was "practically a black supremacist." There is no doubt that Delany's frustration in the 1850s compelled him to espouse what could rightly be construed as racial and black essentialist ideas and schemes. It is also true that he premised his emigration platform on a strong philosophical foundation of racial unity. It is equally true that as part of his emigration propaganda, Delany highlighted social, political, and economic dysfunctions that were clearly racially constructed. Addressing a crowded gathering in Rochester, New York, in 1862, shortly after his return from Africa, Delany emphatically declared that his prime "concern was for the pure black, uncorrupted by Caucasian blood."[11] This is the group that, according to Delany, is directly threatened by American/European hegemonic conspiracy, and, as his second letter ("Trial and Conviction") clearly states, it is precisely the same group that is suffering the brunt of institutional racism within the Republican administration at both the federal and state levels, and, most significantly, it is the group with which Delany is intimately associated by virtue of his "unadulterated blackness."

Delany's analysis acknowledged the reality of race and racial divisions as the basis of arguing for a deracinated society. According to him, "This nation is composed of two great political elements, whites and blacks."[12] From the start of Reconstruction, this reality shaped his advocacy of race-less, color-blind policies and politics. Another consideration for his insistence upon racial harmony cuts deep into his aversion to violence and awareness of the "numerical feebleness" of blacks. He insisted that blacks stood to lose in a racial confrontation. He urged blacks to adopt a policy of reconciliation, one that did not in any way, shape, or form exacerbate racial tension or animosity. For Delany, race was a social reality that could, and should, be transcended in order to have harmonious social relations.

In his speeches, Delany mapped out various strategies of accomplishing this deracination, but overwhelmingly, his proposals entailed sacrifices and concessions that other black leaders found discomforting and unacceptable. For instance, he called for the adaptation of the "peculiar institution" of the South to the changed realities of the post-Civil War era and what he called, the "new state things."[13] This adaptation had to come, he stressed,

> by the clasping of hands, and a combination of the two races in one great southern party, based on the common interest of all the people of both races, inseparably connected, regarding and respecting alike each other's rights, conceding and supporting each other's just and legal claims, promoting peace, friendship and confidence, till we shall be in our domestic

relations only known as one people and one party in interest, developing the rich resources of the soil scarcely yet commenced.[14]

In setting forth this basis for racial harmony and for transcending race, Delany anticipated precisely the same race-effacing and race-transcending paradigm that future generations of black conservatives embraced, exemplified by the Washingtonian ideals that became assertive from the 1890s on. The triple alliance paradigm stands as a shinning testimony to Delany's foresightedness. He presented it as the key to a successful Reconstruction program. It epitomized his vision of racial cooperation and harmony. It foreshadowed the New South movement ideology. Long before white politicians and businessmen talked of sectional harmony, Delany already anticipated the ideology. The only problem with his construct was that it included and envisioned blacks as equal partners, whereas the eventual triumphant New South ideology sacrificed blacks and their interests to consecrate the sectional harmony.

Delany's call for emigration derived from his perception of a global American/European conspiracy against blacks. In thus essentializing race in the nineteenth century, Delany anticipated Du Bois's epic 1903 formulation of race as the central problem of the twentieth century. Early Reconstruction speeches of Delany also inhered strong racial essentialist undertones, loud enough to instill fears among those whites who heard him. Among his contemporaries, Delany was undoubtedly acknowledged as a preeminent exemplar of black pride. John Gaines of Ohio spoke for many when he characterized Delany as the quintessence of black pride. Frederick Douglass is often credited with the remark that he thanked God simply for making him a man, but Delany always thanked God for making him "a black man."[15] In the judgment of Bishop Daniel Payne of the African Methodist Episcopal Church, Delany was simply "too intensely African to be popular and thereby multiplied enemies where he could have multiplied friends."[16] The white abolitionist William Lloyd Garrison once described Delany as "so black as to make his identity with the African race perfect."[17] Delany himself was known to publicly proclaim his "unadulterated blackness" as a badge of honor. His contemporaries believed that the only person who provoked envy from Delany was one darker than he was.[18] In other words, there were strong grounds for proclaiming Delany a racial essentialist.

However, if his career is viewed in its totality, not just isolating the brief nationalist phase, then the racial essentialism for which he became renowned diminishes in significance. The racial lines Delany drew were often ephemeral and utilitarian. Racial unity, black pride, and solidarity were means to an end, not the end. And he was not alone. As established in Chapter 3, even the "radical" New York group of the moral suasionist epoch, including Samuel Cornish (who seemed to favor organizing the black struggle along clearly demarcated racial lines), all adduced utilitarian constructions of race as a reform strategy. Their affirmation of race/color sometimes appeared separatist, yet in reality this was a strategic move driven by integrationist consciousness and aspirations.

There was thus a certain pragmatism and fragility to Delany's conception and utilization of race. His entire nationalism, viewed within a functionalist perspective, underscores his pragmatic and utilitarian approach to race. Delany never envisaged racial pride and solidarity as an absolute and permanent state of black consciousness but as positive consciousness to facilitate the goal of achieving meaningful elevation and empowerment as integral members of the American nation. He acknowledged this utilitarian disposition toward race unambiguously to Garrison, when the latter accused him of harboring caste consciousness in his review of Delany's book, *The Condition*.[19] As much as he loved America and abhorred caste consciousness and any policy of segregation, Delany would "never be reconciled" to a life of subservience. All that he wanted for himself, and for blacks in general, was to be given the same "equal possession and enjoyment of privileges" that whites had. It was largely the failure to achieve this goal that eventually led him to emigration.[20]

Yet Delany never abandoned his belief in the brotherhood and sisterhood of humanity, a value he imbibed in his early moral suasion phase. Even when he underlined race, his ultimate objective was to see this unity reflected in concrete policies that enabled blacks to achieve their potentialities and exercise their rights and privileges as integral members of this community. Establish this, and Delany's race consciousness paradigm disappears. There was nothing absolute, dogmatic, or ideological about Delany's race consciousness. This flexibility allowed him to make the kind of concessions and choices that defined his postbellum career. He thus represents the perfect prototype of August Meier's typology of the typical nineteenth-century black leader—someone who often straddled different ideological spaces and was flexible enough to recognize when compromises were necessary.[21] It would, therefore, be unfair to blame Delany for, or suggest that he was in any way responsible for, the Compromise of 1877, as some critics imply. Draper, for example, argued that by supporting Wade Hampton, Delany "indirectly helped to restore white rule in South Carolina." Victor Ullman was more direct, albeit infused with historical hyperbole:

> Delany certainly did not plan it, but his unremitting efforts to find a formula whereby black and white could live in amity were responsible for the questionable inauguration of Rutherford B. Hayes as 19th President of the United States.
>
> The polite terminology given in the historical texts is that the national election of 1876 was "resolved by a compromise," an agreement between the conservative Republicans of the North and the white Democrats of the South that they would bury the Civil War hatchet. The fact that blacks were buried with it is not mentioned.
>
> In South Carolina, at least, the "sell-out" of the state's electoral votes amounted to Hampton proposing to Hayes . . . "You make me Governor of the State of South Carolina and I'll make you President of the United States." Hampton might never have been in a position to make such a deal if it had not been for Martin R. Delany.[22]

Had Delany seen through the deceitful, perfidious, and fraudulent character of Democratic liberalism, he most certainly would not have staked so much on the movement, his disillusionment with radicalism notwithstanding. He was a victim, perhaps even a prisoner, of his own unqualified faith in the irreversible and progressive course of American national culture.

Delany's adoption of a color-blind ideology in the postbellum phase of his career should, therefore, not be seen as an aberration. That a man who advanced race as the underpinnings of his emigrationist and nationalist schemes in the 1850s should become a deracinated advocate of color-blind ethos from the 1860s on should not surprise anyone. It should be remembered that Delany was a product of the moral suasionist and universalistic culture of the early-nineteenth-century black abolitionist crusade, and as argued, even those abolitionists who prioritized color during this early phase of the black struggle had the overarching objective of achieving an integrative, color-blind social and political order. Color, race, was just a means to the end (integration). Deep in his heart, Delany was a color-blind person, and aspects of his career where he upheld color represented transient and ephemeral reflections of his frustrations. The essential Delany was a man who believed in the universal brotherhood and sisterhood of humanity and who was compelled to develop racial- and color-phobic consciousness by the equally racial- and color-phobic context of his existence.

What we see in the postbellum era, in my judgment, represents the real and essential Delany, more real and essential than the color-conscious and ethnocentric personality popularized in instrumentalist and modern Afrocentric genres. There was, therefore, much more to Delany. The essential Delany was much more pragmatic, compromising, and conservative. As the uses to which he put his racial/ethnic consciousness demonstrate, he was not averse to altering, even reversing, his views and positions whenever his conscience so dictated, and usually the dictates of his conscience were informed by utilitarian considerations. Delany clearly expressed his dislike for ideological straitjackets early in his career in a publication in the *North Star.* "I care little for precedent, and therefore, discard the frivolous rules of formality," he wrote, "conforming always to principle, *suggested by conscience, and guided by the light of reason*" (emphasis added).[23] This in effect is the truism of his career. The decisions and choices Delany made were dictated more by his conscience, guided by the light of his reason, and less by dogmatic subservience to some racial or ideological considerations.

APPENDIX A

"A Political Review"

LETTER FROM MAJOR DELANY TO FREDERICK DOUGLASS

Hon. Fred Douglass

My Dear Sir:

It has been ten years since last we met (in your library at Rochester) to discuss and reconcile ourselves to President Lincoln's war policy. Since then slavery had been overthrown, and no "reunion" of what were, for twenty years or more, the leading colored men of the country who shaped the policy and course of our race which led to disenthralment, having taken place, and consequently no interchange of ideas by counsel, I therefore deem it of importance at the time, to take a political review of South Carolina which I think will apply justly to nearly, if not the whole, of the "reconstructed states" of the South as well as the national government.

When the war ended the colored people of the South had little knowledge of social and political affairs, and had of necessity, to accept such leaders as presented themselves. The first of these were in the persons of various agencies, as school teachers (mostly women), the Christian Commission, Colporteurs and agent to the freedmen's affair (not the Bureau) who aided in directing their social and domestic relations.

When reconstruction commenced, political leaders were greatly required, but few to be had. Southerners (the old masters) studiously opposed and refused to countenance reconstruction, and the freedmen were fearful and would not have trusted them if they could have obtained their aid.

Those who came with or followed the army, with a very few native whites, were the only available political element to be had to carry out the measures of reconstruction.

These were readily accepted by the blacks (by this I include the entire colored people) and the fullest confidence reposed in them. Some were or had been officers in the army. Some private, some sutlers, others peddlers and various tradesmen, others gamblers and even pickpockets and "hangers-on" and "bummers." I am particularly speaking of the whites. Among them were men of refinement, educated gentlemen, and some very good men, but a large part of those active were of the lowest grade of northern society, Negro haters at home, who could not have been elected to any position of honor or trust. Just such men as burnt down Negro orphan asylum and hung Negro men at lamp posts in the New York riot of 1853. In this review, I intend to speak plainly, call things by their right names, and look those of whom I speak directly in the face.

The best and most competent men were chosen to fill the most important positions in state and local government, while the others readily obtained such places as required incumbents. Indeed there was scarcely one so incompetent as not to have been assigned some position of trust.

Positioned in places of power, profit and trust, they soon sought by that guile and deception, known only to demagogues, under the acceptable appellations of Yankee, Republican and Radical, to intrude themselves into the confidence of the blacks, and place themselves at their head as leaders. So insidiously did they do this that it was not discovered by the few colored men of intelligence who held places among them till too late to remedy the fatal evil.

These demagogues laid the foundation of their power upon a basis of the most dangerous political heresy. Deception, lying, cheating, chanting "whatever can be done in politics is fair," and to "beat is the duty in a political contest no matter what means were used to effect it" are among the pernicious precepts of this moral infidelity.

Jealous of the few intelligent colored men among them, they studiously sought to divide the blacks by sowing the seeds of discord among them. This was facilitated by prejudicing the ignorant against the intelligent. These men strove and vied each with the other, regardless of consequence, to place himself in the lead of a community of blacks in both town and country, which in time was reduced to little else than a rabble mob of disorder and confusion. Trained in the Leagues as serfs to their masters, it became dangerous to oppose the teachings of these men of mischief. Because, having been recommended to their confidence at the commencement of reconstruction, their experience and knowledge in public men and matters were too limited to believe anything against them.

A knowledge of this emboldened these men to a persistence in their course of crime and corruption. Hence many otherwise, good men, both white and black, from age, inexperience or weakness were induced to accept the monstrous teachings and join with or follow the lead of these wretched imposters. Their sole object being personal gain, they cared little or nothing for public weal, the interest of the state or people, black or white, nor the Republican cause, upon which they had indecently imposed themselves. This is that which controlled Charleston politics and brought deserved defeat to the Republicans in the recent Municipal election. It was just retribution to a set of unprincipled miscreants, rioting on the people rights under the name of "Republicanism." Honest upright men of all parties, white and black, no longer able to bear it, determined to put down the abominable thing; leading Republicans, who had been standing aloof, taking an active part. Among other things, they taught the simple-minded people that suffrage was inviolably secure, the blacks being in the majority, would always control the affairs of the state in the South; that the 15th Amendment had abolished color and complexion in the United States, and the people were now all of one race. This bare faced deception was so instilled into them that it became dangerous in many instances to go into the country and speak of color in any manner whatever, without the angry rejoinder; "WE don't want to hear that, we are all one color now!"

These ridiculous absurdities were fostered by the demagogues, the better to conceal their own perfidy and keep themselves in the best positions as "Republicanism know no race" they taught.

Another imposition was that colored people did not require intelligent colored leaders; that the Constitution had been purged of color by a Radical Congress, and to be a Republican was all that was required to make a true representative. That mental culture and qualifications were only required by the proud and arrogant, that all who requested those accomplishments were enemies to both black and white, that race representation was making distinctions on account of race and color. By this means they opposed the qualified men among the blacks, encouraged the ignorant and less qualified. They might of necessity take the lead and occupy the best places in the party. These are plain indisputable truths which will not be denied by any upright intelligent Republican, black or white.

Before the introduction of these men among them, there never was a better population, rural or town, out of which to shape a useful political element. Good-hearted, simple-minded, mostly uneducated, they were ready and willing to receive any instruction supposed for their own good, which they anxiously awaited and as eagerly sought. And could they have had the advice of the maturely intelligent, good and virtuous friend of humanity, such as was received and given by us during more than thirty years toilsome battle for liberty and right, there never could have been the cause for the complaint against us as a race now in a measure justifiable.

One most fruitful cause of mischief in the party arose from the age and want of experience on the part of the good white men who assumed the lead in politics—as well as ignorance in the most of them—and the same may be said of their colored colleagues. For the most part young men, where they possessed the required qualifications, they were deficient in experience and knowledge in politics.

To such an extent are they misled that they regularly trained themselves with firearms and marched in companies to political meetings, frequently led by miserable white men. Menacing, threatening, abusing, quarrelling, confusion and frequently rioting are common results of this most disgraceful state of affairs under which we live, all in the name of Republicanism.

The effect upon the people is wonderful. From a polite, pleasant, agreeable, kindly common people, ever ready and obliging, there is now to be met with an ill-mannerly, sullen, disagreeable, unkind, disobliging populace, seemingly filled with hatred and ready for resentment. These changes in the character of the people must have been noticed by every intelligent observer, in contradistinction to their former excellent reputation. Formerly, they were proverbial for their politeness, latterly they are noticed for the absence of it. These people are despoiled of their natural characteristics and shamefully demoralized by renegade intruders.

These strictures had no reference whatever to the intelligent, light-minded, upright gentlemen among the white Republicans, whose examples and precepts have aided in building up society and contributing to the public good, but especially to that class who almost live in the quarters of the country people and hamlets of the towns, among the black populations, keeping them distracted with excitement, who are a curse to the community at large, and a blight in the body politic.

The Social relations of the colored people is another shameful evil, which does more to weaken their strength, neutralize their efforts and divided them in politics than even the graceless intrusion and imposition of white demagogues, because being of their own household, still adhering to an absurdity, a relic of the degraded past, they cling to the assumption of white blood and brown complexion, and to such an extent is this carried, I am told, that old societies have been revived and revised, and absolute provision made against the admission among them of a pure blooded black. Fire, military companies and even churches and graveyards, it is said, are permanently established on this basis. In one church, at least no blacks are to be seen, and in another there is a division between the blacks and browns by different caste.

These distinctions naturally sours the blacks and widen the breach which should never have existed. What a commentary is this on the conditions of the race! Cultivated intelligence and enlightened civilization will alone remedy a humiliating condition of a people now receiving the commiseration of the education world. This canker, this leprosy must be at once healed and by a permanent purification purged from the social system of our people whose vitals it has entered, threatening death to its emaciating victims, now the scoff and derision of the Caucasoid race.

Of a piece with this, is the ridiculous aping objection raised on account of nativity. Do they not know that (unlike the white race which had various established nationalities of the highest civilization throughout the world) we cannot, as a race afford to be divided? That instead of objections, we should welcome with pride the coming among us of people of our own race, of intelligence, culture and responsibility, from whithersover they might come!

This anomalous imitation, not original, but borrowed from the other race, is not confined to class among us, but equally indulged in by many blacks and browns of every social position. Let the people learn this simple, though important lesson: that the rejection of people because of their birth place is social and political death to their race. That without intercourse and accession from abroad, intelligence, like wealth, must be limited and impotent. That the power and glory of the white race consists in their universal intercourse and unlimited recognitions.

But among these are excellent ladies and gentlemen, who, though by affinity and predilection, may belong to such associations, yet they have no sympathy with the motives that induced their formations, and therefore discard them as humiliating and will not be bound by their provisions. And to the credit of the greater of those known as "common people" among the mixed race, they entirely ignore these ridiculous distinctions, studiously refusing to recognize them—the distinction of color being propagated alone by that part known as the "highest class" among them.

To another important point, I would invite your attention—that of the course of the national government. While distinctions in the rights of citizens on account of "race or color" is most pointedly prohibited, distinction on account of color is most definitely made by the government at Washington. It is a fact most noticeable in *executive appointment of colored men, there are none of pure black men, the pure Negro race, but all have been most carefully selected from those having an admixture of white blood. In neither of the departments in Washington is there a single black holding a position above that of porter or lacquey, while in many, if not all of them, except the army and navy—there are those of mixed blood holding positions of clerk-ship—as is just and right—and other equally respectable places. Nor in no appointment requiring qualification by culture in and out of Washington, is there a pure black man or woman to be found, while many such applications have been made, but always rejected. This is no fault of our Brown brother, but that of the government, and the misfortune of the blacks. There may be these two exceptions: An ordinary black man, the keeper of a grogshop; received the appointment of postmaster, across the James River, opposite to Richmond, VA., obtained it is said at the request of a Democratic community. Also it is said that a black man, has received the appointment of Consul-General and Minister residence to the Republic of Liberia, Africa, which required a recommendation from nearly the whole of the Republican members of Senate to obtain the notice of Mr. Secretary of State, Hamilton, Fish! This minister, I am told, persistently refuses to recognize the application of a black for any position. And indeed, I am further informed that his prejudice of color caused the removal of the residence of the accomplished Haitian Minister, Colonel Romain, from Washington to New York City. Other members of the cabinet it is said largely share these feelings against the pure Negro race.*

Nor, out of the six hundred colored people of North have there been any federal appointments in the Northern states to any position above that of messenger or the merest subordinate, except a post office clerkship in Boston and Chicago, one each I believe.

And what is said of Executive appointment at Washington in relation to blacks, the same I think may be safely said of the different state governments, the blacks being studiously neglected, except indeed, to persistently make appointment of incompetent black men, to position which only bring discredit to them and their race. And in not a single instance does it occur to my mind in which a competent black man has received an appointment from a state executive, with a single exception, that of the governor of a far Southern state, who appointed a black man (a special favorite of his) as one of four harbor master—the other being white—he having to employ a white man at hundred dollars a month to do his duties for him, when in the same city there were a number of well qualified black men, not one of whom ever received an office of equal significance. The fact is not ignored of the governor of South Carolina honoring a black man with an appointment of aid-de-camp on his staff, an office purely of honor, yet an honor which any gentleman might except and is duly appreciated by the recipient.

The entire population of the African race is about five million, one-eight of the whole American people. According to the ratio of population, they are entitled to thirty two (32) representatives in Congress, and a corresponding ratio of official appointment. Allowing one and a half million of pure blooded blacks. These, by the foregoing estimate, are entitle to about twenty six (26) representatives, with their ratio of federal offices. And yet these 3-1/2 million of people with their political claims, have been persistently neglected and almost ignored, by both federal and state governments, (except in cases of incompetent blacks for mere political purposes, to conciliate the ignorant blacks) while their more favored brethren of mixed bloods, have received all the places of honor profit and trust, intended to represent the race.

In the name of a common race, for whose liberty and equal right you and I for years have struggled, I now for the first time expose this disparaging injustice and call upon you to aid in righting the wrong. A wrong which longer to endure in silence would be an evidence of conscious inferiority and unworthiness.

Republicanism is simply the "claims to equal rights" established by our fathers in Philadelphia, 1816, by them renewed in 1829 in Cincinnati, Ohio, continued 183-31-31 in Philadelphia; endorsed by their white brethren in 1833 in Boston as the "anti-slavery" and "abolition" of the country, the Free Soil of the Buffalo Convention, 1848, and Pittsburgh Convention 1852 when it was engrafted into politics of Republicanism, at the nomination of Fremont at Rochester, N.Y. 1856, and Lincoln at Chicago 1860.

Anti-slavery, as established by our fathers, and propagated by us and our white friends, had for its basis "justice and equal rights to all men" and for its motto; "Whatsoever ye would that others do unto you, do ye even so to them." This is "anti-slavery" as originally propagated by our brethren, aided by their white friends, continued by us, aided by our white friends and engrafted into politics. This should be Republicanism. Have these principles been adhered to under the dispensation of Republican rule? Have they not been shamefully perverted?

Both of the old parties—Democrats and Whigs—favored slavery, having as their basis the inferiority of the Negro and the right to oppress him and hold him perpetually in bondage, denied of every right but that at the option of the master. Republicanism was intended to supercede these and accord to him the enjoyment of all the rights and privileges of American citizenship.

Under the rallying cry of acting for and representing the "Negro" men of every shade of complexion have attained to places of honor, profit, trust and power in the party, except the real Negro himself—save such places as he had the power which to elect himself who remain today as before emancipation, a political nonentity before the government of the country.

You have now seen the elements of which the party is composed in South Carolina, and its material through the nation. Are these harmonious elements? Does the structure consist of solid materials? Can it stand the storm of political attacks from without, and strife and struggles from within? Is there no repair to be made to the structure, or is it to be left to tumble to pieces by decay and damage, from ill usage? These are questions worthy the attention of the publicist and statesman.

There must be to make it effective a renovating reorganization in this state based upon intelligence, respectability and honesty. The discordant element must become harmonized. One class or race must not be permitted to enjoy privileges of which another is debarred. If this be continued as heretofore, devastation and ruin will come upon the party, when it will cease to exist as it would deserve to be, as no party by whatever name shall exist a single day, which does not accord and practically extend equal rights and their enjoyment to all the citizens, without distinction of race or color.

You and I have spent the best of our lives in the cause of humanity, living to see the overthrow and death of slavery, and universal liberty proclaimed in the land, and it now becomes equally our duty to crush in infancy, the offspring of the monster wherever found.

Preparatory to any action on their part with the other race as a party, the colored people must first become reconciled to themselves as a race, and respect each other as do the whites, regardless of complexion or nativity, making merit only the mark of distinction, as they cannot afford to be divided.

Having settled the above "preparatory" I would lay down the following principles as a basis of all future party actions, by whatever name it may be called, whether Republican or otherwise:

1. Equality before the law to every person of whatever race or color, and strict adherence to the Reconstruction acts bearing upon the same.

2. Colored people must have intelligent leaders of their own race, and white people intelligent leaders of theirs, the two combined to compose the leaders of the party. This must be accepted and acknowledged as the basis of all future political action and necessary to the harmony and safety of both race.

3. All measure in the party must emanate from consultation of the leaders, otherwise such measures may not be respected.

4. Demagogues and disreputable men must be discarded as leaders, and never more be given opportunity to betray their trust and abuse the interests of the people whom they assumed to represent.

I am no candidate nor aspirant for office. I would accept of nothing that made me depend upon the position for my support or cause me to relinquish my personal business. I have spoken simply as **an** *humble citizen, interested in the welfare of the community at large.*

With the above platform to guide any future action, I close my review of the political situation.

Thanking the editor of the Charleston Republican *for the liberal use of this column in granting this publication, I beg to remain, distinguished sir, as ever, Your friend and co-laborer in the cause of humanity.*
Charleston, August 14, 1871.

M. R. Delany
Charleston
August, 14, 1871

SOURCE: The Daily Republican, *August 15, 1871.*

157: F. DOUGLASS TO DELANY

My Dear Sir,

Your well known zeal and ability, and your long devotion to the cause of freedom and equality to all men, will, I am quite sure, obtain for the elaborate letter with which you have honored me, through the columns of the Charleston Daily Republican, *and which is now printed in the columns of the* New National Era, *a thoughtful perusal by intelligent colored men in all parts of this country. While I heartily concur in much that you say in that letter, there are some things in it from which I as heartily dissent. It is, however, due to say that, even where I dissent from your views, I am compelled to respect you boldness, candor, and manly independence in the utterance of your convictions. Especially and sincerely do I thank you for your masterly exposure of the malign influences which surrounded the whole business of reconstruction in South Carolina and the other seceding States. I have, however, no denunciations for the carpetbaggers who assumed the leadership in the matter of reconstruction. Upon the whole, they have done pretty well—at any rate, their prominence was inevitable, and I am disposed to make the best of it. Your narrative is strong and striking, but not strange. The destitution of political knowledge among the newly enfranchised and emancipated people of South Carolina, the sullen contempt and indifference with which the old slave-holding class looked upon all efforts to bring the State into harmonious relations to the National Government, the absence of any middle class among the native white population, possessed of sufficient intelligence and patriotism to take the lead in the needed work of reorganization, the pressing necessity for the early consummation of that work, not only reconcile me to the employment of such hands as were found ready to engaged in that work, but make me thankful that any were found to lead in its performance.*

Better men might have done better work, but the same is true all around the world. The men who lay the foundations of States are not always the most scrupulous. Mingling with the adventurous, ambitious, and daring qualities needed to carry loyal white people into the South at the close of the war, there was doubtless, a tumult of motives—some the highest and best, and others base and selfish. Yet, taken as a whole, the men in whose breasts they dwelt had union, nationality, and liberty in their hears, and were capable in some measure of serving these high interest. At any rate, they were the best that could be had, and we are disposed to give them credit. *The wise, the thoughtful, the men of scrupulous integrity, who stayed quietly at home, avoiding all the hardships and perils of residence in those unfriendly States, should be careful in dealing out censures upon the school masters and school mistresses who hazarded everything.*

As to destitution of political knowledge among the newly emancipated class— what else could have happened? You and I know that one of the worse effects of slavery is to unfit men for freedom. The abject slave to-day may be the haughty and conceited tyrant of to-morrow. The beggar suddenly raised to opulence is more offensively and insufferably insolent than the man reared and educated in wealth. Such is poor human nature. Doomed to ignorance for ages, the Negro could not be expected to cope with the white men about him at the start. If he has been the dupe of designing men it is because of his antecedents. He is subject to the same laws that govern in the case of other men. The bees and butterflies are irresistibly attracted to a garden of sweet flowers, and the cunning and designing are attracted by a crowd of simple men.

The emancipated men of South Carolina have been misled and cheated—they have been made the backs and legs upon which white men ride into power and place. No doubt of it. But the same is true of the laboring classes everywhere—wherever there are backs and legs without brains somebody is bound to ride them. When the crafty and selfish outrage the animal beyond endurance he will rise and plunge, and gyrate and, perhaps, throw the rider; but while he remains only a back and legs somebody will be found with sufficient skill and address to ride the animal.

The colored people of the South are just now going to school. It is hardly worth while to lament that the school is not better than it is. It is the best at hand, and the wisest course is to make the best of it. They cannot expect to get something for nothing. The best things come to any people only through suffering and toil. I rather think that the colored people of the South, notwithstanding the bad precepts they have some-times heard, and the bad political examples set before them by their designing and unscrupulous political and social knowledge, and that they will soon be able to dis-tinguish between a decent man and a demagogue, no matter what disguises he may assume. The outlook in North Carolina is better, and the same, I hope, will be found true of South Carolina not far hence.

I cannot agree with you in denouncing colored me for going armed to political meetings in South Carolina, nor can I agree with you that the practice is an imported one. The habit of carrying deadly weapons in the South belongs to an age considerably earlier than that of the carpet baggers. I may be wrong, but I had supposed that this practice on the part of the newly enfranchised class at the South had been impelled by a dire necessity. It is a bad practice, and one which cannot be commended in a truly civilized community, but everything in this world is relative. Assault compels defense. I shall never ask the colored people to be lambs where the whites insist on being wolves, and yet no man shall out do me in efforts to promote kindness and good will between the races. But I know there can be no peace without justice, and hence the sword.

One other thing: I hardly think you are quite just in what you say of the changed manners of the colored people of South Carolina. It does not seem to me that their degeneracy is so complete as you describe it to be. Were you not M.R. Delany, I should say that the man who wrote thus of the manners of the colored people of South Carolina had taken his place with the old planters. You certainly cannot be among those of the South who prefer the lash-inspired manners of the past. I know too well your own proud and independent spirit, to believe that the manners of an enslaved and oppressed people are more to your taste than those which are born of freedom and independence.

Still, even in what you say on this point, you have the advantage of me. You are on the ground, and may know whereof you affirm. I am, however, disposed to put the best face upon this complaint of yours as upon others. If there be this offensive insolence in the manners of the colored people of South Carolina of which you complain—the result of sudden elevation—time and enlightenment will surely correct the evil. Liberty has its manners as well as slavery, and with those manners true self-respect goes hand in hand with a just respect for the rights and feelings of others. Have patience, my old friend. The white people of the South have more to bear from the change in the Negro's manners than you and I have. It must be very galling to their feelings to see their former slaves, once so humble and cowering in their presence, now passing and repassing without making any one of the old signs of obedience and servitude. But if they can bear this new departure on the part of the blacks, you and I ought to bear our sufferings in silence. All that old-fashioned How-do-Aunty? And Servant-massa manners is out of joint with our times. It was very pleasant in its day. It bespoke condescension on the one side and servile submission on the other, an though pleasanter than the sound of the lash, it was part of slavery. It had a real significance then. It has none now. When the body disappears I would not detain its shadow. But enough on this point.

There is an element of real bitterness in your letter to which I hope you have imparted a coloring deeper than the facts warrant. It is possible that the old enemy of the darker hued people of the West Indies, which has poisoned the life blood of colored society in Haiti, imperiled its independence, and blocked the wheel of its progress has come here also? Can it be that the colored people of South Carolina are going to make such fools of themselves, as to raise such a distinction among themselves based upon a color at a moment when color has just ceased to be a crime in our country, and when human brotherhood is becoming the recognized gospel throughout the world! Are we to have, nay, have we got a caste called the browns in South Carolina? You say we have, and I cannot positively contradict you. If you are right in your facts and specifications, I certainly unite with you in your hottest denunciations of that contemptible and senseless imitation of one of the meanest feelings that ever crept into the human heart.

The white people of this country have in one thing been remarkably consistent. They have hated and persecuted Negro blood wherever they have found it. Except in the State of Ohio, (where a Negro can prove that he is more white man than Negro) the man with the last drop of Negro blood in him is hated and persecuted with all the bitterness visited upon the blackest among us all. They hate the blood wherever they see it, whether in large or small quantity, whether pure or mixed, whether black as midnight or almost white. The whole thing is abominable; but we have more respect for the white man's prejudice and hate than for that of your snuff-colored Negro.

Think of a man putting enmity between the blood that courses in his own veins affecting to despise the one while he respects the other! The thing is almost too absurd for contempt.

While I entirely agree with you that no discrimination should be made against black applicants for office at Washington, because such applicants are black, I am far from agreeing with you that the present Republican administration has made any such discrimination. In fact we know of two clerks in the Departments here who are without doubt as darks as even Mr. Delany would require, and who are as capable and efficient as any others. I am not much of a logician, but I require a little closer connection between premise and conclusion than you have here shown, to consider your conclusion legitimate. There are other reasons than color and race for the limited number of colored clerks employed in the Departments at Washington—reasons which I hope will disappear in time, and which, in fact, are already disappearing. The same causes which gave the leadership in public affairs to white men in South Carolina have given the lion's share of the offices to white men in Washington. As a matter of arithmetic your figures are faultless. The mulattoes, on a solid census basis, ought to have so many offices, the blacks so many, the whites so many, the Germans so many, the Irish so many, and other classes and nationalities should have offices according to their respective numbers. The idea is equal and admirable in theory; but does it not already seem to you a little absurd as a matter of practice? The fact is, friend Delany, these things are not fixed by figures, and while men are what they are cannot be so fixed. According to the census, the colored people of the country constitute one-eight of the whole American people. Upon your statistical principle, the colored people of the United States ought, therefore, not only to hold one-eighth of all the offices in the country but they should own one-eighth the property, and pay one-eighth of all the taxes of the country. Equal in numbers, they should, of course, be equal in everything else. They should constitute one-eighth of the poets, statesmen, scholars, authors, and philosophers of the country. The test should be impartially and stringently applied, if applied at all, and should bear equally in all directions. The Negro in black should mark every octave on the National piano. In every company of eight American authors that can be named we ought to be able to name one black author, and so through all the varied departments of American activity. The Negro should edit just one-eighth of all the newspapers; he should be the author of just one-eighth of all the books written and printed in the Untied States; and, in a word, be one-eighth in everything. Now, my old friend, there is no man in the United States who knows better than you do that equality of numbers has nothing to do with equality of

attainments. You know, too, that natural equality is a very different thing from practical equality; and that though men be potentially equal, circumstances may for a
time cause the most striking inequalities. Look at our newly emancipated people,
read their history of ignorance and destitution, and see their present progress and elevation, and rejoice in the prospect before them. You are too broad not to comprehend,
and too brave to shut your eyes to facts; and in the light of these your octagonal principle certainly will not work.

I note what you say of Hon. Hamilton Fish, the Secretary of State of the United
States, and the removal of Col. Romain, the ex-Haitian Minister, from Washington to
New York, and cannot but think you have done the Secretary of State great wrong in
what you say on that subject. Hamilton Fish may not be an old-fashioned abolitionist,
but he certainly is a gentleman, and incapable of mean and underhand dealing
towards anybody. At any rate, some better witness than "they say," or "it is rumored"
will have to appear before I shall be convinced that your reproaches of this gentleman
and statesman are just.

In conclusion, my dear old friend, let me assure you that I rejoice in every honor
of which you are the recipient, and hold you worthy of all that have been bestowed
upon you, and of still higher promotion. Let me also assure you of my cordial
co-operation with you in all well-directed efforts to elevate and improve our race,
to break down all unjust and mischievous distinctions among them, and secure for
them a just measure of the political privileges now so largely monopolized by our
white fellow-countrymen.

Very truly yours,
Frederick Douglass

SOURCE: The New National Era, *August* 31, 1871.

158: S. N. GALLIARD ON DELANY

GENTLEMEN: In conformity with my promise, I now proceed to give you my
opinion concerning Major Delany's letter. You(r) first question was, "why he
addressed that letter to Mr. Douglass at this time?" I can only impute his motive to
the fact of Mr. Douglass' recent appointment, and my opinion is that he wrote to
him in a public way with the hope that his letter would reach the ear and eye of the
Administration, and it might give him an appointment as a representative of the
"pure black man."

Secondly, Major Delany says that "when reconstruction commenced political leaders were greatly required, but few to be had." Now the question, where was the major? I will tell you. He was in Hilton Head in the capacity of a Bureau agent, and, I learn, busily engaged in selling the cotton, corn and other produce belonging to the poor freemen, which makes him very unpopular with them now. Well, in the year 1867 or 68, I can't remember which, a delegation was appointed by the Republicans of Charleston, after a consultation with the leading men in other counties, to communicate with him (Delany), asking his consent to be placed in a position by which he could become a "leader." He gallantly refused, "saying the time had not come," and did not take any part in the reconstruction of the State. My opinion is he ought to be the last man to growl about "leaders."

Thirdly, you ask my opinion relative to what he says about the "Social relations of the colored people." I believe that social relationship must and will regulate itself. It is a fact that no one will deny, that there are persons who believe that they are superior to others because of a light or brown hue, and are not disposed to associate with "black people." As to "superiority," if they are silly enough to believe that color is the test, then I would leave them to revel in the glories of their mistaken idea. Nobody has a right to find fault with them. I believe that the paragraph in the Major's letter is quite out of place and very impolitic, and has a tendency towards causing an estrangement between the "blacks and browns." Social relationship affects individuals only. Every man has the right to select his own company, and form associations with the same if he chooses.

Politics affects the whole people; therefore, there is such a dissimilarity that while we can afford an estrangement socially, we cannot afford it politically. For the political downfall of one is the downfall of the other. In "Politics" we must work in union. The Major, in probing that old sore, that time alone can cure, is doing the state and country more harm than his philosophical endowments enable him to perceive, for the blacks are just as proud and happy as the browns, or any other color dare to be.

To be rational and politic, if I was the writer, I would advise the voters never to select a man to office who would be likely to discriminate in official patronage or otherwise on account of color. By doing so, every individual will take it in a political aspect, and it is my opinion that this would do more towards harmonizing the conflicting elements, than anything else that could be said or done.

The major says "Black leaders for black men." This reminds me of the diabolical dogma enunciated by Cain, Delany and Co., in the campaign of 1870. That dogma that almost caused the defeat of the Republican party in this (Charleston) county.

The man that would set forth such an unwholesome doctrine must be guilty of one or two evils: If he does it with a view to his own aggrandizement, knowing as he ought the direful consequences that must inevitably accrue from it especially when carried out as preached by the Major and Co., in the last general campaign. Then he must be a . . . And if he does it, not having political sagacity enough to know that it must result detrimentally to the political interests of the black man, then he is insensible to the plainest facts, and unfit to be a "leader." For whilst we are in the majority in this State, we must not forget that we are vastly in the minority in the United States. The moment we inscribe that motto on our banner, (figuratively speaking,) namely! "Black leaders for black men," we will cause such a line (not of sects, as the major says about some imaginary church,) to be drawn, that nothing short of the millennium can erase or destroy it. Our white friends, both north and south, will leave us to "paddle our own canoe" and we, not having sufficient of the necessaries to stem the tide, will drift with the "ebb" into the abyss of political destruction.

Prudence would dictate as a motto "The best Man" be he as black as it is possible to be, or as white as a lily, if he will carry out the principles of Republicanism without fear or favor. Then let him lead or anything else, regardless of his color; there will be no need for division lines. As a party, keep in view that maxim, "United we stand, divided we fall."

I was asked what I thought of the Major as an aspirant for office. I don't know if it is your purpose to act or propose him for an office, but in case it be so, I should say, judging from the anxiety manifested last fall whilst a candidate for the United States Senate, that he would accept an office, though he would have to "depend upon it for a support."

Yours respectfully,
S. N. Gailliard

SOURCE: Daily Republican, *August 22, 1871.*

APPENDIX B

"Trial and Conviction"

Charleston, South Carolina,
February 28th, 1876.
Hon. Frederick Douglass,
Washington, District of Columbia.

My Dear Sir and Friend,

When we last met in 1872, the situation in the South, and my position there, was along and earnest theme between us, and I think then, we did not materially differ, as to the duties and policy of our race as a part of the fixed industrial and political elements. The constantly increasing and alarming intrusion of the worst class of white political adventurers from the North, was with us, a subject of the deepest interest.

So long as the black man can be made to serve the purposes of this class, he may consider himself secure, but the moment he ceases to do this, he becomes the subject of resentment and opposition, if not attack and punishment. To these adventurers, he at once becomes offensive. Such, as an individual, I have ever been, and in a series of short articles, in this pamphlet, I propose to lay before the country, the true character of so called radicalism, as it exists in the state of South Carolina, and the alarming extent to which it has gone, in subverting the rights and liberties of the people, especially those who oppose them whether white or black, as exhibited in my own case.

In the worst of times of ANTE BELLUM days, during the existence of an institution that was national and recognized by the constitution, defended by the North and South, supported by the Supreme Court and Treasury, Army and Navy of the country, you and I could write, speak of, and oppose the policies and parties which supported it, boldly and fearlessly. But since the overthrow of that institution and the power of those who supported it, we dare not oppose the infamies of radical rule under these adventurers and new masters of the whole people, without the fear of the loss of liberty, by ignominious convictions, through conspiracy and perjury. And you must remember, that our race it is, which is made the instruments of this most intolerable state of affairs in the hands of a class through the state, worse than that of the abominable gang of ruffians, who, during their civil war, undertook to draw up and try as criminals, the respectable people of London. It is not republicanism that is doing this, but imposters, intruders, villains by the name.

My dear Douglass: It is due to the joint position once occupied by you and I in the cause of the rights of man and our common country; to the honors which I have received in foreign lands, to the honors received in our own country, especially those of the suffrage on one half of the people of South Carolina for the second office in their sovereignty, an honor which any man might well covet; it is due to the distinguished chief magistrate, who has honored me with the official position which, I now occupy, to vindicate an unsullied reputation against as vile and bare-face a conspiracy as ever disgraced civilization. An outrage only to be reconciled with the character of those of who originated it and loaned their aid in carrying it out.

The rights of the people are always insecure, when the ignorant, venal, low and vulgar, bet the power in their own hands.

First Offence:

During the session of the Constitutional Convention at Columbia, 1867, a young member offered a resolution claiming for our race the nominee in the next National Convention for the Vice Presidency of the United States.

On seeing this in the telegraphic news of the first paper which reached me, I at once wrote the following letter, (taken from the New York Daily Tribune, Tuesday, August 6th, 1867:

Those who demanded that the Vice-Presidency should be offered to the Blacks will learn from the sensible and patriotic letter of Major Delany, a colored soldier, that the "one sentiment among the old line leading men" of that race is that "no such nonsense should for a moment be entertained." "Our enemies," he says, "would desire no heavier nor stronger club with which to break the heads of our friends, and knock out our brains than this.

————*Tribune:*

The following letter is addressed to the Rev. H. H. Garnet, Pastor, Shiloh Presbyterian Church, New York, by Major Delany, a colored soldier:

My Dear Sir:

In such times as these, it requires men of the greatest practical experience, acquired ability, mature intelligence, and discretional wisdom, to speak and act for the race now an integral part and essential element in the body politic of the nation. Therefore, I do most sincerely hope that you and other leading minds among our people may take your stand, speak out, and define your true sentiments in relation to the great points now agitating the public mind, especially the black man's claim to office.

The great principle always advocated by our leading men has been to claim for us, as a race all the rights and privileges belonging to an American citizen of the most favored race. But I do not think that those who have so long, so steadily, and determinedly stood up as you and others of us have done, even to a national concession of these claims, ever contemplated taking any position among our fellow-citizens, till we, at least, should be READY and QUALIFIED. It follows as a matter of course that MORE than we should be ready, before it is POSSIBLE to attain to such positions. I am sure that upon this point, there will be but one sentiment among the old-line leading men of our race, contemporaneous with us, when the subject is placed before them.

I have been induced to pen this letter to you by seeing in the telegraph proceedings of the Columbia, S.C. Convention a claim put forth by Mr.————in behalf of our race, for the Vice-Presidency of the United States. I hope no such nonsense for a moment will be entertained. Our enemies would desire no heavier nor stronger club to break the heads of our friends and knock out our brains than this. We are not children, but men comprehending the entire situation, and should at once discountenance anything that would seemingly make us cat's paw and ridiculous in the eyes and estimation of the political intelligence of the world. Let colored men be satisfied to take things like other men, in their natural course and time, prepare themselves in every particular for municipal positions, and they may expect to attain to some other in time.

Mr.————is a young man of 27 or 28 years of age, and consequently without any political experience, except such as acquired since the war commenced and therefore may be excused for so palpable a political blunder. I am a personal friend of his, therefore, take the liberty of speaking frankly about him.

I am Sir, for our race and country at large,

Your Friend,

M. R. Delany

Hilton, Head, S.C., July 27, 1867.

Second Offence:

At a caucus of the colored members of the State Nominating Convention, 1868, then sitting in Charleston, it was decided upon to nominate a colored man for Congress, and Mr. L. S. Langley was assigned the duty of corresponding with then person designated. At the time, Reconstruction was incomplete, and the state of the black race was undetermined, the feelings of the common people of the great North, North-West and West, still seething and wrankling with emotions of the war, were in no mood to tolerate any such advanced move as this, when in reply to this, I sent the following letter to Mr. Langley, (taken from Charleston, Daily News, of Saturday, March 21st, 1868). Of this letter, there have been many misconceptions, and some silly and mischievous ones:

> The following letter from M. R. Delany, an intelligent and well educated colored man, who lately held the commission of Major in the United States army, and who is now, we believe, an ATTACHE of the Freedmen's Bureau has been sent to us for publication. As a manifesto from a Negro leader, disclosing authoritatively the purposes of the Radical party, with regard to the black race in the future, it is very interesting and significant:

Bureau Sub-District, Charleston

Headquarters, Hilton Head

Hilton, Head, S.C. February, 5th, 1868.

L.S. Langley, Esq., Member, Constitutional

Convention, South Carolina, Charleston, S.C.

Dear Sir:

Your favor of the 3rd inst., in reply to my letter to you of the 26th ult., was received by last night's mail.

In reply to your request to permit my name to be put in nomination as a candidate for Congress from the Second Congressional District, composed of Charleston, Beaufort, Colleton and Barnwell, permit me to offer you my unfeigned and heartfelt *thanks for the compliment thereby paid, confidence reposed and deference shown, because prompted by motives in strict accordance (as I know your delegation is aware) with my sense of propriety and fitness of things; acquired ability, qualified by adaptation, age and experience.*

It is scarcely necessary for me to repeat what you have frequently known me to express the greatest possible discretion and prudence in these first steps in the incipiency of the enfranchisement of our race in this country. Every step taken by us should be fraught with prudence and caution, lest thereby an error prejudicial to the efforts of our friends in and out of the councils of the nations, and fatal to our cause, might be committed.

It is not necessary to our claims as American citizens, nor important to the accomplishment of that end, that a black man at this period be a representative in the national halls of legislation. This, let me insist with emphasis the nation (the American people generally), are not ready for. And this sentiment, however undesirable, must be yielded to by us. And when they are ready for it, of course, there will be no objection, and consequently no harm done, and should they never become ready, then that will be the end of the whole matter.

Let our great and good hearted friend, Wendell Phillips, outside of the councils, claim what he pleases—it is right. His sentiments are as essential to the political life of the nation, as oxygen to animal life. And same also with the great and good statesmen inside of the council.

But too much of one at the wrong time, would assuredly produce the extinction of animal life; and too much of the other at an improper time, in like manner, prove the destruction of our hopes and cherished political issues of our friends.

Whatever they may claim at present as our rights, they do so as white men, a part and parcel of the dominant race, who desire to express for the nation, sentiments of generosity toward the black race, for their fidelity, patriotism, and deeds of military valor in the recent life struggle of the country. This they can afford to do. But we should not presume by reason of this or our numbers, to assume these positions to ourselves.

I regret the expressions of approbation in my letter of the 28th of January, of your and Mr. Whipper's course in Convention, of liberality and leniency toward the late oppressors of our race; but am as I was in regard to the Vice-Presidency, entirely opposed at this period of political experience of the country, to any person identified with the black race entering any council of the nation as a member.

I therefore most respectfully decline the proffered honor of your nomination— an honor as complimentary to me as it is liberal and generous in you to offer it.

Be pleased to make known my views in full to your delegation, with my heartiest thanks for their high consideration, and accept the warmest regards, with much.

I have the honor to be, Sir,
Your most obedient servant,
M. R. Delany.

Third Offence:

I was sent in March or April, 1868 to attend the great Ratification Meeting, held at the Epping Hall, now U.S. Court Room, when all the candidates for states offices would be present.

As might be expected, at that meeting there were much though well meant, doubtless, ill-timed and extravagant advice, I by a designed arrangement of some friends, at my own request, being kept till near the last, that I might learn the spirit and disposition of the speakers.

I advised my own race to moderation of action and sentiments, in all that they said and did, reminding them, that we were only one sixth of the entire population of the country, that the white people are the ruling element of the nation, and must take the first rank, and would have the first and choice places, though we would get some; that in conceding rights to us, they had no intention to surrender their own; that whatever we claim for ourselves, we should take care not to interfere with the rights of others. That we must not in finding room for ourselves undertake to elbow the white people out of their places.

At the conclusion of my speech, there was a buzz in the great throng, and on passing out, many murmurs of disapproval of what I had said, spoiling many of the misguided radical harangues made that night, one gentleman, now a prominent leader, expressing himself aloud, saying: "that man should never be permitted to hold office in this state!" The crowd of colored people speaking with expressions of disapprobation of what I had said to them, because their radical leaders present, made them believe, that it was against their interests and rights. The adventurers even made them believe, that I was against my own race, and had been sent to the meeting by the old planters in their interests. And such was my third offense, as they designedly interpreted.

Fourth Offence:

My fourth offence, consisted of a "Political Review", a letter addressed to you through the columns of the Charleston Daily Republican, dated August, 14th, 1871, from which the following are a few extracts.

When reconstruction commenced, political leaders were greatly required, but few to be had. Southerners (the old masters) studiously opposed and refused to countenance reconstruction, and the freedmen were fearful and would not have trusted them if they could have obtained their aid.

Those who came with or followed the army, with a very few native whites, were the only available political element to be had to carry out the measures of reconstruction.

These were readily accepted by the blacks (by this I include the entire colored people) and the fullest confidence reposed in them. Some were or had been officers in the army. Some private, some, sutlers. others peddlers and various tradesmen, others gamblers and even pickpockets and "hangers-on" and "bummers". I am particularly speaking of the whites. Among them were men of refinement, educated gentlemen, and some very good men, but a large part of those active were of the lowest grade of northern society, Negro haters at home, who could not have been elected to any position of honor or trust. Just such men as burnt down Negro orphan asylum and hung Negro men at lamp posts in the New York riot of 1853. In this review, I intend to speak plainly, call things by their right names, and look those of whom I speak directly in the face.

The best and most competent men were chosen to fill the most important positions in state and local government, while the others readily obtained such places as required incumbents. Indeed there was scarcely one so incompetent as not to have been assigned some position of trust.

Positioned in places of power, profit and trust, they soon sought by that guile and deception, known only to demagogues, under the acceptable appellations of Yankee, Republican and Radical, to intrude themselves into the confidence of the blacks, and place themselves at their head as leaders. So insidiously did they do this that it was not discovered by the few colored men of intelligence who held places among them till too late to remedy the fatal evil.

These demagogues laid the foundation of their power upon a basis of the most dangerous political heresy. Deception, lying, cheating, chanting "whatever can be done in politics is fair", and to "beat is the duty in a political contest no matter what means were used to effect it" are among the pernicious precepts of this moral infidelity.

Jealous of the few intelligent colored men among them, they studiously sought to divide the blacks by sowing the seeds of discord among them. This was facilitated by prejudicing the ignorant against the intelligent. These men strove and vied each with the other, regardless of consequence, to place himself in the lead of a community of blacks in both town and country, which in time was reduced to little else than a rabble mob of disorder and confusion. Trained in the Leagues as serfs to their masters, it became dangerous to oppose the teachings of these men of mischief. Because, having been recommended to their confidence at the commencement of reconstruction, their experience and knowledge in public men and matters were too limited to believe anything against them.

A knowledge of this emboldened these men to a persistence in their course of crime and corruption. Hence many otherwise, good men, both white and black, from age, inexperience or weakness were induced to accept the monstrous teachings and join with or follow the lead of these wretched imposters. Their sole object being personal gain, they cared little or nothing for public weal, the interest of the state or people, black or white, nor the Republican cause, upon which they had indecently imposed themselves. This is that which controlled Charleston politics and brought deserved defeat to the Republicans in the recent Municipal election. It was just retribution to a set of unprincipled miscreants, rioting on the people rights under the name of "Republicanism". Honest upright men of all parties, white and black, no longer able to bear it, determined to put down the abominable thing; leading Republicans, who had been standing aloof, taking an active part. Among other things, they taught the simple-minded people that suffrage was inviolably secure, the blacks being in the majority, would always control the affairs of the state in the South; that the 15th Amendment had abolished color and complexion in the United States, and the people were now all of one race. This bare faced deception was so instilled into them that it became dangerous in many instances to go into the country and speak of color in any manner whatever, without the angry rejoinder; "WE don't want to hear that, we are all one color now!".

These ridiculous absurdities were fostered by the demagogues, the better to conceal their own perfidy and keep themselves in the best positions as "Republicanism know no race" they taught.

Another imposition was that colored people did not require intelligent colored leaders; that the Constitution had been purged of color by a Radical Congress, and to be a Republican was all that was required to make a true representative. That mental culture and qualifications were only required by the proud and arrogant, that all who requested those accomplishments were enemies to both black and white, that race representation was making distinctions on account of race and color. By this means they opposed the qualified men among the blacks, encouraged the ignorant and less qualified. They might of necessity take the lead and occupy the best places

I the party. These are plain indisputable truths which will not be denied by any upright intelligent Republican, black or white.

These strictures have no reference whatever to the intelligent, high-minded, upright gentlemen among the white Republicans, whose examples and precepts have aided in building up society and contributing to the public good; but especially, to that class who almost live in the quarters of the country people, and hamlets of the towns, among the black population, keeping them distracted with excitement, who are a curse to the community at large, and a blight in the body politic.

Fifth Offence:

The *fifth offense,* consisted in a pamphlet said to have been written by me, called "Political Battle Axe, For the use of the Colored Men of the state of South Carolina in the year 1872, by Kush." Even this, was referred to in court on the trial.

This pamphlet, was very widely circulated, was found in all parts of the state, and seems to have been simultaneously scattered through every county. Though it had an unknown author, it was at once attributed to me, created quite a sensation, much interest, and general murmuring. It had incorporated at the conclusion, a Constitution for the political guidance of a society called, "The Young Men's Progressive Association."

And this seems really to have been the first effective entering wedge in the ranks of reckless radical republicanism in the state. As quickly following the appearance of the "Battle Axe" a "Progressive Association" among the young men was organized, and immediately thereafter, a scheme was set on foot, a committee of three hundred organized, a correspondence entered into with a learned and distinguished gentleman of the state of an opposition candidate, and all the details of a bolt completed, being the first suggestion of such a move in our state. This was politically known as the "Willard Movement" and gave great dissatisfaction to the regulars. "Vengeance" was then sworn against me.

Sixth Offence:

My sixth offense was embodied in two letters addressed to a distinguished gentleman of the black race occupying a high place in the state, (whom I refrain from naming here, as he took umbrage at the liberty of addressing my letter to him at the time) dated Feb. 10th, and March 17th, 1874, in which I advocated, general amnesty, cumulative voting or minority representation, and cooperation in political actions by whites and blacks of the state, as the only guarantee against a displacement of *the blacks by emigration, which would most certainly be encouraged to neutralize the political misrule of republicanism*

Seventh Offence:

The letter written by me the same year, in reply to a committee of colored citizens, requesting my views in relation to a colored mayor for Charleston, in which I told them that the credit of the city would be blasted by destroying confidence everywhere in our financial and commercial relations. The state having been ruined under the suffrage of the colored race, the city of Charleston was the only part of it left, that gave us credit abroad, advising against any such movement, as the most impolitic that could at the time be set on foot.

The Crowning Offence:

The "crowning act of infamy", an offense never to be forgotten, and sworn to be punished, was that on the fourth day of October, 1874, I dared receive the unanimous endorsement of the Conservative Convention sitting in Columbia, as the nominee for Lieutenant-Governor on the Independent Republican ticket, cooperating with conservatives. This was an offense unbearable, a sin never to be forgiven, and only to be remitted for by the most condign punishment.

The Aggravating Offence:

After the election, in which the state came well nigh being carried for the co-operatives, reducing the majority from forty thousand to ten, I went to New York City, and under the auspices of the most distinguished gentlemen for positions, wealth, and education, in the most select and Aristocratic Hall in the great Metropolis (Irving Hall). I addressed a meeting presided over by Col. William Cullen Bryant, editor, scholar, poet and statesman, supported by the equally venerable Hon. Peter Cooper, the millionaire, Philanthropist, proprietor and donor of the great Cooper Institute, and many other distinguished gentlemen without regard to politics.

From this aggravation of a sin (the Conservative nomination) there was no redemption this side of the grave, and punished I must be even unto death!

Though seven years to this time have elapsed, since mustered out of my four years service as a major commanding the United States army, they have persistently opposed and prevented my nomination or appointment to any office, either state or federal, till I received the nomination of the Independent Republicans, and Conservatives, to the high and honorable position of Lieutenant-Governor of the state, 1974, and four months since, the office of Trial Justice, which I now hold. Crush me to earth, they were determined upon, and all because I could not be used, was above their influence, and would as I ever shall, oppose dishonesty, corruption and imposition upon the people's rights, under the disguised mockery of politics and law, "he has gone far enough, he shall be put down!" they said as I passed by the City Hall one day, shortly after returning from the North, the "Solicitor" was heard to bet that he would have me in the Penitentiary, in two weeks after the meeting of the Court!

I shall not forget in this connection to acknowledge the generous course of Gen. H. G. Worthington, the Collector of the Port of Charleston, in tendering and appointing me, as inspector of customs, which I held till relinquished to run for the above mentioned office. This he did, in the face of the opposition of these very pretended Republicans.

Tenth and Most Irritating Offence:

In the last Municipal election for Mayor and other officers of Charleston, I took an active part, conducting a weekly paper, as the representative organ of the colored population, against fraud, and in favor of good government, closely contesting every inch of ground, and determinedly disputing every claim put forth. The close of the contest gave us the city government.

Many were the cunning and plausible devices brought in to this contest, well adapted to deceive, all of which were met and dispersed, routing our opponents with surprise and dismay, dispelling every hope of carrying the state, because of their failure in carrying the city.

In this, I was charged with having dealt a heavy hand, and for so grave an offense, I must pay the severest penalty known to the criminal law excepting death. And that would have been the penalty, could it legally have been inflicted.

Grand Larceny:

January 1871, I entered into a general business of land agency, and land and note brokerage. The buying of state and county claims and pay certificates, was a general business at that time, the investment being considered safe and good.

In April of that year, I was called upon to act as the Agent of Mrs. E. B. Richardson, and aid her in getting out letters of administration on the estate of her father, Telemachus Baynard, who died on John's Island. I did so, becoming an appraiser, with two other gentlemen, legally chosen.

On visiting the place to appraise the property, when about to return, we were informed that there were to hundred dollars in money in the house, said to be funds belonging to a religious society, of which the deceased was a trustee, holding the funds. The money was given in trust to me as the agent of Mrs. Richardson, to be accounted for to the society, at the same time it was stated, there had been much wrangling and quarrelling about the money. The men claiming to be trustees wanting to take it without responsibility, while the widow of the deceased refused to give it till her daughter came and took out letters of administration.

There had been as reported to me quite a stir among the members of the society concerning the funds, many objecting to them being delivered to the persons who made the demand. Several called upon me at different times, begging me to retain the money, till their dispute was settled. Using my discretion in the matter, I determined to secure it by investing it in county claims which at the time I was daily buying, for which I never paid less, but frequently more than fifty cents on the dollar. This I did, but supposing at the time, that the money would be realized in the fall of the fiscal year, as was expected by all who dealt at the time in this class of paper which mainly consisted in the monthly salaries of county employees, such as constables, deputy coroners, many of the deputy sheriffs, witnesses at courts, and jurors, till the rule of court by Judge Graham compelled the payment of jurors on the presentation of their tickets at the counter of the county treasurer, as the judge's was paid.

After waiting in expectation and promises which are well remembered by all of the people of this county for these back payments, till the order came that none could be paid till special appropriation for the payment would be made by the legislature, and they began to depreciate to fifteen and twenty cents on the dollar. I had an injunction sued out and judgment, on one thousand and fifty one dollars, all held in trust by me for others (except eighty dollars) for the express purpose of securing these funds at par and with interest, so that not a dollar of the assets could be lost by depreciation in value.

Mr. Sheriff Mackey who was a lawyer, obtained the injunction for me, at the same time that he obtained one for himself on twelve thousand or more dollars, these being the first suits entered against the county for those deficiencies.

An appropriation for these back claims, as is well known to all, was made, and all remember the first installment of sixty thousand dollars reported. And though mine was the second judgment on file in the Commissioner's and Treasurer's office, Col. Mackey received his twelve thousand dollars, and the remainder of the forty eight thousand was exhausted, and not a cent paid on the one thousand and more *dollars due to my claim. Another sixty thousand of that appropriation was received by the treasurer, and all paid out as before. And up to the present, from year to year, appropriations have been made for back claims against the county, and every other creditor preferred, when a simple rule of court as the late Hon. Judge Graham frequently promised, would only be necessary to obtain the payment of that judgment, in which is the sum of two thousand dollars of money belonging to the Wesley Society, which was the cause of this suit for Breach of trust and Grand Larceny.*

And this material fact I desire to impress upon the public mind, that I never did use the money, invested it for safe keeping as the agent of the administratrix into whose hands it fell, till the people who claimed it settled their dispute, and secured it by injunction, and judgment to prevent the contingency of a loss, and IT IS THERE NOW SECURED by judgment, in the office of the Clerk of the Court.

I never claimed that judgment only as an agent in trust for others, and not as a party in interest, except eighty dollars as stated.

I subsequently offered to transfer from the judgment to the trustee Messrs. Brown and Rivers, the amount of the money I received, but they as frequently declined to accept saying that, "they did not understand these things." At one time in the summer of 1874, I took Mr. Brown to the door of the office of the Clerk in the Court House, to make the transfer, but he turned away saying that he would "see me again."

During the same season Dr. Webster (the head of this whole matter) called on me at the Custom House where I was an Inspector of Customs, when I went directly to the Court House with him to make the transfer to the amount of the money invested, where the judgment or claims on file were shown to him by Mr. Lee, one of the clerks. Mr. Winkler being out just at the time, but Mr. Webster seeming satisfied as was thought, at seeing that there was a judgment secured, would not wait.

There are two other material points of fact to which I invite the public attention, to the last of which Mr. Lee, the clerk referred to will testify.

The encumbrance of two hundred dollars placed upon the judgment by a law firm against me, was done without my knowledge or consent, and evidently in anticipation of this suit to embarrass me. I protest that I knew nothing about it and the parties who entered it know that I did not. Yet it was declared to the jury that I had it done in my own interest and had actually sold this to satisfy a debt against me. The transfers made to Messrs. A. G. Coleman, E. G. Schwartz and Sampson Green, it was declared from the same source to the jury, were portions of the judgment sold off by me to these parties, when they were all original claimants in the judgment to the amount received by each of them, I holding for the two first on their own account, and on account of Sampson Green for Mrs. Richardson, the administratrix.

To the latter, A. T. Smythe, Esq., can confirm, as Green, through him, sued on his transcript from the judgment, when he satisfied himself that I was not his debtor, but simply the agent of another. And to conclude this part of my statements, I should not neglect to say, that to Messrs. Campbell and Whaley, through whom Mr. Webster sued for the Church, I several times offered and urged them to accept of a transfer from the judgment to them, their share of the money claimed by the trustees, but they declined to settle the matter in that way. But I believe that they never obtained judgment against me. That perhaps is the reason they declined to accept the transfer.

I should here state that the same person, Dr. Webster, sent me a postal card of intimidation (Political) stating that he was coming out with a newspaper, and if I did not comply with his demand in paying the money, he would attack my character. He did so, as during the canvas, a few weeks later, about ten days before the election, he published a letter in his paper, over his own initials, accusing me with robbing a Church! This letter was hastily read at all of their political gatherings.

The Law Suit:

I left New York after the middle of May of last year, *1875*, after spending some weeks North endeavoring to enlighten the people of both races as to the true state of our political affairs, the causes, the character of the people whom we desire to come into the state, and those whom we did not want. My course and position while absent were well known at home, because the leading papers wherever I spoke, noticed my speeches, some of which were noticed here as I am informed.

I had arrived but a short time in Charleston, till this suit was entered in a Trial Justice office against me for Breach of Trust and Grand Larceny by this Rev. Alonzo W. Webster, D.D., he making two or three black men make the affidavit, these black men being local preachers under him, he being the president elder.

From October *1875*, it was continued to the next or February term of the Court of General Sessions, *1876*.

The Trial . . . Paneling a Jury:

A handsome little black child, about four or five years of age was led by a black man, an employee of the Sheriff's office, into the court room, and seated on a chair at the table. The solicitor entered immediately after announcing that he was ready.

The child was stood up on the chair by the same black official who led it into the court room, and directed to take a ballot, when with child-like innocence it was bent to thrust in his hand, when it was seized by the official with an admonition, which did not require to be repeated, as at each drawing the child carefully inserted *its hand leaning and peeping into the hat that it might be certain not to disturb the arrangement till the panel was complete. In this case a special panel was drawn, though I was willing to accept of either of the two fixed juries Nos. 1 and 2, as they stood on the general panel or venire. I never before understood a packed jury.*

The Testimony:

It is not my purpose here to sift the testimony of those who were trained to swear against me, as the fact that I was convicted on the statements herein set forth of my transactions in the money matter, makes its won comment beyond a controversy. A more shameful misstatement, misrepresentation, and barefaced perversion of truth, never was perpetrated in a court of justice. Falsehood after falsehood was declared by one of the witnesses, and shamefully reiterated by the counsel for the prosecution. It is enough to make one shudder and the flesh to creep on its bones, to contemplate the reckless perversion of truth, exhibited on that occasion. It was a deep seated conspiracy, with a determination to crush me, and every thing was resorted to, in furtherance of that end.

The Solicitors:

The state, the nation, the world at large should know, the point at which the Charleston Bar, of which a Wardlaw, a Duncan, an O'Neil, a Petigru, and such lights of learning and literature, with their compeers both dead and living, once members, has arrived in the progress of such legal management as that of the present prosecuting attorney.

This functionary, without comparison, I venture to state, in Belle letters literature and forensic eloquence, a specimen of which I shall give, that people abroad may understand the character of those by whom we are now mastered; commenced his pleading by the declaration, that of fourteen years at the bay, it was the happiest moment of his life. That he never felt so strong in all his life before, because he had for the first time before him, the very character he wanted.

Then, in a tirade of an unbroken stain of full one half hour, of low, coarse and vulgar abuse, of sneers and jeers, of jibes and butts, and mockery, at my pretended respectability, integrity, morality, learning and veracity; placing himself squarely before me, with extended arm, his fingers nearly touching my nose, with all the vehemence which he could command, he three times exclaimed as I give it here, increasing the emphasis to the climax as he observed the smiles of sanction in the countenances of his jury as they glanced with nods of the head at each other: "You tell a DAMNED INFERNAL LIE! It is a DAMNED INFERNAL LIE!! You are a DAMNED INFERNAL LIAR!!!" This was the language of the solicitor of the Charleston Bar, in open court, in a plea which by his own admission, was the greatest thing that he ever made, and the happiest hour of his life! What have not the Charlestonians been reduced to? Have they a Modoc Indian at the head of their Bar?

The Jury:

The following is the list of names of the jury which convicted me, all respectable men, one of whom stooped whispering into the ear of a lawyer who passed out from the jury box: "He's good for the penitentiary!" They returning in less than ten minutes with a verdict of guilty.

E. R. Cowperthwait, Foreman
Daniel B. Dupont
D. P. Johnstone
Edward Weston
John Cross
Thomas M. Holmes
Alva Gage
Benjamin Moncriff
Edward N. Wilson
Henry Artope
Benjamin S. Roper
G. W. Klinck.

There was one remarkable coincidence about these gentlemen, all of them happened to be those who are opposed to the election of Mayor Cunningham, whom I supported, and did much toward the defeat of the candidate which they supported. And some of them were candidates for offices of honor or profit, on their side hence, I had aided in their defeat! History shall have their names. Their verdict was a foregone conclusion. Those in capitals are all colored men. ALBUS ET NIGER OMNIA FRATER NOBILE.

The Sentence:

Some time was spent on the day of sentence in searching out points of law on the motion made by my learned and able counsel, E. E. Seabrook, Esq. I requested the sentence if it had to come, as his honor was refused the motions.

"I should prefer to find some law if possible to avert a sentence. Indeed, it will give me a great deal of pleasure if I could!" said the Judge. "But it would only be nominal," said his honor, "as to take an appeal to the Supreme Court, has made a sentence necessary."

There was but one object on the part of those who brought on this base and shameful prosecution at the head of whom was this man Webster, and this so called solicitor, which was to disgrace me so in the estimation of the respectable native white citizens who had supported me for the second office in the state, that they would henceforth discard me, and by the telling of the blacks that I was sent to the state's prison, I could never again have political influence enough to check them in their deception and imposition.

With the same faithful adherence to the cause of universal liberty as in ANTE BELLUM days, shall I continue to advocate the rights of the whole people of the state, without regard to race, color, or politics, if doing so, it shall necessitate the driving of such wretches into their native haunts, never more to be seen among respectable men.

Personal:

I believe that his honor the Judge, was deceived from the first by this solicitor, and did not till after judgment, really understand the true state of the case.

And I here take pleasure in recording the generous course of Col. Bowen, the Sheriff, who refrained from the exercise of his official authority over me during the entire trial. Also to his gentlemanly assistant, the first deputy Sheriff, Mr. Dingle, who treated me in like manner. And to Mr. John Bonnin, sub-deputy, for uniform attentions in the court room during the entire proceedings, also to Mr. Dover, a sub-deputy. Both of the latter being men of my own race.

A conspiracy to send an innocent respectable citizen to the state prison for the purpose of disgracing and humiliating him to destroy his political influence, is one of the greatest as well as the meanest and most cowardly outrages ever perpetrated in a civilized country; and the men who could aid in so vile an act, are capable of anything dishonorable to accomplish their ends.

They are moral assassins, unequalled by any KU-KLUX however vile, cruel and revolting; the creatures and offshoots of a terrible conspiracy, a hydra-headed monster, whose heart is in Orangeburg, and its body entwined and coiled through every community in the state, with its vilest hideous head in Charleston.

This conspiracy is in waiting for the citizens, whom those vile wretches hate, and have attempted upon others and failed, I being their first victim. The outrage is fearful and too monstrous to be a reality. The serpent must be driven from its lair.

Now let them succeed and go on in this last scheme of prosecution of theirs to hold the reigns of power, and keep their feet on the people of the South, by using our race as the political instrument of their oppression, let them continue to promote strife between the races, the eye of the whole North and West being already turned in this direction, and their minds made up, and the first occasion for the murmur of a conflict of races, and the whole country will rise up and rush to arms with such force and power, that Sherman's invasion compared with which, would be but children's school play.

Extermination will be their theme
Their watch-word, "Every Negro in the grave!"
Until from Withlacooche's stream
To where the Rio Grande laves;
One simultaneous war cry,
Will burst upon the midnight air;
And rouse the black man, but to die!
Midst weeping, wailing and despair!

When our race, shall only be remembered among the things of the past! And it is for us, I mean the colored men of leading intelligence, to avert this dreadful; this fearful thing in time.

M. R. Delany
To Hon. Frederick Douglass

NOTES

INTRODUCTION

1. *North Star*, June 2, 1848.
2. Ibid.
3. Ibid.
4. Victor Ullman, *Martin R. Delany: The Beginnings of Black Nationalism*. Boston: Beacon Press, 1971. Robert Khan, "The Political Ideology of Martin Delany" *Journal of Black Studies*, June 1984. Harold Cruse, *The Crisis of the Negro Intellectual*. New York: William Morrow, 1967. Vincent Harding, *There Is A River: The Black Struggle for Freedom in America*. New York: Vintage Books, 1983; see also his *The Other American Revolution*. Los Angeles: Center for Afro-American Studies, University of California at Los Angeles, 1980. Sterling Stuckey, *The Ideological Origins of Black Nationalism*. Boston: Beacon Press, 1972.
5. August Meier and Elliot Rudwick, *Black History and the Historical Profession, 1915–1980*. Urbana: The University of Illinois Press, 1986, chs. 2, 3. John H. Franklin, "On the Evolution of Scholarship in Afro-American History" in Darlene Clark Hine ed., *The State of Afro-American History: Past, Present, and Future*. Baton Rouge: Louisiana State University Press, 1986, 13–24. William H. Harris, "Trends and Needs in Afro-American Historiography" Ibid., 139–156. Robert L. Harris, "Coming of Age: The Transformation of Afro-American Historiography" *Journal of Negro History* 66, no. 2, summer 1962. Earl Thorpe, *Mind of the Negro: An Intellectual History of Afro-America*. New York: Negro University Press, 1970. Harold Cruse, "Black Studies: Interpretation, Methodology and the Relationship to Social Movements" *Afro-American Studies* 2, 1971, 15–51. Sterling Stuckey, "Twilight of Our Past: Reflections on the Origins of Black History" in John A. Williams and Charles F. Harris, eds., *Amistad 2: Writings on Black History and Culture*. New York: Vintage books, 1971. Vincent Harding, "Beyond Chaos: Black History and the Search for the New Land," in John A. Williams and Charles F. Harris, eds., *Amistad 1: Writings on Black History and Culture*. New York: Vintage Books, 1970.
6. To be a conservative, such as Martin Delany was, in the context of Radical Reconstruction was to stand in opposition to the ideas and programs of the Radical Republican administration, especially in relation to the political enfranchisement of blacks and the accompanying social implications. I refer to Delany as a conservative precisely because of his vocal and harsh opposition to Radical Reconstruction. He never disguised his dislike for, and disagreement with, what he perceived and characterized as the irrational, radical, provocative,

and conflict-driven political agenda of the black–Republican Party alliance after the Civil War. But Delany's ideas also betrayed sensibility to pragmatic realities. He frequently appealed to other black leaders to de-emphasize traditional party and racial loyalties in preference for new relationships mandated by utilitarian considerations—that is, considerations that, in his judgment, would bring immediate benefits to blacks, regardless of the ideological context or implications. For example, his advice to blacks to embrace their erstwhile oppressors because blacks stood more to gain economically from such a relationship than in the Republican alliance was born of awareness of the economic strength of the old slave-owning class, the political vicissitudes of the Civil War and Reconstruction notwithstanding.

7. Martin R. Delany, "Trial and Conviction." Charleston, 1876, (unpublished pamphlet). Copy in the Charleston Historical Society Library.
8. Ibid., 17.
9. Frank (Frances) Rollin, *Life and Public Services of Martin R. Delany*. Boston: Lee and Shepard, 1868, 171.
10. Martin R. Delany, "A Political Review," *Daily Republican*, August 15, 1871. See also his "Trial and Conviction."
11. *Douglass's Monthly*, August 1862, 695.
12. Martin Delany to Frederick Douglass, Pittsburgh, July 1, 1850. *North Star*, July 11, 1850.
13. "M. R. Delany." *North Star*, May 19, 1848.
14. "Letter From York." *North Star*, December 15, 1848.
15. Martin R. Delany, "American Civilization: Treatment of the Colored People in the United States" *North Star*, March 30, 1849.
16. Ibid.

CHAPTER ONE

Black Biography: From Instrumentalism to Functionalism

1. Theodore Draper, "The Father of American Black Nationalism" *New York Times Review of Books*, March 12, 1970.
2. Theodore Draper, *The Rediscovery of Black Nationalism*. New York: Viking Press, 1970, 40.
3. Ibid.
4. Ibid.
5. "An Exchange on Black History" *New York Times Review of Books*, May 21, 1970. See also "Exchange on Black Nationalism" *New York Times Review of Books*, December 3, 1970.
6. "An Exchange on Black History," 37.
7. Ibid.
8. Ibid., 39.
9. Ibid., 38.
10. Draper, *The Rediscovery*; also "The Father of American Black Nationalism."
11. Earl Thorpe, *The Mind of the Negro: An Intellectual History of Afro-America*. New York: Negro University Press, 1970, 443.
12. Earl Thorpe, *Black Historians: A Critique*. New York: William Morrow, 1971, 113.
13. Carter G. Woodson, *The Education of the Negro Prior to 1861*. New York: A and B Books, 1919; *African Heroes and Heroines*. Washington, D.C.: Associated

Publishers, 1939; *The African Background Outlined.* Washington, D.C.: ASNLH, 1936; *The Miseducation of the Negro.* Washington, D.C.: Associated Publishers, 1923; *The Negro as a Businessman.* Washington, D.C.: Associated Publishers, 1929; *The Negro In Our History.* Washington, D.C.: ASNLH, 1922.

14. Benjamin Brawley, *A Short History of the American Negro.* New York: Macmillan, 1939; *A Social History of the American Negro.* New York: Macmillan, 1921; *Negro Builders and Heroes.* Chapel Hill: University of North Carolina Press, 1937; *The Negro Genius.* New York: Dodd, Mead, 1937; and *Early Negro American Writers.* Chapel Hill: University of North Carolina Press, 1835.

15. W. E. B. Du Bois, *The Suppression of the African Slave Trade to the United States of America, 1638–1870.* New York: Longmans, 1896; *The Philadelphia Negro.* Philadelphia: University of Pennsylvania Press, 1899; *The Souls of Black Folk.* Chicago: A. C. McClurg, 1903; *The Gift of Black Folk.* Boston: Startford, 1924; *Black Reconstruction.* New York: Harcourt Brace, 1935; *The World and Africa.* New York: Viking Press, 1947.

16. John W. Burgess, *Reconstruction and the Constitution, 1866–1876.* New York: 1902. William A. Dunning, *Reconstruction, Political and Economic, 1865–1877.* New York: Harper, 1907. Walter F. Fleming, *The Sequel of Appomattox.* New Haven: 1919. James F. Rhodes, *History of the United States from the Compromise of 1850 to the McKinley-Bryan Campaign of 1896,* 8 vols., New York: Macmillan, 1904–1920. Claude G. Bowers, *Tragic Era: The Revolution After Lincoln.* Boston: 1929. Ulrich B. Phillips, *American Negro Slavery.* New York: 1918.

17. W. E. B. Du Bois, *Black Reconstruction in America 1860–1880.* New York: Atheneum, 1983 (originally published in 1935). See also his earlier "Reconstruction and Its Benefits" *American Historical Review,* 15, 1910, 781–799.

18. Du Bois, *Black Reconstruction,* 723.

19. Benjamin Quarles, *Frederick Douglass.* New York: Atheneum, 1968 (originally published Washington, D.C.: Association Press, 1948); *The Negro in the Civil War.* New York: Russell and Russell, 1953; *The Negro in the American Revolution.* Chapel Hill: University of North Carolina Press, 1961; *Lincoln and the Negro.* New York: Oxford University Press, 1962; *The Negro in the Making of America.* Chapel Hill: University of North Carolina Press, 1961; *Black Abolitionists.* London: Oxford University Press, 1968. John Hope Franklin, *From Slavery to Freedom: A History of African Americans.* 7th ed. New York: McGraw-Hill, 1994 (originally published in 1947), which has become a classic; *Reconstruction: After the Civil War.* Chicago: University of Chicago Press, 1961; *The Militant South.* Cambridge: Harvard University Press, 1956; *The Emancipation Proclamation.* New York: Anchor Books, 1965.

20. James W. C. Pennington, *A Textbook of the Origin and History of the Colored People.* Hartford, Conn.: 1841. William C. Nell, *Colored Patriots of the American Revolution.* Boston: R. F. Wallcut, 1855; also his *Services of Colored Americans in the Wars of 1776 and 1812.* Boston: Prentiss and Sawyer, 1855. William Still, *The Underground Railroad.* Philadelphia: Porter and Coats, 1872. George Washington Williams, *A History of the Negro Race in America from 1619 to 1880.* New York: Putnam and Sons, 1883; also his *The Negro in the Americas.* Washington, D.C.: Howard University, 1940; *A History of the Negro Troops in the War of the Rebellion, 1861–1865.* New York: Harper and Brothers, 1888.

21. August Meier and Elliot Rudwick, eds., *Black History and the Historical Profession 1915–1980.* Urbana: University of Illinois Press, 1986, chap. 5.

22. Vincent Harding, "Beyond Chaos: Black History and the Search for the New Land" in John A. Williams and Charles F. Harris, eds., *Amistad 1: Writings on Black History and Culture*. New York: Vintage Books, 1970, 275.
23. Ibid., 278–279.
24. Ibid., 280.
25. Sterling Stuckey, "Twilight of Our Past: Reflections on the Origins of Black History" in John A. Williams and Charles F. Harris, eds., *Amistad 2: Writings on Black History and Culture*. New York: Vintage Books, 1971, 277–278.
26. Ibid., 289.
27. Ibid., 288.
28. Peter Walker, *Moral Choices: Memory, Desire and Imagination in Nineteenth Century American Abolitionism*. Baton Rouge: Louisiana State University Press, 1978.
29. Victor Ullman, *Martin R. Delany: The Beginnings of Black Nationalism*. Boston: Beacon Press, 1971, chap. 25.
30. Vincent Harding, *There Is a River: The Black Struggle For Freedom in America*. New York: Vintage Books, 1983.
31. Draper, "The Father of American Black Nationalism."
32. Bill McAdoo, "Pre-Civil War Black Nationalism" *Progressive Labor*, 5, June–July 1966.
33. Ibid., 40.
34. Ibid., 42–43.
35. Walker, *Moral Choices*, 214. Also see Philip Foner, *Frederick Douglass: A Biography*. New York: Citadel, 1964. Benjamin Quarles, *Frederick Douglass*. New York: Atheneum, 1967.
36. Walker, *Moral Choices*, 222.
37. E. Waldo Martin, *The Mind of Frederick Douglass*. Chapel Hill: University of North Carolina Press, 1985. William McFeely, *Frederick Douglass*. New York: W. W. Norton, 1991.
38. Thomas Holt, *Black Over White: Negro Political Leadership in South Carolina during Reconstruction*. Urbana: University of Illinois Press, 1977. Edmond L. Drago, *Black Politicians and Reconstruction in Georgia: A Splendid Failure*. Baton Rouge: Louisiana State University Press, 1982. Howard N. Rabinowitz, *Southern Black Leaders of the Reconstruction Era*. Urbana: University of Illinois Press, 1982. David C. Rankin, "The Politics of Caste: Free Colored Leadership in New Orleans During the Civil War" in Robert R. Macdonald et al., eds., *Louisiana's Black Heritage*. New Orleans: Louisiana State Museum, 1979, 125–138; also his "The Origins of Negro Leadership in New Orleans During Reconstruction" in Rabinowitz, *Southern Black Leaders*.
39. Rabinowitz, *Southern Black Leaders*.
40. August Meier, "Afterword: New Perspectives on the Nature of Black Political Leadership during Reconstruction" in Rabinowitz, *Southern Black Leaders*, 402.

CHAPTER TWO

Delany Historiography

1. Ralph Ellison, *Invisible Man*. New York: Vintage Books, 1952, 3.
2. Idus Newby, "Historians and Negroes" *Journal of Negro History* 54, no. 1, January 1969.

3. Ibid.
4. Maxwell Whiteman, "Introduction" in *Afro-American History Series 3: The Black Intellectuals*. Pennsylvania: Scholarly Resource Inc., n.d.
5. W. E. B. Du Bois, "A Forum of Facts and Opinions" *Pittsburgh Courier*, July 25, 1936.
6. Paul M. Gaston, *The New South Creed: A Study in Southern Mythmaking*. New York: Vintage Books, 1973, 178–179. Michael C. C. Adams, *Our Masters the Rebels: A Speculation on Union Military Failures in the East, 1861–1865*. Cambridge: Harvard University Press, 1978, 178–179. The theme of the nation's fascination with the South is also addressed in Thomas L. Connelly and Barbara L. Bellows, *God and General Longstreet: The Lost Cause and the Southern Mind*. Baton Rouge: Louisiana State University Press, 1982.
7. Idus Newby, "Historians and the Negroes." Also Ulrich B. Phillips, "The Central Themes of Southern History" *American Historical Review*, 34, October 1928, 30–45. Wilbur J. Cash, *The Mind of the South*. New York, 1941. William A. Dunning, *Reconstruction, Politics and Economics, 1865–1877*. New York: Harper, 1907. Ulrich B. Phillips, *American Negro Slavery*. New York, 1918. Walter F. Flemming, *The Sequel of Appomattox*. New Haven, 1919. These historians treat the black presence in America as insignificant and blacks as mere passive objects. Addressing the American Historical Association in 1929, Phillips claimed that the central theme of Southern history has been whites' determination to maintain a biracial society. Southernism, he argued, arose from "a common resolve indomitably maintained" that the South "shall be and remain a white man's country." See his, *The Course of the South to Secession*. New York: Appleton-Century, 1939, 152.
8. Samuel DuBois Cook, "A Tragic Conception of Negro History" *Journal of Negro History* 45, October 1960, 225.
9. The Sambo personality, made popular by Stanley Elkins in his book *Slavery: A Problem in American Institutional and Intellectual Life* (Chicago: University of Chicago Press, 1959), depicts slaves as childlike, spineless, docile, and submissive, totally dependent on their masters, whose absolute control and authority they accepted, without any inclination or disposition to engage in self-determinist acts.
10. Frank (Frances) Rollin, *Life and Public Services of Martin R. Delany*. Boston: Lee and Shepard, 1868, 23. Frank A. Rollin was the pen name of Frances Rollin. Originally from Santo Domingo, Rollin was one of five sisters prominent in the South Carolina black society. She taught at a Freedmen's Bureau school in Beaufort. Delany had once helped her file complaints against the captain of the *Pilot Boy*, a steamer that ran from Charleston to the Sea Islands. In violation of an order against discrimination on railroads and steamboats, the captain had refused her first-class ticket. Through Delany's help, Rollin filed a complaint, and the captain was fined $250. Delany became her hero. When later she confided in him that her career goal was to be a writer, he offered to help by letting her write his life story. After weeks of interviews, Rollin published *Life and Public Services* in 1868. Soon after she married William J. Whipper, a Pennsylvania lawyer who had moved south in 1866. See Dorothy Sterling, *The Making of an Afro-American: Martin R. Delany*. New York: Doubleday, 1971, 279–281.
11. James T. Holly, "In Memoriam" *AME Church Review*, October 1886, 119–120.
12. Ibid., 120–121.

13. Ibid.
14. For a more recent analysis of this genre, see William L. Van deBurg, *New Day in Babylon: The Black Power Movement and American Culture, 1965–1975.* Chicago: University of Chicago Press, 1992. Also John T. McCartney, *Black Power Ideologies: An Essay in African-American Political Thought.* Philadelphia: Temple University Press, 1992.
15. Martin R. Delany, "Political Destiny of the Colored Race on the American Continent" in Rollin, *Life and Public Services*, 335.
16. Theodore Draper, "The Fantasy of Black Nationalism" *Commentary* 48, Third Quarter, 1969; "The Father of American Black Nationalism" *New York Times Review of Books*, March 12, 1970; *The Rediscovery of Black Nationalism.* New York: The Viking Press, 1970.
17. Draper, *The Rediscovery*, 21, 21–47.
18. Sterling Stuckey, *The Ideological Origins of Black Nationalism.* Boston: Beacon Press, 1972, 3–7. He also made reference to a nationalistic song sung by slaves in Charleston, South Carolina, in 1813. See "A Hymn of Freedom: South Carolina," *Journal of Negro History* 50, January 1965.
19. Victor Ullman, *Martin R. Delany: The Beginnings of Black Nationalism.* Boston: Beacon Press, 1971. Dorothy Sterling *The Making of an Afro-American: Martin R. Delany.* New York: Doubleday, 1971.
20. Cyril E. Griffith, *The African Dream: Martin R. Delany and the Emergence of Pan-Africanist Thought.* University Park: Pennsylvania Sate University Press, 1975. Also his, "Martin R. Delany and the African Dream 1812–1885," Ph.D., diss., Michigan State University, 1973.
21. Floyd J. Miller, "The Father of Black Nationalism: Another Contender," *Civil War History*, 17, December 1971; "Search For a Black Nationality: Martin Robison Delany and the Emigrationist Alternative," Ph.D., diss., University of Minnesota 1975; *The Search for a Black Nationality: Black Emigration and Colonization, 1787–1863.* Urbana: University of Illinois Press, 1975.
22. Nell I. Painter, "Martin R. Delany: Elitism and Black Nationalism" in Leon Litwack and August Meier, eds., *Black Leaders of the Nineteenth Century.* Urbana: University of Illinois Press, 1988, 170.
23. Nell I Painter, "Martin Delany: A Black Nationalist in Two Kinds of Time" *New England Journal of Black Studies*, 8, 1989, 37–47.
24. Ibid.
25. Ibid., 45.
26. Painter, "Martin R. Delany: Elitism and Black Nationalism" in Litwack and Meier eds., *Black Leaders*, 170.
27. Painter, "Martin Delany: A Black Nationalist in Two Kinds of Time," 46.
28. Vincent Harding, *There Is A River: The Black Struggle for Freedom in America.* New York: Vintage Press, 1983; also his *The Other American Revolution.* UCLA: Center for Afro-American Studies, 1980.
29. Harold Cruse, *The Crisis of the Negro Intellectual.* New York: William Morrow, 1967.
30. Robert M. Khan, "The Political Ideology of Martin Delany" *Journal of Black Studies*, June 1984, 415–440.
31. Louis Rosenfeld, "Martin Robison Delany (1812–1885): Physician, Black Separatist, Explorer, Soldier" *Bulletin of the New York Academy of Medicine*, second series, vol. 65, no. 7, September 1989, 816.
32. Ibid.

33. Mike Sajna, "Martin Delany: Father of Black Nationalism" *Greensburg Tribune-Review*, February 25, 1990.
34. Mia Bay, *The White Image in the Black Mind: African-American Ideas about White People, 1830–1925*. New York: Oxford University Press, 2000, 220.
35. Ibid.
36. Ibid., 221.
37. Ibid., 226.
38. Ibid., 64.
39. Ibid., 96.
40. Robert S. Levine, *Martin Delany, Frederick Douglass and the Politics of Representative Identity*. Chapel Hill: University of North Carolina Press, 1997.
41. Martin R. Delany, *The Principia of Ethnology: The Origin of the Races and Color*. Baltimore: Black Classic Press, 1991 (originally published in 1879 in Philadelphia by Harper and Brother).
42. Tunde Adeleke, "Race and Ethnicity in Martin R. Delany's Struggle" *Journal of Thought* 29, no. 1, spring 1994: 19–50.
43. Tunde Adeleke, "Afro-Americans and Moral Suasion: The Debate in the 1830s and 1840s" *Journal of Negro History* 83, spring 1998.
44. Robert Levine, *Martin Delany, Frederick Douglass*, 24–25.
45. Tunde Adeleke, "Afro-Americans and Moral Suasion."
46. Edna B. McKenzie, "Doctor, Editor, Soldier: On Pittsburgh's Very Own Martin R. Delany" *Post Gazette*, February 5, 1992.
47. Carmen J. Lee, "Marker Honors Black Doctor: Friend of Frederick Douglass was Newspaper Publisher" *Post Gazette*, May 11, 1991.
48. Edna McKenzie, "Remarks at Marker Dedication 5/11/91" (unpublished paper), Historical Society of Western Pennsylvania, Pittsburgh, Pennsylvania.
49. Ibid.
50. Ibid. "Augustine" was the pseudonym Delany used in a series of articles in the *Colored American* in the 1830s.
51. Ibid.
52. Louis Rosenfeld, "Martin R. Delany," *Bulletin of the New York Academy of Medicine*, 816.
53. Edna McKenzie, "Doctor, Editor, Soldier."
54. Sajna, "Martin Delany: Father of Black Nationalism." Also Althea Fonville, "Pittsburgher was Father of Black Nationalism" in *Pittsburgh Courier*, February 14, 1976; and her "Pittsburgher Was Father of Black Nationalism" ibid., February 15, 1975.
55. Nathan I. Huggins, "Afro-American History: Myths, Heroes, Reality" in Nathan Huggins, Martin Kilson, and Daniel Fox, eds., *Key Issues in the Afro-American Experience*, vol. 1. New York: Harcourt Brace, 1971, 12.
56. Ibid.
57. Ibid., 12–13.
58. Louis R. Harlan, "Tell It Like It Was: Suggestions on Black History" in James C. Curtis and Lewis L. Gould, eds., *The Black Experience in America: Essays*. Austin: University of Texas Press, 1970, 172.
59. Ibid., 184.
60. E. Waldo Martin, *The Mind of Frederick Douglass*. Chapel Hill: University of North Carolina Press, 1985. Litwack and Meier, *Black Leaders of the Nineteenth Century*. John Hope Franklin, *George Washington Williams:*

A Biography. Chicago: University of Chicago Press, 1985. William S. McFeely, *Frederick Douglass*. New York: W. W. Norton, 1991. John H. Franklin and August Meier, eds., *Black Leaders of the Twentieth Century*. Urbana: University of Illinois Press, 1982. Howard N. Rabinowitz ed., *Southern Black Leaders of the Reconstruction Era*. Urbana: University of Illinois Press, 1982.

61. August Meier, "Afterward: New Perspectives on the Nature of Black Political Leadership during Reconstruction" in Rabinowitz, *Southern Black Leaders*.

62. Martin R. Delany, *Eulogy on the Life and Character of the Rev. Fayette Davis* (pamphlet) Pittsburgh, September 2, 1847. Pittsburgh: Benj. Franklin Peterson, Mystery Office, 1847, 5.

CHAPTER THREE

First Integrationist Phase: Moral Suasion, 1830–1849

1. James O. Horton, *Free People of Color: Inside the African American Community*. Washington, D.C.: Smithsonian Institution Press, 1993. Leonard P. Curry, *The Free Black in Urban America, 1800–1850: The Shadow of the Dream*. Chicago: University of Chicago Press, 1981. Leon Litwack, *North of Slavery: The Negro in the Free States 1790–1860*. Chicago: University of Chicago Press, 1961.

2. Robert McColley, *Slavery and Jeffersonian Virginia*, 2nd ed. Urbana: University of Illinois Press, 1973, chap. 3.

3. Frank (Frances) Rollin, *Life and Public Services of Martin R. Delany*. Boston: Lee and Shepard, 1868, chaps. 1 and 2. Dorothy Sterling, *The Making of an Afro-American: Martin R. Delany 1812–1885*. New York: DaCapo, 1996, chaps. 1–3 (originally published in 1971).

4. Rollin, *Life and Public Services*, 33–37; Sterling, *The Making of an Afro-American*, chap. 3.

5. A. J. White Hutton, *Some Historical Data Concerning the History of Chambersburg*. Chambersburg, Pa.: Franklin Repository, 1930, 33.

6. W. E. B. Du Bois, *The Philadelphia Negro*. Philadelphia: 1899, 257–304.

7. Rollin, *Life and Public Services*, 40.

8. Gerald Sorin, *Abolitionism: A New Perspective*. New York: Praeger, 1972. James Stewart, *Holly Warriors: The Abolitionists and American Slavery*. New York: Hill and Wang, 1976. Carlton Mabee, *Black Freedom: The Nonviolent Abolitionists From 1830 Through the Civil War*. London: Macmillan, 1970. William E. Gienapp, "Abolitionism and the Nature of Ante-Bellum Reform" in Donald M. Jacobs ed., *In Courage and Conscience: Black and White Abolitionists in Boston*. Bloomington: Indiana University Press, 1993. Stanley Harrold, *American Abolitionists*. New York: Longman, 2001.

9. "Minutes and Proceedings of the Second Annual Convention" in Howard H. Bell, ed., *The Proceedings of the National Negro Conventions, 1830–1864*. New York: Arno Press and the New York Times, 1969, 34.

10. "Minutes of the Fourth Annual Convention" in Bell, *The Proceedings*, 7.

11. Tunde Adeleke, "The Religious Dimensions of Martin R. Delany's Struggle" *Journal of American and Canadian Studies* 10, autumn 1992; also his "Afro-Americans and Moral Suasion: The Debate in the 1830s and 1840s" *Journal of Negro History*, spring 1998.

12. Howard H. Bell, "The American Moral Reform Society 1836–1841" *Journal of Negro Education* 27, winter 1958, 34.
13. Richard P. McCormick, "William Whipper: Moral Reformer" *Pennsylvania History* 43, January 1976, 31.
14. Floyd J. Miller, *The Search for Black Nationality: Black Emigration and Colonization, 1787–1863*. Urbana: University of Illinois Press, 1975; also his "The Father of Black Nationalism: Another Contender" *Civil War History* 17, December 1971. Dorothy Sterling, *The Making of an Afro-American*. Victor Ullman, *Martin R. Delany: The Beginnings of Black Nationalism*. Boston: Beacon Press, 1971.
15. Howard H. Bell, *A Survey of the Negro Convention Movement 1830–1861*. New York: Arno Press and the New York Times, 1969. Tunde Adeleke, "Afro-Americans and Moral Suasion: The Debate in the 1830s and 1840s" *Journal of Negro History* 83, spring 1998. William H. Pease and Jane H. Pease, "The Negro Convention Movement" in Nathan Huggins, Martin Kilson and Daniel Fox, eds., *Key Issues in the Afro-American Experience*, vol. 1. New York: Harcourt Brace, 1971.
16. Adeleke, "Afro-Americans and Moral Suasion."
17. Bell, *A Survey of the Negro Convention*; also his "The American Moral Reform Society"; and *The Proceedings of the National Negro Conventions, 1830–1864*.
18. Philip S. Foner and George E. Walker, eds., *Proceedings of the Black State Convention, 1840–1865*, vol. 1. Philadelphia: Temple University Press, 1979, 117.
19. Adam D. Simmons, "Ideologies and Programs of the Negro Anti-Slavery Movement 1830–1861." Ph.D. diss., Northwestern University, 1983, 87. James B. Stewart, *William Lloyd Garrison and the Challenge of Emancipation*. Arlington Heights, Ill.: Harlan Davidson, 1992. John L. Thomas, *The Liberator, William Lloyd Garrison: A Biography*. Boston: Little Brown, 1963.
20. Foner and Walker, *The Proceedings*, 118.
21. Ibid.
22. Ibid.
23. Ibid., 135–136.
24. Ibid., 135.
25. *Colored American*, December 9, 1837, 2.
26. Ibid.
27. *Ibid.*, December 16, 1837, 2; February 16, 1839; May 2, 1839.
28. *Ibid.*, May 3, 1838; August 15, 1839, 21; February 16, 1839, 2.
29. Ibid., May 3, 1838, 54; February 16, May 2, 1839.
30. Foner and Walker, *The Proceedings*, 135. Martin Delany, *The Condition, Elevation, Emigration, and Destiny of the Colored People of the United States*. Baltimore: Black Classic Press, 1993 (originally published in 1852), 95–96. Charles S. Johnson, "The Rise of the Negro Magazine" *Journal of Negro History* 13, no. 1, January 1928, 9. *Colored American*, September 16, 1837, 2.
31. McCormick, "William Whipper," 28–29.
32. Ibid.
33. Ibid.
34. *Colored American*, August 26, 1837, 2; September 9, 1837, 2; January 8, 1837, 2.
35. Ibid.
36. William Whipper, "Non-violence to Offensive Aggression" *Colored American*, September 16, 1837, 1.

37. Ullman, *Martin R. Delany*, 41.
38. Ibid., 26–27. Sterling, *The Making of an Afro-American*, 42–43.
39. McCormick, "William Whipper"; Adeleke, "Afro-Americans and Moral Suasion."
40. Sterling, *The Making of an Afro-American*, 80–81. Rollin, *Life and Public Services*, chap. 5. Also *Pennsylvania Freeman*, August 20, 1846, 3.
41. *North Star*, November 17, 1848, 2; April 7, 1848, 2; January 7, 1848, 2–3; December 15, 1848, 3; April 28, 1848, 2; January 2, 1848, 3.
42. Ibid., June 5, 1849, 2; May 6, 1848, 2.
43. Ibid., January 5, 1849, February 6, 1848, March 9, April 7, 1848, April 14, 1848.
44. Ibid., March 16, 1849, 2; December 15, 1848; Delany, *The Condition*, 37–38.
45. Delany, *The Condition*, chap. 4; *North Star*, April 7, 1848, 3; October 6, 1849, 2; January 5, 1849.
46. *North Star*, April 18, 1848; April 28, 1848; May 6, 1848, 2; June 5, 1849, 2; April 12, 20, 1849.
47. Ibid., January 5, 1849.
48. Ibid., October 6, 1849, 2; April 7, 1848, 3.
49. Ibid., December 15, 1848.
50. Ibid., February 16, 1849, 2; see Delany's series, "Domestic Economy" *North Star*, March 23, 1849, 2; April 13, 1849, 2; April 20, 1849, 2.
51. *North Star*, April 20, 1849.
52. Ibid.
53. Tunde Adeleke, "Religion in Martin R. Delany's Struggle" *Religious Humanism* 27, no. 2, spring 1993.
54. Ibid.
55. Ibid.
56. Tunde Adeleke, "The Religious Dimensions of Martin R. Delany's Struggle" *Journal of American and Canadian Studies* 10, autumn 1992, 27–28.
57. Ibid.
58. Ibid.
59. Ibid., 28–29.
60. Ibid.
61. Ibid.
62. Delany, *The Condition*, 37–39, 42, chaps. 4 and 5; "Domestic Economy" *North Star*, March 16, 1849; April 13, 1849. Adeleke, "The Religious Dimensions" 30–31.
63. Delany, *The Condition*, 39.
64. *North Star*, November 17, 1848, 2; April 7, 1848, 2; January 7, 1848, 2–3; December 15, 1848, 3; April 28, 1848, 2; January 2, 1848, 3.
65. Ibid., December 15, 1848, 3.
66. Ibid., May 6, 1848, April 13, 1849, April 20, 1849.
67. Delany, *The Condition*, 42.
68. Ibid., chap. 5.
69. Ibid.
70. Ibid.
71. Ibid., 43.
72. Ibid., 44.
73. Ibid., chap. 5.
74. Ibid., 44–45.
75. *North Star*, January 2, 1848, 3.
76. Ibid., December 15, 1848, 3.
77. Ibid.

78. Delany's report from Sandusky, Ohio, June 1, 1848. *North Star,* June 14, 1848.
79. Adam D. Simmons, "Ideologies and Programs of the Negro Antislavery Movement." Ph.D., diss., Northwestern University, 1983, 32.
80. *North Star,* April 13, 1849, 2.
81. Simmons, "Ideologies and Programs" 34.
82. Charles Godfrey LeLand, *Memoirs.* New York, 1893, 216. Also E. M. Geffen, "Violence in Philadelphia in the 1840s and 1850s" *Pennsylvania History* 4, October 1969.
83. "Minutes of the State Convention of the Colored Citizens of Pennsylvania, Convened at Harrisburg, December 13–14, 1848" in Foner and Walker, *The Proceedings,* 118–138.
84. Ibid.
85. Ibid.
86. Ibid., 124–125.
87. For a detailed analysis of the concept herrenvolk democracy, see George Frederickson, *The Black Image in the White Mind: The Debate on Afro-American Character and Destiny, 1817–1914.* New York: Harper and Row, 1971. Pierre Van den Berghe, in *Race and Racism: A Comparative Perspective,* New York: John Wiley, 1967, used the term "herrenvolk democracy" to describe contexts such as the United States and apartheid South Africa that are democratic for the master race but tyrannical for the subordinate group.
88. "Minutes of the State Convention of the Colored Citizens of Pennsylvania," 123–124.
89. Ibid., 124.
90. McCormick, "William Whipper," 37.
91. Ibid.
92. *North Star,* June 29, 1849, 1.
93. Benjamin Quarles, *Frederick Douglass.* Washington, D.C.: Associated Publishers, 1948, 83–84.
94. Philip S. Foner, ed., *The Life and Writings of Frederick Douglass,* vol. 5., *Supplementary.* New York: International Publishers, 1975, 70–71.
95. *North Star,* March 23, 1849, 2.
96. Martin Delany, "American Civilization: Treatment of the Colored People," *North Star,* March 30, 1849.
97. Ibid.
98. Dred Scott was an illiterate slave of John Emerson of Missouri who was later taken to Illinois and the section of Wisconsin Territory covered by the Missouri Compromise and was later returned to Missouri. When Emerson died, Scott, who was inherited by Emerson's brother, John Sanford, sued in the lower court of Missouri for his freedom on the grounds that residence in a free state had made him a free man. In 1848, the Missouri supreme court struck down his suit. After a series of failures in the state courts, in 1854 Scott took his case to the United States Supreme Court. In its epochal decision rendered on March 6, 1857, the majority, led by Chief Justice Roger Taney, rejected Scott's appeal on the grounds that Scott's suits had no *locus standi,* since blacks were not citizens of the United States, and consequently, residence in a free state did not confer freedom. Second, the Court held that blacks had no rights that whites were bound to respect. See Don E. Fehrenbacher, *The Dred Scott Case: Its Significance in American Law and Politics.* New York: Oxford University Press, 1978. Also Paul Finkelman, ed., *Dred Scott v. Sanford: A Brief History*

with Documents. New York: Bedford Books, 1997. The 1854 Kansas-Nebraska Act had opened the possibility of expansion of slavery into an area from which it had been prohibited by the Missouri Compromise.

99. Don E. Fehrenbacher, *The South and Three Sectional Crises.* Baton Rouge: Louisiana State University Press, 1980.
100. Foner and Walker, *The Proceedings.*
101. Rollin, *Life and Public Services,* 76.
102. Delany, *The Condition,* chap. 16.
103. "Letter From Mr. Delany," *Frederick Douglass' Paper,* April 11, 1853.
104. Ibid.
105. "Remarks," Ibid.
106. "The Letter of M. R. Delany," *Frederick Douglass' Paper,* May 6, 1853.
107. Martin Delany, "Political Aspect of the Colored People of the United States" *Provincial Freeman,* October 13, 1855. Also his "Political Events" *Provincial Freeman,* July 5, 1856.
108. Delany, "Political Aspect." Also Delany, *The Condition,* and "Political Destiny of the Colored Race on the American Continent" in Rollin, *Life and Public Services,* 327–367.
109. Delany, "Political Aspect." Also, "Dr. Delany on Africa" *Weekly Anglo-African,* January 25, 1862; Dr. Delany to James McCune Smith (Important Movement), *Weekly Anglo-African,* January 4, 1862; Dr. Delany to Prof. M. H. Freeman (On Haitian Emigration), *Weekly Anglo-African,* February 1, 1862; Delany to Frederick Douglass, *Douglass' Monthly,* September 1862; S. N. Geers, "Brooklyn Affairs" *Weekly Anglo-African,* November 2, 1861; "Dr. M. R. Delany" *Douglass' Monthly,* August 1862; Martin Delany, "The Moral and Social Aspect of Africa" *Liberator,* May 1, 1863.
110. Delany, "Political Destiny" 335.
111. Tunde Adeleke, *UnAfrican Americans: Nineteenth Century Black Nationalists and the Civilizing Mission.* Lexington: University Press of Kentucky, 1998.

CHAPTER FOUR

Second Integrationist Phase: 1863–1874

1. Martin R. Delany, *The Condition, Elevation, Emigration and Destiny of the Colored People of the United States.* Baltimore: Black Classic Press, 1993, 154–155 (originally published in 1852).
2. Ibid.
3. Delany to Frederick Douglass, Pittsburg, March 22, 1853. *Frederick Douglass' Paper,* April 11, 1853.
4. Ibid. See also "Letter From M. R. Delany" *Frederick Douglass' Paper,* April 11, 1853.
5. The most recent projection of this image is in Mia Bay, *The White Image in the Black Mind: African-American Ideas About White People, 1830–1925.* New York: Oxford University Press, 2000. Cyril E. Griffith, *The African Dream: Martin R. Delany and the Emergence of Pan-Africanist Thought.* University Park: Pennsylvania State University Press, 1975. Also Sterling Stuckey, *The Ideological Origins of Black Nationalism.* Boston: Beacon Press, 1972.
6. Delany, *The Condition.*

7. Philip S. Foner, ed., *The Life and Writings of Frederick Douglass*, vol. 5, *Supplementary*. New York: International Publishers, 1975, 202.

8. Philip S. Foner and George Walker, eds., *Proceedings of the Black State Conventions, 1840–1865*. Philadelphia: Temple University Press, 1980, vols. 1 and 2. See also Howard Bell, *A Survey of the Negro Convention Movement, 1830–1861*. New York: Arno Press, 1969. "Convention of the Colored Persons of Pennsylvania," *Pennsylvania Freeman*, October 23, 1952, 1.

9. "Proceedings of the First Convention of the Colored Citizens of the State of Illinois, Chicago, October 6–8, 1853" in Foner and Walker, *Proceedings*, vol. 2, 60.

10. Frederick Douglass, "Prejudice Against Color" *North Star*, June 13, 1850, 2.

11. Martin R. Delany, "Political Destiny of the Colored Race on the American Continent" in Frank (Frances) Rollin, *Life and Public Services of Martin R. Delany*. Boston: Lee and Shepard, 1868, 327–367.

12. *Provincial Freeman*, October 13, 1855, 97–98.

13. Ibid.

14. Floyd J. Miller, *The Search For a Black nationality: Black Emigration and Colonization, 1787–1863*. Urbana: University of Illinois Press, 1975, 165–167.

15. *Chatham Tri-Weekly Planet*, 4, 1857, 2. Jonathan W. Walton, "Blacks in Buxton and Chatham, Ontario, 1830–1890: Did the 49th Parallel Make a Difference?" Ph.D. diss. Princeton, 1979, 71–87. Memorandum of Deed of Purchase in Chatham" Delany Files, London, Ontario, Cross Cultural Learner's Center. "Editorial" *Provincial Freeman*, May 16, 1856, February 23, 1856. Victor Ullman, *Martin R. Delany: the Beginnings of Black Nationalism*. Boston: Beacon Press, 1971, 193. Donald Simpson, "Blacks in Ontario," Ph.D. diss., University of Western Ontario, 1971.

16. *Provincial Freeman*, July 5, 1856, 46.

17. Richard Blackett, "Martin Delany and Robert Campbell: Black Americans in Search of an African Colony" *Journal of Negro History* 62, no. 1, January 1977. A. H. M. Kirk-Green, "America in the Niger Valley: A Colonization Centenary" *Phylon*, 22, 4, 1962. Martin R. Delany, "Official Report of the Niger Valley Exploring Party" in Martin Delany and Robert Campbell, *Search for a Place: Black separatism and Africa, 1860*. Ann Arbor: University of Michigan Press, 1971, 26–148.

18. The desire for homogenization through the removal or elimination of blacks was a significant component of Civil War nationalism. See George M. Frederickson, *The Black Image in the White Mind: The Debate on Afro-American Character and Destiny, 1817–1914*. New York: Harper and Row, 1971, chaps. 5 and 6.

19. Ibid., 150–151. *United States Congress, House Select Committee on Emigration and Colonization Report*, Washington D.C., 37th Congress, 2nd Session, December 2, 1861–July 17, 1862, 1–83. This report advocated colonization on the grounds that "the highest interest of the white race" required that they have sole possession of "every acre of our present domain." Ibid., 151. Also Charles H. Wesley, "Lincoln's Plan for Colonizing the Emancipated Negroes" *Journal of Negro History* 4, 1, January 1919.

20. James McPherson, *The Negro Civil War: How American Negroes Felt and Acted during the War*. New York: Vintage Books, 1965, 77–97. Blacks angrily opposed colonization. See *Anglo-African Magazine*, January 5, 12, 1861. On Delany's opposition to the Haytian colonization scheme, see *Douglass's Monthly*, September 1862, 179. *Weekly Anglo-African*, February 1, 1862.

21. Wilson J. Moses, *The Golden Age of Black Nationalism, 1850–1925*. New York: Oxford University Press, 1978. Theodore Draper, *The Rediscovery of Black Nationalism*. New York: Viking Press, 1970. Griffith, *The African Dream*; Floyd J. Miller, *The Search for a Black Nationality: Black Emigration and Colonization, 1787–1863*. Urbana: University of Illinois Press, 1975.

22. Martin R. Delany, *A Series of Four Tracts on National Polity*. Charleston, S.C.: Republican Book and Job Office, 1870, 9.

23. Rollin, *Life and Public Services*, 137. Also *Douglass's Monthly*, April 1861, 444.

24. Rollin, *Life and Public Services*, 140–141.

25. Ibid., chap. 19.

26. Ibid., 169–171.

27. Ibid., 181.

28. Ibid., 211–212.

29. Delany to the Secretary of War, Chicago, Illinois, December 15, 1863, in Delany File, London, Ontario, CCLC. Also Ira Berlin, Joseph Reidy, and Leslie Rowland, eds., *Freedom: A Documentary History of Emancipation, 1861–1881*. Series 11. *The Black Military Experience*. Cambridge: Cambridge University Press, 1982, 101–102.

30. Berlin, Reidy, and Rowland, *Freedom*, 181–226.

31. William H. Wiggins, *O Freedom! Afro-American Emancipation Celebrations*. Knoxville: University of Tennessee Press, 1987.

32. Walter L. Fleming, ed., *Documentary History of Reconstruction: Political, Military, Social, Religious, Educational and Industrial, 1865–1906*, vol. 1. New York: McGraw-Hill, 1966, 195–196.

33. Martin R. Delany, "Trial and Conviction." Charleston, 1876, 3 (unpublished pamphlet). Copy in the Charleston Historical Society Library.

34. Ibid., 6. Also his "A Political Review" *Daily Republican*, August 15, 1871.

35. Delany, *A Series of Four Tracts*, 12–13.

36. Ibid.

37. Edward Magdol, "Martin R. Delany Counsels Freedmen, July 23, 1865" *Journal of Negro History*, 56, October 1971, 303–307. Also Berlin, Reidy, and Rowland, *Freedom*, 739–741; Martin Delany, "Prospects of the Freedmen on Hilton Head" in Rollin, *Life and Public Services*, 230–242. Long before the end of war, blacks had demonstrated their eagerness for land and their determination to acquire land either individually or collectively in the Sea Islands. But the presence of Northern speculators proved a stumbling block. These land speculators, or "new masters," were more interested in exploiting black labor than in helping to consolidate black freedom through economic power. See Willie Lee Rose, *Rehearsal for Reconstruction: The Port Royal Experiment*. New York: Vintage Books, 1967. Lawrence N. Powell, *New Masters: Northern Planters During the Civil War and Reconstruction*. New Haven, Conn.: Yale University Press, 1980. Delany frequently alerted freedmen to the presence of land speculators. Laura M. Towne noted in her diary entry for Sunday, August 3, 1865, an "unwise" speech by Delany "a few Sundays ago" that got blacks so excited against Edward S. Philbrick. See Rupert Sargent Holland, ed., *Letters and Diary of Laura M. Towne*. Cambridge: Harvard University Press, 1912, 165. Philbrick was one of several Northern land speculators who participated in the Port Royal experiment and opposed land sales to blacks. He personally operated about twelve plantations. See Elizabeth W. Pearson, ed., *Letters From Port Royal Written At the Time of the Civil War*. Boston: W. B. Clarke, 1906, viii.

38. Magdol, "Martin R. Delany."
39. Delany, "Prospects".
40. Delany, "Political Economy" *North Star*, March 16, 1849; *The Condition*, 46.
41. Delany, "Prospects," 238.
42. Magdol, "Martin R. Delany."
43. Blacks desperately wanted land. They believed that the lands they toiled on as slaves rightfully belonged to them. They were prepared to purchase lands individually or by pooling their resources together communally. For a discussion of this "homestead ethics" among the freedmen, see James M. McPherson, "The Ballot and Land for the Freedmen, 1861–1865" in Kenneth Stampp and Leon F. Litwack, eds., *Reconstruction: An Anthology of Revisionist Writings*. Baton Rouge: Louisiana State University Press, 1969. Martin Abbot, "The Freedmen's Bureau and Its Carolina Critics" in *Proceedings of the South Carolina Historical Association*, 1962. LaWanda Cox, "The Promise of Land for the Freedmen" *Mississippi Valley Historical Review*, 45, December 1958. Martin Abbott, "Free Land, Free Labor and the Freedmen's Bureau" *Agricultural History*, 30, October 1956. Milfred C. Fierce, "Black Struggle for Land During Reconstruction" *Black Scholar*, February 1974. Elizabeth Bethel, *Promisedland: A Century of Life in A Negro Community*. Philadelphia: Temple University Press, 1981. Edward Magdol, *A Right to the Land: Essays on the Freedmen's Community*. Westport, Conn.: Greenwood Press, 1977. Claude F. Oubre, *Forty Acres and a Mule: The Freedmen's Bureau and Black Land Ownership*. Baton Rouge: Louisiana State University Press, 1978. W. E. B. Du Bois, *The Souls of Black Folk: Essays and Sketches*. Chicago: A. C. McClurg, 1903, chap. 2.
44. Rollin, *Life and Public Services*, 238. See also Delany, "Trial and Conviction," 9.
45. Delany, "Prospects," 230–241.
46. Ibid., 238.
47. Martin Delany, "Triple Alliance: The Reconstruction of the South, The Salvation of its Political Economy" in Rollin, *Life and Public Services*, 242–243.
48. "Third Offense" in "Trial and Conviction," 7. Also his "A Political Review"; Delany to Rev. Henry H. Garnet, July 27, 1867" in "Trial and Conviction," 4–5.
49. *News and Courier*, September 21, 22, 1876. Also Bernard E. Power, "Black Charleston: A Social History, 1822–1865" Ph.D., diss., Northwestern University, 1982, chap. 3.
50. George R. Bentley, *A History of the Freedmen's Bureau*. Philadelphia: University of Pennsylvania Press, 1965, 1–30.
51. Oubre, *Forty Acres and a Mule*. Magdol, *A Right to the Land*. Fierce, "Black Struggle for Land."
52. *Anti-slavery Reporter*, vol. 13, no. 7, July 1, 1865, 192.
53. Leon F. Litwack argued that "nothing in the experience of the slaveowning class had prepared it to deal with blacks as free workers, and in many respects it was less equipped to make the transition to freedom than its former slaves," hence the vehemence with which members of this class opposed black land-ownership. See his "The Ordeal of Black Freedom" in Walter J. Fraser and Winifred B. Moore, eds., *The Southern Enigma: Essays on Race, Class and Folk Culture*. Westport, Conn.: Greenwood Press, 1983, 5–9. For more on the reluctance of Southern whites to adjust to the postwar realities, see Glennon Graham, "From Slavery to Serfdom: Rural Black Agriculturalists in South Carolina, 1865–1900" Ph.D., diss., Northwestern University, 1982, chaps. 1–3.

Eric Foner, *Nothing But Freedom: Emancipation and Its Legacy*. Baton Rouge: Louisiana State University Press, 1983.

54. James McPherson, *The Negro Civil War: How American Negroes Felt and Acted During the War*. New York: Vintage Books, 1965, 295, 296–297. Also his "The Ballot and Land for Freedmen," 146–148.

55. For more on General Sherman's Field Order and its impact see Walter L. Fleming, *Documentary History of Reconstruction*, vol. 1. New York: McGraw-Hill, 1966, 350–358.

56. Ibid., 168–169.

57. Delany, "Prospects".

58. Rollin, *Life and Public Services*, 242–243. Also, 2–Martin Delany, Freedmen's Bureau Papers in War records Office, National Archives, Washington, D.C. Records of the Assistant Commissioners of the State of South Carolina, BRFAL, 1865–1870, Microcopy 869, National Archives.

59. Martin Delany, Freedmen's Bureau Report for May 1868, BRFAL Microcopy no. 849, roll 32, 773–779.

60. Rollin, *Life and Public Services*, 243–244.

61. Ibid., 245–251.

62. Ibid., also 260–262; According to Glennon Graham, Southern whites did not consider themselves in need of "Reconstruction." Blacks were the ones in need of Reconstruction. This sort of attitude greatly informed white responses to blacks and explained the paternalistic and racist dispositions. See his "From Slavery to Serfdom." Also C. W. Tebeau, "Some Aspects of Planter-Freedman Relations, 1865–1880" *Journal of Negro History*, 21, no. 2, April 1936. James H. Croushore and David M. Potter, eds., *John William De Forest: A Union Officer in the Reconstruction*. New Haven, Conn.: Yale University Press, 1948. According to John De Forest, "Many of the planters seemed to be unable to understand that work could be other than a form of slavery, or that it could be accomplished without some prodigious binding and obligating of the hireling of the employer," Ibid., 28.

63. Rollin, *Life and Public Services*, 252–254.

64. Ibid., 256.

65. Ibid., also 263.

66. Delany, "Trial and Conviction," 7. Also *Daily Republican*, June 24, August 20, 1870.

67. *Daily Republican*, June 24, 1870.

68. Rollin, *Life and Public Services*, 238.

69. Wilbur J. Cash, *The Mind of the South*. New York: Vintage Books, 1941.

70. Lacy K. Ford, "One Southern Profile: Modernization and the Development of White Terror in York County, 1856–1876." Master's thesis, University of South Carolina, 1976, xi, 53–54.

71. Alrutheus A. Taylor, *The Negro in South Carolina during the Reconstruction*. Washington: ASALH, 1924, 42. Perry's policy declared in force the laws enacted prior to secession and restored all officials in power before the collapse of the Confederacy. Francis Simkins and Robert Woody, *South Carolina during Reconstruction*. Gloucester, Mass.: Peter Smith, 1966, 33–35. Also John S. Reynolds, *Reconstruction in South Carolina*. New York: Negro University Press, 1969, chap. 1.

72. The new constitutions reasserted state rights and developed the infamous "black codes" as a means of subordinating blacks to the new form of bondage.

Simkins and Woody, *South Carolina during Reconstruction*, 38–40. Taylor, *The Negro in South Carolina*, 42–47, 50–51. Also Herbert Aptheker, "South Carolina Negro Convention, 1865" *Journal of Negro History*, 31, January 1945, 91–92. *New York Tribune*, November 29, 1865, 1, 8.

73. Aptheker, "South Carolina Negro Convention," 93–95.
74. Ibid. Also, "Proceedings of the South Carolina Conventions," in Foner and Walker, *Proceedings*, vol. 2, 284–304.
75. A South Carolinian (Belton O'Neall Townsend) "South Carolina Morals" *Atlantic Monthly*, April 1877, 470.
76. "Exchange Between Johnson and Negro Spokesmen on Suffrage" in LaWanda Cox and John Cox, eds., *Reconstruction, the Negro and the New South* (Documents). Columbia: University of South Carolina Press, 1973, 20–29. See also their *Politics, Principle, and Prejudice 1865–1866: Dilemma of Reconstruction America*. New York: Atheneum, 1976, 151–171.
77. "Exchange Between Johnson and Negro Spokesmen on Suffrage," 20–29.
78. The desire for homogenization through the removal or elimination of the blacks was a significant component of Civil War nationalism. See Frederickson, *The Black Image in the White Mind*, chaps. 5, 6.
79. Ibid., 150–151. Also United States Congress, House Select Committee on Emancipation and Colonization Report, Washington, DC., 37th Congress, 2nd Session, December 2, 1861–July 17, 1862, 1–83. This report advocated colonization on the ground that "the highest interests of the white race" required that they have sole possession of "every acre of our present domain." George Frederickson, *The Black Image in the White Mind*, 151. Also Charles H. Wesley, "Lincoln's Plan for Colonizing the Emancipated Negroes" *Journal of Negro History* 4, no. 1, January 1919.
80. Rollin, *Life and Public Services*, 281–283.
81. Peggy Lamson, *The Glorious Failure: Black Congressman Robert Brown Elliott and the Reconstruction in South Carolina*. New York: W. W. Norton, 1973, 42.
82. Taylor, *The Negro in South Carolina*, 52–53. Walter L. Fleming, ed., *Documentary History of Reconstruction: Political, Military, Social, Religious, Educational and Industrial, 1865–1906*, vol. 1. New York: McGraw Hill, 1966, 197, 478–479.
83. Simkins and Woody, *South Carolina during Reconstruction*, chap. 3.
84. Ibid.
85. Ibid., chaps. 4, 5. Also *Proceedings of the Constitutional Convention of South Carolina*, vol. 1. New York: Arno Press, 1968. House Miscellaneous Document No. 81, serial 1349, "Resolutions of the Constitutional Convention of South Carolina, 1868" 40th Congress, 2nd Session.
86. John S. Reynolds, *Reconstruction in South Carolina*. New York: Negro University Press, 1969, 74–76. Also Fleming, *Documentary History*, 455–456.
87. Taylor, *The Negro in South Carolina*, 187. Lamson, *The Glorious Failure*, 64–65. For more on the notion that blacks were naturally inferior and therefore deserved to be enslaved, see *Charleston Mercury*, November 27, 1866.
88. Lamson, *The Glorious Failure*, 64–65. See also "The Appeal of the South Carolina Democrats to Congress" in LaWanda Cox and John Cox, eds., *Reconstruction, the Negro and the New South*. Columbia: University of South Carolina Press, 1973, 228–236. Also he letters of Jas. H. Campbell to the Aiken Democratic Club, in the Dawson Pamphlet Collection, University of North Carolina, Chapel Hill.

89. *Daily Phoenix*, April 14, 1868. The letters of Jas. H. Campbell. Letter of Col. Thomas to the colored people informing them that suffrage was not a right that blacks should aspire to. As a leading member of the Newberry Democratic Club, Thomas expressed the racist consciousness of party comrades that South Carolina was a white man's state and ought to remain so. Ibid.

90. *Daily Phoenix*, April 26, 1868.

91. Letters of Jas. H. Campbell. Also *Daily Phoenix*, April 14, 1868.

92. *Charleston Mercury*, April 4, 1866.

93. Letters of Jas. H. Campbell.

94. "Speech of Col. J. F. Thomas at a Democratic Convention," *Daily Phoenix*, April 10, 1868, February 26, 1868.

95. John Hammond Moore, ed., *The JUHL Letters to the Charleston Courier: A View of the South, 1865–1871*. Athens: University of Georgia Press, 1974, 113.

96. *Daily Phoenix*, April 15, 1868, April 22, 1868. Also *Platform of the Union Reform Party and the Address of the Executive Committee to the people of the State* (pamphlet). Columbia: Daily Southern Guardian, 1870, in the Dawson Pamphlets Collection.

97. *Daily Phoenix*, April 26, 1868. The minutes of the Democratic Party of Charleston show a determined effort to win blacks away from the Republican connection through efficient organizational procedures. Democratic Party, Charleston, Minutes 1868, Mss. South Caroliniana Library, Columbia. At the same time, the Democratic garrison at Abbeville "itched to get a shot at the Negroes." Despite the presence of a company of troops, the garrison beat and stabbed several blacks. This information is in a letter of Edward Crossland to his mother, in the Crossland Papers, South Caroliniana Research library. In the state legislature, Democratic sympathizers voted to abolish the political disabilities imposed by the Fourteenth Amendment. Ellison Summerfield Keiff (FL 1876) MP, vol. Bd. 1867–76. Mss. South Caroliniana.

98. *Daily Phoenix*, April 26, 1868, May 5, 1868.

99. Ibid., February 26, 1868, April 10, 1868.

100. Ibid., April 22, 1868.

101. *Daily Republican*, August 28, 1869.

102. This is clearly suggested in his letter to Henry H. Garnet where he rejected Wendell Phillips call for a black Vice-President. See his "Trial and Conviction," 4–5. Also "Delany to L. S. Langley" Ibid., 6–7; *On National Polity* (pamphlet), 10.

103. *Daily Phoenix*, April 14, 1868, April 22, 1868. See also the Letters of Jas. H. Campbell; Letter of Col. Thomas to the Colored People.

104. Delany, "A Political Review."

105. Ibid.

106. Delany to Rev. Henry H. Garnet, in "Trial and Conviction."

107. Delany, "A Political Review."

108. Delany to Rev. Henry H. Garnet, in "Trial and Conviction."

109. Ibid.

110. Ibid.

111. Delany to L. S. Langley, February 5, 1868, in "Trial and Conviction," 6–7.

112. Ibid.

113. Ibid.

114. "Colored Officials" *New York Times*, August 21, 1867.

115. Ibid.

116. Ibid.
117. Ibid.
118. Ibid.
119. Ibid.
120. Ibid.
121. Ibid.
122. Ibid.
123. Fides, "Thoughts for the Colored People" *Daily Phoenix*, April 12, 1868.
124. Ibid.
125. Ibid.
126. Delany, "Trial and Conviction."
127. Ibid.
128. Ibid.
129. Ibid.
130. Joseph A. Alvarez, *From Reconstruction to Revolution: The Struggle for Equality*. New York: Atheneum, 1971, 3–49. Also William Gillette, *Retreat From Reconstruction, 1869–1879*. Baton Rouge: Louisiana State University Press, 1978. Eric Foner, *Reconstruction: America's Unfinished Revolution*. New York: Harper and Row, 1988.
131. *Daily Republican*, June 24, 1870, July 5, 1870. Delany made similar demands in his "*A Series of Four Tracts*."
132. *Daily Republican*, June 29, 1870, June 30, 1870.
133. Ibid., June 24, 1870, July 7, 1870, July 27, 1870. Also Ullman, *Martin R. Delany*, 411–415.
134. Delany to William Coppinger, August 18, 1880, in American Colonization Society Papers, Washington D.C.
135. *Daily Republican*, August 28, 1869; February 5, 1876. "Conservative Republicanism" could be defined as an attempt by conservatives to use Radical Republican means to attain conservative ends. An example was the attempt by the Democrats to co-opt the platform of the Radical Republicans in order to win over blacks and defeat Radical Reconstruction. It could also mean an attempt by a Republican to use conservative means or voice conservative sentiments to achieve a political goal. Delany used this technique. For the platform of the Union Reform Party, see *Daily Republican*, July 6, 1870. *Daily Republican*, February 5, 1876. Also Robert H. Woody, "South Carolina Election of 1870" *North Carolina Historical Review* 8, 1931.
136. *Daily Republican*, July 28, 1870, July 27, 1870. Francis L. Cardozo, "Address Before the Grand Council of the Union Leagues, July 27, 1870" *Journal of Negro History* 61, no. 2, April 1976.
137. Robert DeLarge demanded justice for blacks and the full exercise of the franchise at a mass meeting of Republicans in Charleston. *Daily Republican*, June 24, 1870. Rev. Cain also advocated equal representation of the races. Ibid., July 28, 1870; also June 24, 1870, July 5, 1870.
138. Ibid., June 24, 1870, June 27, 1870, July 7, 1870.
139. Ibid., June 30, 1870.
140. Ibid., July 5, 1870.
141. Ibid., July 21, 1870.
142. "Speech of Lieut. Col. Delany." Ibid., 24, 1870.
143. Ibid.
144. Ibid.

145. Ibid. July 25, 1870.
146. "A Card." Ibid., August 16, 1870.
147. Ibid.
148. "Speech of Col. Delany." Ibid., August 20, 1870.
149. Ibid.
150. Ibid., June 24, 1870, July 7, 1870. Also R. H. Woody, "South Carolina Elections." Taylor, *The Negro in South Carolina*, 198.
151. Ullman, *Martin R. Delany*, 420.
152. Delany, "Trial and Conviction"; Delany, "Homes For the Freedmen" *Daily Republican*, May 2, 1870, 2. He wrote three letters on this theme. He sent one to Senator Henry Wilson of Massachusetts and the other two to Daniel L. Eaton, an official of the Freedmen's Bank in Washington, D.C. The Boston Public Library has all three letters.
153. Delany, "Homes For the Freedmen."
154. Delany, "A Political Review" *Daily Republican*, August 15, 1871. Also in *New National Era*, August 31, 1871, 3.
155. Ibid.
156. Ibid.
157. Ibid.
158. Ibid.
159. Ibid.
160. Ibid.
161. Ibid.
162. "Major Delany's Letter to Frederick Douglass" *News and Courier*, August 18, 1871.
163. "Letter of M. R. Delany Addressed to Frederick Douglass" *News and Courier*, August 17, 1871; "Major Delany's Letter to Frederick Douglass" Ibid., August 19, 1871. Also *News and Courier*, August 17, 1871, August 18, 1871, August 19, 1871.
164. "Letter of M. R. Delany Addressed to Frederick Douglass" Ibid., August 17, 1871.
165. Ibid.
166. "Major Delany's Letter to Frederick Douglass" Ibid., August 18, 1871.
167. "Major Delany's Letter to Frederick Douglass" Ibid., August 19, 1871.
168. "Major Delany's Letter" *New National Era*, October 12, 1871.
169. George Rable, *But There Was No Peace: The Role of Violence in the Politics of Reconstruction*. Athens: University of Georgia Press, 1984. Also Simkins and Woody, *South Carolina during Reconstruction*.
170. *New National Era*, August 31, 1871.
171. Ibid.
172. Ibid., July 26, 1871.
173. *Daily Republican*, June 22, 1871.
174. Ibid.
175. *Proceedings of the Southern States Convention of Colored Men, Held in Columbia, S.C., October 18–25*. Columbia: Carolina Printing Company, 1871.
176. Ibid., 20.
177. Ibid., 23.
178. Ibid., 30–31.
179. Ibid., 40.
180. Ibid., 31.

181. Ibid., 32.
182. *New National Era*, August 10, 1871.
183. Simkins and Woody, *South Carolina during Reconstruction*, 466. Blesser, *The Promised Land*.
184. Rev. R. Cain to Gov. Franklin J. Moses, May 18, 1873, Franklin J. Moses Papers, Box 4, Folder 3, South Carolina Department of Archives and History (SCDAH).
185. Martin R. Delany, "South Carolina Obligations 1" *New York Times*, September 25, 1872.
186. Delany, "South Carolina Obligations 2" *New York Times*, September 30, 1872.
187. Ullman, *Martin R. Delany*, 430.
188. Diary of Josephus Woodruff, Ms., South Carolina Department of Archives and History, Columbia.
189. Ullman, *Martin R. Delany*, 435–436. Delany to Coppinger, August 18, 1880.
190. R. H. Cain to Gov. Franklin J. Moses, May 8, 1873. Franklin J. Moses Papers, Box 4, folder 3, SCDAH.
191. Ibid.
192. R. H. Woody, "Franklin J. Moses: Scalawag Governor of South Carolina" *North Carolina Historical Review*, 10, April 1933.
193. "Minority Representation: Delany to Hon. J. J. Wright" *New York Times*, February 21, 1874.
194. *New York Times*, February 21, 1874.
195. Ibid.
196. Walter Allen, *Governor Chamberlain's Administration in South Carolina: A Chapter of Reconstruction in the Southern States*. New York: Negro University Press, 1969, 284.
197. This "population bogey" has been a veritable weapon of the state conservatives since the inception of Radical Reconstruction. *Daily Phoenix*, February 26, 1868, April 10, 1868; also Letters of Jas. H. Campbell to the Aiken Democratic Club, in the Dawson Pamphlet Collection, University of North Carolina, Chapel Hill; also in the South Carolina Historical Society collection, Charleston. Speech of Col. J. F. Thomas at a Democratic Convention, *Daily Phoenix*, April 10, 1868.
198. F. L. Cardozo, "South Carolina: The Political Situation" *New York Times*, June 16, 1874; also *New York Times*, June 21, 1874, June 22, 1874.
199. F. L. Cardozo, "South Carolina: The Political Situation" *New York Times*, February 16, 1874. Also Foner, *Reconstruction*, 424.
200. Joel Williamson, *After Slavery: The Negro in South Carolina during Reconstruction 1861–1877*. Chapel Hill: University of North Carolina Press, 1965, 332.
201. Simkins and Woody, *South Carolina during Reconstruction*, 470–473. Also W. E. B. Du Bois, *Black Reconstruction in America 1860–1880*. New York: Atheneum, 1983, chap. 10 (originally published in 1935). "Independent Republican Party: M.P. 1874" Mss. South Caroliniana Research Library, Columbia. Thomas Holt, *Black Over White: Negro Political Leadership in South Carolina during Reconstruction*. Urbana: University of Illinois Press, 1979, chapter 8.
202. "Independent Republican Party." Also Holt, *Black Over White*.
203. *Daily Phoenix*, April 15, 1868, April 22, 1868. *Platform of the Union Reform Party* (pamphlet). Columbia, S.C.: Daily Southern Guardian, 1870.

Robert H. Woody, "South Carolina Election of 1870" *North Carolina Historical Review* 8, 1981. Taylor, *The Negro in South Carolina*, 198.

204. Foner, *Reconstruction*, chap. 9. Michael Perman, *Reunion Without Compromise: The South and Reconstruction, 1865–1868*. Cambridge: Cambridge University Press, 1973, chap. 3. For a detailed study of Democratic liberalism, see Lawrence Grossman, *The Democratic Party and the South: Northern and National Politics, 1868–1892*. Urbana: University of Illinois Press, 1976. Also *News and Courier*, October 16, 1874.

205. "Conservatives and Republicans in a Common Cause" *News and Courier*, October 2, 1874.

206. Ibid.

207. "The Independent Republican State Nominating Convention, Hibernian Hall" *News and Courier*, October 3, 1874.

208. Ibid.

209. Ibid.

210. Ibid.

211. "The Independent State Convention" *News and Courier*, October 5, 1874.

212. Ibid.

213. Ibid.

214. "A Rousing Ratification Meeting Last Night" *News and Courier*, October 7, 1874.

215. Ibid.

216. Ibid.

217. Ibid.

218. Ibid.

219. Ibid.

220. Ibid.

221. Ibid.

222. "A Voice from the Mountains" *News and Courier*, October 16, 1874.

223. Ibid.

224. Simkins and Woody, *South Carolina during Reconstruction*, 348–349.

225. "A Cause of Fair Dealing and Peace in Chester" *News and Courier*, October 24, 1874.

226. *News and Courier*, October 16, 1874.

227. Ibid., October 7, 1874.

228. Ibid.

229. Ibid. Also Simkins and Woody, *South Carolina during Reconstruction*, 473.

230. Ibid.

231. Ibid., 473.

232. Foner, *Reconstruction*, 456.

233. Grossman, *The Democratic Party and the South*, 45–49.

234. Ullman, *Martin R. Delany*, 456.

CHAPTER FIVE
Third Integrationist Phase: 1875–1877

1. Martin R. Delany, "Trial and Conviction." Charleston, 1876, 10 (unpublished pamphlet). Copy in the Charleston Historical Society Library.

2. Ibid.

3. Ibid.

4. *New York Daily Tribune,* March 6, 1875, 7.

5. Ibid.

6. Eric Foner, *Reconstruction: America's Unfinished Revolution, 1863–1877.* New York: Harper and Row, 1988, 524–553.

7. Ibid. Also Delany, "Trial and Conviction," 15.

8. Delany, "Trial and Conviction."

9. Ibid., 10.

10. Ibid.

11. Ibid., 10–11.

12. Ibid.

13. Victor Ullman, *Martin R. Delany: The Beginnings of Black Nationalism.* Boston: Beacon Press, 1971, 465.

14. Ibid., 468.

15. A South Carolinian (Belton O'Neall Townsend) "The Political Condition of South Carolina," *Atlantic Monthly,* February 1877, 181. The Democrats, in fact, began a forceful reorganization of their party in response to the circuit judge's election. They would resist any attempts to seat Moses and Whipper as judges. "Out of the sin and sorrow of the judicial election shall be born, if we dare and do, a new South Carolina," they declared. *News and Courier,* December 29, 1875; also December 28, 1875, December 30, 1875, and January 21, 1876.

16. Martin R. Delany, "Trial and Conviction," 15.

17. Ibid., 11–15. Also *News and Courier,* March 23, 1876, 2.

18. Delany, "Trial and Conviction," 15–16.

19. Ibid.

20. Ibid.

21. Ibid.

22. "The Charges Against M. R. Delany" *News and Courier,* March 23, 1876.

23. Ibid.

24. Delany, "Trial and Conviction."

25. Ibid.

26. Ibid.

27. Ibid., 3.

28. Ibid.

29. Ibid.

30. Ibid., 4–11.

31. Ibid., 18.

32. Ibid.

33. Frederick Douglass, *Life and Times of Frederick Douglass.* New York: Collier Books, 1895, 482.

34. Ibid.

35. Rev. N. N. Hunter to Delany, April 22, 1876, in Daniel H. Chamberlain Papers, Box 12, folder 2, South Carolina Department of Archives and History (SCDAH).

36. R. S. Tharin to Gov. Chamberlain, June 1, 1876, in Daniel H. Chamberlain Papers, Box 12, folder 34, SCDAH.

37. C. C. Bowen to Gov. Chamberlain, April 3, 1876, in Daniel H. Chamberlain Papers, Box 11, folder 33, SCDAH.

38. J. P. Reed, "The State vs. Martin R. Delany, April 27, 1876," Daniel Chamberlain Papers, Box 14, folder 16, SCDAH.
39. George E. Johnston and Aaron Logan to Gov. Chamberlain, August 19, 1876. Daniel H. Chamberlain Papers, Box 14, folder 4, SCDAH.
40. R. Jones to Delany, July 3, 1876, Daniel H. Chamberlain Papers, Log Book, vol. 4, SCDAH.
41. Delany to R. Jones, July 7, 1876, Daniel H. Chamberlain Papers, Box 13, folder 13, SCDAH.
42. Ibid.
43. "The State vs. M. R. Delany" Daniel H. Chamberlain Papers, Box 14, folder 16, SCDAH.
44. Delany to Gov. Chamberlain, September 1, 1876, Ibid., Box 14, folder 18.
45. Ibid.
46. Ibid. Delany is requesting a prepaid thousand-mile railroad ticket to pay for his travels.
47. *News and Courier*, October 3, 1874, October 7, 1874.
48. Richland Democratic Club Minutes: Scrapbook 1876–1880. Mss. South Caroliniana Research Library, Columbia. Also Delany to Rev. Garland H. White, September 18, 1876. *News and Courier*, September 19, 1876.
49. Delany to Rev. Garland H. White.
50. Ibid.
51. *New York Times*, April 7, 1876,1. Also April 8, 1876, 1.
52. Ibid., June 15, 1876.
53. Delany to Rev. Garland H. White.
54. *Daily Register*, July 15, 1876, 2; July 20, 1876. An Address to the People of the United States Adopted at *A Conference of Colored Citizens, Held at Columbia, South Carolina, July 20–21, 1876*. Columbia, S.C.: Republican Printing Company and State Printers, 1876 (pamphlet). According to one authority, the Hamburg riot finally solidified white Carolinians behind a straight-out platform. George B. Tindall, *South Carolina Negroes, 1877–1900*. Columbia: University of South Carolina Press, 1952, chap. 1.
55. Ibid., 10. There were also bloody riots in Charleston. See *Charleston Riots of 1876* (pamphlet), 34, of the Dawson Pamphlets, University of North Carolina Library, Chapel Hill.
56. *Richland Democratic Club, Minute: Scrapbook*. South Caroliniana Research Library, Columbia.
57. Ibid.
58. *News and Courier*, December 18, 1875. According to one authority, "by 1876 only the idea of reconstruction remained to be destroyed, reconstruction itself already had fallen in almost all southern states." Joseph Alvarez, *From Reconstruction to Revolution: The Black Struggle for Equality*. New York: Atheneum, 1972, 41. John Hammond Moore, ed., *The JUHL Letters to the Charleston Courier: A View of the South, 1865–1871*. Athens: University of Georgia Press, 1974, 362.
59. Joel Williamson, *After Slavery: The Negro in South Carolina during Reconstruction, 1861–1877*. Chapel Hill: University of North Carolina Press, 417.
60. *Daily Register*, Columbia, September 28, 1876. Also A South Carolinian (Belton O'Neal Townsend), "The Political Condition of South Carolina" *Atlantic Monthly*, February 1877, 183–184. *Reconstruction Scrapbook, 1865–1877*,

Mss. South Caroliniana Research Library, Columbia; also Robert McKay Scrapbook, 1865–1887, Mss. Ibid.

61. Delany to Rev. Garland White, *News and Courier*, September 19, 1876.

62. *News and Courier*, October 10, 1876; also October 13, 1876.

63. Ibid.

64. Ibid.

65. "The Campaign in the City" *News and Courier*, October 14, 1876.

66. Ibid.

67. Ibid.

68. Ibid.

69. "Union of the Two Races: What Prevents It?" *Daily Register*, (Columbia), September 28, 1876.

70. Ibid.

71. *Daily Register*, September 28, 1876. Also A South Carolinian (Belton O'Neal Townsend), "The Political Condition of South Carolina," *Atlantic Monthly*, February 1877, and *Reconstruction Scrapbook*.

72. *News and Courier*, October 10, 1876, 4, September 19, 1876, 4; October 14, 1876, 4; October 13, 1876, 4. *Daily Register*, September 28, 1876.

73. Rupert Sargent Holland, ed., *Letters and Diary of Laura M. Towne*. Cambridge: Harvard University Press, 1912, 254.

74. On the role of violence in Reconstruction, see George C. Rable, *But There was No Peace: The Role of Violence in the Politics of Reconstruction*. Athens: University of Georgia Press, 1984; Ida Waller Pope, "Violence as a Political Force in the Reconstruction South" Ph.D., diss., University of Southwestern Louisiana, 1982. Allen W. Trelease, *White Terror: The Ku Klux Klan Conspiracy and Southern Reconstruction*. New York: Harper and Row, 1971. Otto H. Olsen, "The Ku Klux Klan: A Study in Reconstruction Politics and Propaganda" *North Carolina Historical Review*, 3, summer 1962. Francis B. Simkins, "The Ku Klux Klan in South Carolina, 1868–1871" *Journal of Negro History*, 12, no. 4, October 1927. Herbert Shapiro, "The Ku Klux Klan During Reconstruction: The South Carolina Episode" *Journal of Negro History*, 49, January 1964. Although violence played a crucial role, there was, however, an equally strong ideological dimension to the success of redemption in 1876. Joel Williamson argued that a strong revival of the age-old paternalistic ethics contributed to the success of the Democrats in 1876. The white Carolinian worldview of a hierarchical social order in which black occupied the lowest wrung of the ladder was undermined but not totally destroyed by the Civil War and radical Reconstruction. As the prospect of redemption brightened in the 1870s, white Carolinians revived the idea, clothed in a paternalistic robe. Black prosperity and survival they argued depended upon surrender to the leadership of the superior white race. They promised "almost everything" to blacks in a South Carolina ruled by Democrats. But a large part of this "liberal" and paternalistic rhetoric was uttered in "calculated bad faith." See Joel Williamson, *The Crucible of Race: Black-White Relations in the American South since Emancipation*. London: Oxford University Press, 1984, 79–88.

75. W. E. B. Du Bois, *Black Reconstruction in America, 1860–1880*. New York: Harcourt Brace, 1935, 428. Orville Vernon Burton, "Ungrateful Servants? Edgefield Black Reconstruction: Part 1 of the Total History of Edgefield County, South Carolina" Ph.D., diss., Princeton University, 1976.

76. Alfred B. Williams, *Hampton and His Red Shirts: South Carolina Deliverance in 1876*. Charleston: Walker, Evans and Cogswell, 1935, 260–261. *News and*

Courier, October 1, 1876, 3; October 17, 18, 1876. Henry T. Thompson, *Ousting the Carpetbaggers from South Carolina*. New York: Negro University Press, 1962, 120.

77. Delany, "Trial and Conviction," 11–16.
78. Ibid., 10–16.
79. Theodore Draper, "The Father of American Black Nationalism" *New York Times Review of Books*, March 12, 1970.
80. Delany to Garrison, May 14, 1852, *Liberator*, May 21, 1852.
81. Martin Delany, *A Series of Four Tracts on National Polity*. Charleston, S.C.: Republican Book and Job Office, 1870 (pamphlet).
82. Delany, "Citizenship" *National Era*, March 10, 1870.
83. Belton O'Neal Townsend, "The Result in South Carolina" *Atlantic Monthly*, 41, January 1878, 2–3. On the subject of fraud, see, *Recent Election in South Carolina: Testimony Taken by the Select Committee on the Recent Election in South Carolina*. House Miscellaneous Document no. 31, 44th Congress, 2nd Session. Washington, D.C.: Government Printing Office, 1877. Also *South Carolina in 1876. Testimony as to the Denial of the Elective Franchise in South Carolina At the Elections of 1875 and 1876*. Senate Miscellaneous Documents, no. 48, 44th Congress, 2nd Session, 3 vols. Washington, D.C., 1877. *Report of the Joint Investigation Committee on Public Frauds and Election of Hon. J. J. Patterson to the United States Senate Made to the General Assembly of South Carolina at the Regular Session, 1877–1878*. Columbia: Calvo and Patton State Printers, 1878. According to Joel Williamson, although no authoritative data exists, the great mass of blacks remained loyal to the Republican Party. See his *After Slavery*, 411.

CHAPTER SIX

Final Years: 1878–1885

1. "A Progressive Age" *News and Courier*, July 23, 1877, 4.
2. Belton O'Neal Townsend, "The Result in South Carolina," *Atlantic Monthly*, 41, January 1878, 2–3.
3. Thomas Holt, *Black Over White: Negro Political Leadership in South Carolina During Reconstruction*. Urbana: University of Illinois Press, 1977, 211. *News and Courier*, November 29, 1877, 2; January 15, 2. See Hampton Family Papers, Mss. Folder 90, South Caroliniana Research Library, Columbia; Wade Hampton 111, 1818–1902, 4 Mps. 10, 11, January 1877–1925, April 1878, July 1878. South Caroliniana Research Library, Columbia.
4. Holt, *Black Over White*.
5. Martin W. Gary to Hugh, March 10, 1878; Martin Witherspoon Gary Papers, Mss. South Caroliniana Research Library, Columbia.
6. Martin W. Gary to Hugh, May 3, 1878, Martin Witherspoon Gary Papers, Ibid. General Butler to Gary, April 3, 1878, Mss. Ibid; J. S. Hudson to Gary, January 14, 1878, Mss. Ibid.; Ellis G. Taylor to Gary, August 19, 1878. Mss. Ibid.
7. J. H. Hudson to Gary, September 7, 1878, Mss. South Caroliniana Research Library, Columbia.
8. Ibid.
9. Wade Hampton Papers, Box 5, folder 41, South Carolina Department of Archives and History (SCDAH), Columbia.

10. *News and Courier*, November 5, 1877; William H. Shirley Jr., "A Black Republican Congressman during the Democratic Resurgence in South Carolina: Robert Smalls, 1876–1882," Master's thesis, University of South Carolina, 1970, 33.
11. Townsend, "The Result in South Carolina," 6–9.
12. Ibid.
13. Ibid.
14. Richard Cain to William Coppinger, January 25, 1877, in Martin Delany File, London (Ontario) Cross Cultural Learner's Center. Also in American Colonization Society Papers, Library of Congress, Washington, D.C.
15. Cain to Coppinger, February 12, 1877. Ibid.
16. *News and Courier*, July 16, 1877, 4.
17. Ibid., April 16, 1878.
18. St. Julian Jervey to S. J. Robinson, Esq., February 15, 1878. Wade Hampton Papers, Box 9, folder 39, SCDAH.
19. Wade Hampton Papers, Box 10, folder 14, SCDAH.
20. Delany to Wade Hampton, Wade Hampton Papers, Letters Received, Box 10, folder 29, SCDAH.
21. Wade Hampton Papers, Letters Received, Box 10, folder 30, SCDAH.
22. Idus Newby, *The Development of Segregationist Thought*. Homewood, Ill.: Dorsey Press, 1968.
23. Martin Delany, *Principia of Ethnology: The Origin of Race and Color*. Philadelphia: Harper and Brother, 1879.
24. Robert S. Levine, *Martin Delany, Frederick Douglass and the Politics of Representative Identity*. Chapel Hill: University of North Carolina Press, 1977, 234.
25. Ibid., 235.
26. Mia Bay, *The White Image in the Black Mind: African-American Ideas about White People, 1830–1925*. New York: Oxford University Press, 2000, 96.
27. *Liberator*, May 1, 1863.
28. Delany, *Principia*, chaps. 1–5.
29. Ibid., Preface.
30. Ibid., chaps. 1–5.
31. Ibid., chaps. 8–12.
32. Ibid., chaps. 13–18.
33. Ibid., chap. 18.
34. Ibid.
35. Ibid., 92.
36. Ibid.
37. Ibid., 92–93.
38. Ibid., 91–92.
39. Martin Delany to William Coppinger, August 18, 1880, American Colonization Society Papers.
40. Martin Delany to Hon. J. H. Latrobe, American Colonization Society Papers.
41. Ibid.
42. Ibid.
43. Delany to William Coppinger, August 18, 1880, American Colonization Society Papers.
44. Ibid.
45. Ibid.
46. Ibid.

47. Delany to William Coppinger, December 18, 1880, American Colonization Society Papers.
48. Ibid.
49. Dorothy Sterling, *The Making of an Afro-American: Martin Robison Delany*. New York: Da Capo Press, 1996, 326–328. (originally published by Doubleday in 1971.)
50. *Douglass's Monthly*, August 1862, 695.
51. Sterling, *The Making of an Afro-American*, 327.
52. *Xenia Gazette*, January 7, 1885.

CONCLUSION

1. Martin Delany, "Trial and Conviction." Charleston, 1876, (unpublished pamphlet) 10–11.
2. Victor Ullman, *Martin R. Delany: The Beginnings of Black Nationalism*. Boston: Beacon Press, 1971, ix.
3. Martin R. Delany, *A Series of Four Tracts on National Polity*. Charleston, S.C.: Republican Book and Job Office, 1870.
4. Martin R. Delany, "Citizenship" *National Era*, March 10, 1870.
5. *Daily Republican*, July 5, 1870. Delany espoused this utilitarian conception of politics in several speeches, see ibid., June 24, 1870, July 15, 1870.
6. *Daily Republican*, July 25, 1870, 2.
7. *News and Courier*, September 21, 1876, September 22, 1876. Also Bernard E. Powers, "Black Charleston: A Social History, 1822–1865," Ph.D. diss., Northwestern University, 1982.
8. Ibid. A South Carolinian (Belton O'Neall Townsend) "The Political Condition in South Carolina" *Atlantic Monthly*, February 1877, 184–185.
9. Ibid., 185–186.
10. Ullman, *Martin R. Delany*. Nell I. Painter, "Martin R. Delany: Elitism and Black Nationalism" in Leon Litwack and August Meier eds., *Black Leaders of the Nineteenth Century*. Urbana: University of Illinois Press, 1988, 149–172.
11. "Dr. M. R. Delany" *Douglass' Monthly*, August 1862.
12. Martin Delany, "The Black Man's Political Movement" (letter to Rev. Garland H. White), September 18, 1876, *News and Courier*, September 19, 1876.
13. Ibid.
14. Ibid.
15. Frank (Frances) Rollin, *Life and Public Services of Martin R. Delany*. Boston: Lee and Shepard, 1868, 19.
16. Daniel A. Payne, *Recollections of Seventy Years*. Nashville, Tenn.: AME, 1898, 160–161.
17. *Liberator*, May 7, 1852.
18. Rollin, *Life and Public Service*, 19–22.
19. *Liberator*, May 7, 1852.
20. "Letter From Dr. Delany" *Liberator*, May 21, 1852.
21. August Meier, "Afterward: New Perspectives on the Nature of Black Political Leadership During Reconstruction" in Howard N. Rabinowitz ed., *Southern Black Leaders of the Reconstruction Era*. Urbana: University of Illinois Press, 1982, 393–405.
22. Victor Ullman, *Martin R. Delany*, 458.
23. *North Star*, June 16, 1848.

BIBLIOGRAPHY

ARCHIVAL SOURCES

Amistad Research Center, Tulane University, New Orleans.
American Missionary Association Papers.
Martin R. Delany Papers.
Cross Cultural Learner's Center, London, Ontario, Canada.
Martin R. Delany Papers.
Kent County Historical Society, Chatham, Ontario, Canada.
Martin R. Delany Papers.
The Library of Congress, Washington, D.C.
American Colonization Society Papers.
Moreland-Spingarn Research Center, Howard University, Washington, D.C.
Martin R. Delany Papers.
South Carolina Department of Archives and History, Columbia.
Daniel H. Chamberlain Papers.
Diary of Josephus Woodruff.
Franklin J. Moses Papers.
Martin R. Delany, Freedmen's Bureau Papers.
Wade Hampton Papers.
South Carolina Historical Society, Charleston.
Martin R. Delany Papers.
South Caroliniana Research Library, University of South Carolina, Columbia.
Democratic Party, Charleston, Minutes 1868.
Edward Crossland Papers.
Elizabeth A. Summers Papers.
Ellison Summerfield Keiff (FL1876) MP.
Francis Warrington Dawson Papers.
Independent Republican Party: MP. 1874.
Martin Witherspoon Gary Papers.
Reconstruction Scrapbook, 1865–1877.
Richland Democratic Club Minutes: Scrapbook 1876–1880.
Robert McKay Scrapbook.
Wade Hampton III, 1818–1902, 4 MPS. January 1877–1925, April 1878,
    July 1878.
Wade Hampton Family Papers.
War Records Office, National Archives, Washington, D.C.
Martin Delany, Correspondence, Recruiting Posters, Military Records.

Martin Delany, Freedmen's Bureau Papers. Records of the Assistant Commissioners for the State of South Carolina. Bureau of Refugees, Freedmen and Abandoned Lands (BRFAL), 1865–1870; Microcopy 869.
Martin Delany, Freedmen's Bureau Reports for May 1868. BRFAL, Microcopy 849, roll32.
Xenia Public Library, Xenia, Ohio.
Martin R. Delany Papers.

GOVERNMENT PUBLICATIONS

House Miscellaneous Document Number 81. Serial 1349. Resolutions of the Constitutional Convention of South Carolina, 1868. 40th Congress, 2nd Session.
Recent Election in South Carolina: Testimony Taken by the Select Committee on the Recent Election. House Miscellaneous Document Number 31, 44th Congress, 2nd Session. Washington, D.C., 1877.
Report of the Joint Investigation Committee on Public Frauds and Election of Hon. J. J. Patterson to the United States Senate Made to the General Assembly of South Carolina at the Regular Session, 1877–1878. Columbia, S.C.: Calvo and Patton State Printers, 1878.
South Carolina in 1876. Testimonies to the Denial of the Elective Franchise in South Carolina at the Election of 1875 and 1876. Senate Miscellaneous Document Number 48, 44th Congress, 2nd Session, 3 vols. Washington, D.C., 1877.
United States Congress, House Select Committee on Emigration and Colonization Report. Washington, D.C. 37th Congress, 2nd Session, December 2, 1862–July 17, 1862.

PAMPHLETS

A Conference of Colored Citizens, Held at Columbia, S.C. July 20–21, 1876. Columbia, S.C.: Republican Printing Company and State Printers, 1876.
Charleston Riots of 1876. Dawson Pamphlets Collection, Wilson Library, University of North Carolina, Chapel Hill.
Platform of the Union Reform Party and the Address of the Executive Committee to the People of the State. Columbia, S.C.: Daily Southern Guardian, 1870. Dawson Pamphlets Collection.
Proceedings of the Southern States Convention of Colored Men, Held in Columbia, S.C., October 18–25, 1870. Columbia, S.C.: Carolina Printing, 1871. Dawson Pamphlets Collection.
The Letters of Jas H. Campbell to the Aiken Democratic Club. Dawson Pamphlets Collection.

NEWSPAPERS/PERIODICALS

AME Church Review, 1886.
Anglo-African Magazine (New York), 1859–1861.
Anti-Slavery Reporter (New York), 1865.

Charleston Mercury, 1865–1868.
Charleston News and Courier, 1865–1878.
Chatham Daily News, 1955.
Chatham Tri-Weekly Planet, 1857–1859.
Colored American (New York).
Daily Phoenix (Columbia, S.C.), 1868–1871.
Daily Register (Columbia, S.C.), 1876.
Daily Republican (Charleston, S.C.), 1869–1872.
Douglass's Monthly (New York), 1859–1862.
Frederick Douglass' Paper (New York), 1852–1855.
Liberator (Boston), 1835–1859.
New National Era (Washington, D.C.), 1870–1871.
New York Daily Tribune, 1875.
New York Times, 1865–1877.
New York Tribune, 1865–1877.
North Star (New York), 1847–1849.
Pennsylvania Freeman, 1846–1852.
Pennsylvania History.
Pittsburgh Courier, 1936.
Pittsburgh Mystery, 1843–1844.
Post Gazette (Pittsburgh).
Provincial Freeman (Chatham, Ontario), 1853–1857.
Weekly Anglo-African (New York), 1859–1862.

BOOKS

Adams, Michael C. C. *Our Masters the Rebels: A Speculation on Union Military Failures in the East, 1861–1865*. Cambridge: Harvard University Press, 1978.
Adeleke, Tunde. *UnAfrican Americans: Nineteenth Century Black Nationalists and the Civilizing Mission*. Lexington: University Press of Kentucky, 1998.
Allen, Walter. *Governor Chamberlain's Administration in South Carolina: A Chapter of Reconstruction in the Southern States*. New York: Negro University Press, 1969.
Alvarez, Joseph A. *From Reconstruction to Revolution: The Struggle for Equality*. New York: Atheneum, 1971.
Bay, Mia. *The White Image in the Black Mind: African-American Ideas About White People, 1830–1925*. New York: Oxford University Press, 2000.
Bell, Howard H. *The Proceedings of the National Negro Conventions, 1830–1864*. New York: Arno Press and the New York Times, 1969.
———. *A Survey of the Negro Convention Movement, 1830–1861*. New York: Arno Press and the New York Times, 1969.
Bentley, George R. *A History of the Freedmen's Bureau*. Philadelphia: University of Pennsylvania Press, 1965.
Berlin, Ira, Joseph Reidy, and Leslie Rowland, eds. *Freedom: A Documentary History of Emigration, 1861–1881*. Series 11, *The Black Military Experience*. Cambridge: Cambridge University Press, 1982.
Bethel, Elizabeth R. *Promiseland: A Century of Life in a Negro Community*. Philadelphia: Temple University Press, 1981.
Bowers, Claude. *Tragic Era: The Revolution After Lincoln*. Boston, 1929.

Brawley, Benjamin. *A Social History of the American Negro*. New York: Macmillan, 1921.

———. *Early Negro American Writers*. Chapel Hill: University of North Carolina Press, 1935.

———. *The Negro Genius*. New York: Dodd, Mead, 1937.

———. *Negro Builders and Heroes*. Chapel Hill: University of North Carolina Press, 1937.

———. *A Short History of the American Negro*. New York: Macmillan, 1939.

Burgess, John W. *Reconstruction and the Constitution, 1866–1876*. New York, 1902.

Cash, Wilbur J. *The Mind of the South*. New York, 1941.

Connelly, Thomas L., and Barbara L. Bellows. *God and General Longstreet: The Lost Cause and the Southern Mind*. Baton Rouge: Louisiana State University Press, 1982.

Cox, LaWanda, and John Cox, eds. *Reconstruction, the Negro and the New South (Documents)*. Columbia: University of South Carolina Press, 1973.

———. *Politics, Principle, and Prejudice, 1865–1866: Dilemma of Reconstruction America*. New York: Atheneum, 1976.

Croushore, James H., and David M. Potter, eds. *John William De Forest: A Union Officer in Reconstruction*. New Haven, Conn.: Yale University Press, 1948.

Cruse, Harold. *The Crisis of the Negro Intellectual*. New York: William Morrow, 1967.

Curry, Leonard P. *The Free Black in Urban America, 1800–1850: The Shadow of the Dream*. Chicago: University of Chicago Press, 1981.

Delany Martin R. *Eulogy on the Life and Character of the Rev. Fayette Davis*. Pittsburgh: Benj. Franklin Peterson, 1847.

———. *The Condition, Elevation, Emigration, and Destiny of the Colored People of the United States*. 1852. Baltimore: Black Classic Press, 1998.

———. *A Series of Four Tracts on National Polity*. Charleston, S.C.: Republican Book and Job Office, 1870.

———. *Principia of Ethnology: The Origins of the Races and Color*. 1879. Baltimore: Black Classic Press, 1991.

———. *Official Report of the Niger Valley Exploring Party*. New York: Thomas Hamilton, 1861.

———. "Trial and Conviction." Charleston, 1876.

Douglass, Frederick. *Life and Times of Frederick Douglass*. New York: Collier Books, 1895.

Drago, Edmund, L. *Black Politicians and Reconstruction in Georgia: A Splendid Failure*. Baton Rouge: Louisiana State University Press, 1982.

Draper, Theodore. *The Rediscovery of Black Nationalism*. New York: Viking Press, 1970.

Du Bois, William E. B. *The Suppression of the African Slave Trade to the United States of America, 1638–1870*. New York: Longman, 1896.

———. *The Philadelphia Negro*. Philadelphia: University of Pennsylvania Press, 1899.

———. *The Souls of Black Folk*. Chicago: A. C. McClurg, 1903.

———. *The Gift of Black Folk*. Boston: Stratford, 1924.

———. *Black Reconstruction in America, 1860–1880*. New York: Harcourt Brace, 1935.

———. *The World and Africa*. New York: Viking Press, 1947.

Dunning, William A. *Reconstruction, Political and Economic, 1865–1877.* New York: Harper, 1907.

Elkins, Stanley, *Slavery: A Problem in American Institutional and Intellectual Life.* Chicago: 1959.

Fehrenbacher, Don E. *The Dred Scott Case: Its Significance in American Law and Politics.* New York: Oxford University Press, 1978.

———. *The South and Three Sectional Crises.* Baton Rouge: Louisiana State University Press, 1980.

Finkelman, Paul, ed. Dred Scott v. Sanford: *A Brief History With Documents.* New York: Bedford Books, 1997.

Fleming, Walter F. *The Sequel of Appomattox.* New York: 1919.

———. ed., *Documentary History of Reconstruction: Political, Military, Social, Religious, Educational and Industrial, 1865–1906.* Vol. 1. New York: McGraw-Hill, 1966.

Foner, Eric. *Reconstruction: America's Unfinished Revolution.* New York: Harper and Row, 1988.

Foner, Philip, S. *Frederick Douglass: A Biography.* New York: Citadel, 1964.

———. ed., *The Life and Writings of Frederick Douglass.* Vol. 5., *Supplementary.* New York: International Publishers, 1975.

Foner, Philip S., and George Walker, eds., *Proceedings of the Black State Conventions, 1840–1865.* Vol. 1. Philadelphia: Temple University Press, 1980.

Franklin, John Hope. *The Militant South.* Cambridge: Harvard University Press, 1956.

———. *Reconstruction: After the Civil War.* Chicago: University of Chicago Press, 1961.

———. *The Emancipation Proclamation.* New York: Anchor Books, 1965.

———, and August Meier, eds., *Black Leaders of the Twentieth Century.* Urbana: University of Illinois Press, 1982.

———. *George Washington Williams: A Biography.* Chicago: University of Chicago Press, 1985.

———. *From Slavery and Freedom: A History of African Americans.* 7th ed. New York: McGraw Hill, 1994.

Fraser, Walter J, and Winifred B. Moore, eds. *The Southern Enigma: Essays on Race, Class and Folk Culture.* Westport, Conn.: Greenwood Press, 1983.

Frederickson, George. *The Black Image in the White Mind: The Debate on Afro-American Character and Destiny, 1917–1914.* New York: Harper and Row, 1971.

Gaston, Paul M. *The New South Creed: A Study in Southern Mythmaking.* New York: Vintage Books, 1973.

Gillette, William. *Retreat from Reconstruction, 1869–1879.* Baton Rouge: Louisiana State University Press, 1978.

Griffith, Cyril E. *The African Dream: Martin R. Delany and the Emergence of Pan-Africanist Thought.* University Park: Pennsylvania State University press, 1975.

Grossman, Lawrence. *The Democratic Party and the South: Northern and National Politics, 1868–1892.* Urbana: University of Illinois Press, 1976.

Harding, Vincent. *The Other American Revolution.* Los Angeles: Center for Afro-American Studies, University of California at Los Angeles, 1980.

———. *There Is a River: The Black Struggle for Freedom in America.* New York: Vintage Books, 1983.

Harold, Stanley. *American Abolitionists.* New York: Longman, 2000.

Hine, Darlene Clark, ed. *The State of Afro-American History: Past, Present and Future*. Baton Rouge: Louisiana State University Press, 1986.

Holland, Rupert, ed. *Letters and Diary of Laura M. Towne*. Cambridge: Harvard University Press, 1912.

Holt, Thomas. *Black Over White: Negro Political Leadership in South Carolina during Reconstruction*. Urbana: University of Illinois Press, 1977.

Horton, James O. *Free People of Color: Inside the African American Community*. Washington, D.C.: Smithsonian Institution Press, 1993.

Huggins, Nathan I. *Key Issues in the Afro-American Experience*. Vol. 1. New York: Harcourt Brace, 1971.

Hutton, A. J. White, *Some Historical Data Concerning the History of Chambersburg*. Chambersburg: Franklin Repository, 1930.

Jacobs, Donald M, ed. *In Courage and Conscience: Black and White Abolitionists in Boston*. Bloomington: Indiana University Press, 1993.

Lamson, Peggy. *The Glorious Failure: Black Congressman Robert Brown Elliott and the Reconstruction in South Carolina*. New York: W. W. Norton, 1973.

Levine, Robert S. *Martin Delany, Frederick Douglass and the Politics of Representative Identity*. Chapel Hill: University of North Carolina Press, 1977.

Litwack, Leon. *North of Slavery: The Negro in the Free States, 1790–1860*. Chicago: University of Chicago press, 1961.

———, and August Meier, eds. *Black Leaders of the Nineteenth Century*. Urbana: University of Illinois Press, 1988.

Mabee, Carlton. *Black Freedom: The Nonviolent Abolitionists from 1830 through the Civil War*. London: Macmillan, 1970.

Macdonald, Robert R., et al. *Louisiana's Black Heritage*. New Orleans: Louisiana State Museum, 1979.

Magdol, Edward. *A Right to the Land: Essays on the Freedmen's Community*. Westport, Conn.: Greenwood Press, 1977.

Martin, Waldo E. *The Mind of Frederick Douglass*. Chapel Hill: University of North Carolina Press, 1985.

McCartney, John T. *Black Power Ideologies: An Essay in African-American Political Thought*. Philadelphia: Temple University Press, 1992.

McColley, Robert. *Slavery and Jeffersonian Virginia*. 2nd ed. Urbana: University of Illinois Press, 1973.

McFeely, William. *Frederick Douglass*. New York: W. W. Norton, 1991.

McPherson, James. *The Negro Civil War: How American Negroes Felt and Acted during the War*. New York: Vintage Books, 1965.

Meier, August, and Elliot Rudwick. *Black History and the Historical Profession, 1915–1980*. Urbana: University of Illinois Press, 1986.

Miller, Floyd J. *The Search for Black Nationality: Black Emigration and Colonization, 1787–1863*. Urbana: University of Illinois Press, 1975.

Moore, John Hammond, ed. *The JUHL Letters to the Charleston Courier: A View of the South, 1865–1871*. Athens: University of Georgia Press, 1974.

Moses, Wilson J. *The Golden Age of Black Nationalism, 1850–1925*. New York: Oxford University Press, 1978.

Nell, William C. *Colored Patriots of the American Revolution*. Boston: R. F. Walcut, 1855.

———. *Services of Colored Americans in the Wars of 1776 and 1812*. Boston: Prentiss and Sawyer, 1855.

Oubre, Claude F. *Forty Acres and a Mule: The Freedmen's Bureau and Black Land Ownership*. Baton Rouge: Louisiana State University Press, 1978.

Payne, Daniel A. *Recollections of Seventy Years*. Nashville, Tenn.: AME, 1898.

Pearson, Elizabeth W., ed. *Letters from Port Royal Written at the Time of the Civil War*. Boston: W. B. Clarke, 1906.

Pennington, James W. C. *A Textbook of the Origin and History of the Colored People*. Hartcourt, Conn., 1841.

Perman, Michael. *Reunion without Compromise: The South and Reconstruction, 1865–1868*. Cambridge: Cambridge University Press, 1973.

Phillips, Ulrich B. *American Negro Slavery*. New York, 1918.

————. *The Course of the South to Secession*. New York: Appleton-Century, 1939.

Powell, Lawrence. *New Masters: Northern Planters during the Civil War and Reconstruction*. New Haven, Conn.: Yale University Press, 1980.

Quarles, Benjamin. *The Negro in the Civil War*. New York: Russell and Russell, 1953.

————. *The Negro in the American Revolution*. Chapel Hill: University of North Carolina Press, 1961.

————. *The Negro in the Making of America*. Chapel Hill: University of North Carolina Press, 1961.

————. *Lincoln and the Negro*. New York: Oxford University Press, 1962.

————. *Black Abolitionists*. London: Oxford University Press, 1968.

————. *Frederick Douglass*. 1948. New York: Atheneum, 1968.

Rabinowitz, Howard N. *Southern Black Leaders of the Reconstruction Era*. Urbana: University of Illinois Press, 1982.

Rable, George. *But There Was No Peace: The Role of Violence in the Politics of Reconstruction*. Athens: University of Georgia Press, 1984.

Reynolds, John S. *Reconstruction in South Carolina*. New York: Negro University Press, 1969.

Rhodes, James F. *History of the United States from the Compromise of 1850– to the McKinley-Bryan Campaign of 1896*. New York: Macmillan, 1904–1920.

Rollin, Frank A. *Life and Public Services of Martin R. Delany*. Boston: Lee and Shepard, 1868.

Rose, Willie Lee. *Rehearsal for Reconstruction: The Port Royal Experiment*. New York: Vintage Books, 1967.

Simkins, Francis, and Robert Woody. *South Carolina during Reconstruction*. Gloucester, Mass.: Peter Smith, 1966.

Sorin, Gerald. *Abolitionism: A New Perspective*. New York: Praeger, 1972.

Stampp, Kenneth, and Leon F. Litwack, eds. *Reconstruction: An Anthology of Revisionist Writings*. Baton Rouge: Louisiana State University Press, 1969.

Sterling, Dorothy. *The Making of an Afro-American: Martin R. Delany*. New York: Doubleday, 1971.

Stewart, James B. *Holly Warriors: The Abolitionists and American Slavery*. New York: Hill and Wang, 1976.

————. *William Lloyd Garrison and the Challenge of Emancipation*. Arlington Heights, Ill: Harlan Davidson, 1992.

Still, William. *The Underground Railroad*. Philadelphia: Porter and Coats, 1876.

Stuckey, Sterling. *The Ideological Origins of Black Nationalism*. Boston: Beacon Press, 1972.

Taylor, Alrutheus A. *The Negro in South Carolina during the Reconstruction*. Washington, D.C.: ASNLH, 1924.

Thomas, John L. *The Liberator, William Lloyd Garrison: A Biography*. Boston: Little Brown, 1963.

Thompson, Henry T. *Ousting the Carpetbaggers from South Carolina*. New York: Negro University Press, 1962.

Thorpe, Earl. *Mind of the Negro: An Intellectual History of the Afro-America*. New York: Negro University Press, 1970.

———. *Black Historians: A Critique*. New York: William Morrow, 1971.

Trelease, Allen W. *White Terror: The Ku Klux Klan Conspiracy and Southern Reconstruction*. New York: Harper and Row, 1971.

Ullman, Victor. *Martin R. Delany: The Beginnings of Black Nationalism*. Boston: Beacon Press, 1971.

Van de Burg, William L. *New Day in Babylon: The Black Power Movement and American Culture, 1965–1975*. Chicago: University of Chicago Press, 1992.

Van den Berghe, Pierre. *Race and Racism: A Comparative Perspective*. New York: John Wiley, 1967.

Walker, Peter. *Moral Choices: Memory, Desire, and Imagination in Nineteenth Century American Abolitionism*. Baton Rouge: Louisiana State University Press, 1978.

Williams, Alfred B. *Hampton and His Red Shirts: South Carolina Deliverance in 1876*. Charleston, S.C.: Walker, Evans and Cogswell, 1935.

Williams, George Washington. *A History of the Negro Race in America from 1619–1880*. New York: Putnam and Sons, 1883.

———. *A History of the Negro Troops in the War of the Rebellion, 1861–1865*. New York: Harper and Brothers, 1888.

———. *The Negro in the Americas*. Washington, D.C.: Howard University Press, 1940.

Williamson, Joel. *After Slavery: The Negro in South Carolina during Reconstruction 1861–1877*. Chapel Hill: University of North Carolina Press, 1965.

———. *The Crucible of Race: Black-White Relations in the American South since Emancipation*. London: Oxford University Press, 1984.

Williams, John A., and Charles F. Harris, eds. *Amistad 1: Writings on Black History and Culture*. New York: Vintage Books, 1970.

———. *Amistad 2: Writings on Black History and Culture*. New York: Vintage Books, 1971.

Woodson, Carter G. *The Education of the Negro Prior to 1861*. New York: A & B Books, 1919.

———. *The Negro in Our History*. Washington, D.C.: ASNLH, 1922.

———. *The Miseducation of the Negro*. Washington, DC: Association Publishers, 1923.

———. *The Negro as a Businessman*. Washington, D.C.: Association Publishers, 1929.

———. *The African Background Outlined*. Washington, D.C.: ASNLH, 1936.

———. *African Heroes and Heroines*. Washington, D.C.: Associated Publishers, 1939.

ARTICLES

Abbot, Martin. "The Freedmen's Bureau and its Carolina Critics." *Proceedings of the South Carolina Historical Association* (1962).

———. "Free Land, Free Labor, and the Freedmen's Bureau." *Agricultural History* (October 30, 1956).

Adeleke, Tunde. "The Religious Dimensions of Martin R. Delany's Struggle." *Journal of American and Canadian Studies* 10 (autumn 1992).

———. "Race and Ethnicity in Martin R. Delany's Thought." *Journal of Thought* 29, no. 1 (spring 1994).

———. "Afro-Americans and Moral Suasion: The Debate in the 1830s and 1840s." *Journal of Negro History* 80, no. 111 (spring 1998).

Aptheker, Herbert. "South Carolina Negro Convention, 1865." *Journal of Negro History* 31 (January 1945).

Bell, Howard H. "Convention of the Colored Persons of Pennsylvania." *Pennsylvania Freeman*, October 23, 1952.

———. "The American Moral Reform Society, 1836–1841." *Journal of Negro Education* 25, no. 11 (winter 1958).

Blackett, Richard. "Martin Delany and Robert Campbell: Black Americans in Search of an African Colony." *Journal of Negro History* 60, no. 11 (January 1977).

Cardozo, Francis L. "South Carolina: The Political Situation." *New York Times*, February 16, 1874.

———. "South Carolina: The Political Situation." *New York Times*, June 16, 1874.

———. "Address Before the Grand Council of the Union Leagues, July 27, 1870." *Journal of Negro History* 61, no. 2 (April 1976).

Cook, Samuel Dubois. "A Tragic Conception of Negro History." *Journal of Negro History* 45 (October 1960).

Cox, LaWanda. "The Promise of Land for Freedmen." *Mississippi Valley Historical Review* 45 (December 1958).

Cruse, Harold. "Black Studies: Interpretation, Methodology and the Relationship to Social Movements." *Afro-American Studies* 2 (1971).

Delany, Martin R. "American Civilization: Treatment of the Colored People in the United States." *North Star*, March 30, 1849.

———. "Political Aspect of the Colored People of the United States." *Provincial Freeman*, October 13, 1855.

———. "Political Event." *Provincial Freeman*, July 5, 1856.

———. "Political Destiny of the Colored Race on the American Continent." In *Life and Public Services of Martin R. Delany*, ed. Frank Rollin. Boston: Lee and Shepard, 1868.

———. "Citizenship." *National Era*, March 10, 1870.

———. "Homes for Freedmen." *Daily Republican*, May 2, 1870.

———. "A Political Review." *Daily Republican*, August 15, 1871.

———. "South Carolina Obligations." *New York Times*, September 25, 1872.

———. "South Carolina Obligations." *New York Times*, September 30, 1872.

Douglass, Frederick. "Prejudice Against Color." *North Star*, June 13, 1850.

Draper, Theodore. "The Father of American Black Nationalism." *New York Times Review of Books*, March 12, 1970.

———. "The Fantasy of Black Nationalism." *Commentary* 48 (1969).

Du Bois, William E. B. "Reconstruction and Its Benefits." *American Historical Review* 15 (1910).

———. "A Forum of Facts and Opinions." *Pittsburgh Courier*, July 25, 1936.

"An Exchange on Black History." *New York Times Review of Books*, May 21, 1970.

"Exchange on Black Nationalism." *New York Times Review of Books*, December 3, 1970.

Fierce, Milfred C. "Black Struggle for Land during Reconstruction." *Black Scholar* (February 1974).

Fonville, Althea. "Pittsburgher Was Father of Black Nationalism." *Pittsburgh Courier*, February 15, 1975.

———. "Pittsburgher Was Father of Black Nationalism." *Pittsburgh Courier*, February 14, 1976.

Franklin, John Hope. "On the Evolution of Scholarship in Afro-American History." In *The State of Afro-American History: Past, Present and Future*, ed. Darlene Clark Hine. Baton Rouge: Louisiana State University Press, 1986.

Geffen, Elizabeth M. "Violence in Philadelphia in the 1840s and 1850s." *Pennsylvania History* 4 (October 1969).

Gienapp, William E. "Abolitionism and the Nature of Ante-Bellum Reform." In *In Courage and Conscience: Black and White Abolitionists in Boston*, ed. Donald M. Jacobs. Bloomington: Indiana University Press, 1993.

Harding, Vincent. "Beyond Chaos: Black History and the Search for the New Land." In *Amistad 1: Writings on Black History and Culture*, ed. John A. Williams and Charles F. Harris. New York: Vintage Books, 1970.

Harlan, Louis R. "Tell It Like It Was: Suggestions on Black History." In *The Black Experience in America: Essays*, ed. James G. Curtis and Lewis L. Gould. Austin: University of Texas Press, 1970.

Harris, Robert L. "Coming of Age: The Transformation of Afro-American Historiography." *Journal of Negro History* 65, nos. 1, 2 (summer 1962).

Harris, William H. "Trends and Needs in Afro-American Historiography." In *The State of Afro-American History: Past, Present, and Future*, ed. Darlene Clark Hine. Baton Rouge: Louisiana State University Press, 1986.

Holly, Theodore J. "In Memoriam." *AME Church Review* (October 1886).

Huggins, Nathan I. "Afro-American History: Myths, Heroes, Reality." In *Key Issues in the Afro-American Experience*, ed. Nathan Huggins, Martin Kilson and Daniel Fox. Vol. 1. New York: Harcourt Brace, 1971.

Johnson, Charles S. "The Rise of the Negro Magazine." *Journal of Negro History* 13, no. 1 (January 1928).

Khan, Robert. "The Political Ideology of Martin Delany." *Journal of Black Studies* (June 1984).

Kirk-Green, A. H. M. "Americans in the Niger Valley: A Colonization Centenary." *Phylon* 22, no. 4 (1962).

Lee, Carmen J. "Marker Honors Black Doctor: Friend of Frederick Douglass Was Newspaper Publisher." *Post Gazette*, May 11, 1991.

Litwack, Leon F. "The Ballot and Land for Freedmen 1861–1865." In *Reconstruction: An Anthology of Revisionist Writings*, ed. Kenneth Stampp and Leon F. Litwack. Baton Rouge: Louisiana State University Press, 1969.

———. "The Ordeal of Black Freedom." In *The Southern Enigma: Essays on Race, Class and Folk Culture*, ed. Walter J. Fraser and Winifred B. Moore. Westport, Conn.: Greenwood Press, 1983.

Magdol, Edward. "Martin R. Delany Counsels Freedmen, July32, 1865." *Journal of Negro History* 56 (October 1971).

McAdoo, Bill. "Pre-Civil War Black Nationalism." *Progressive Labor* 5 (June–July 1966).

McCormick, Richard P. "William Whipper: Moral Reformer." *Pennsylvania History* 10, no. 1111 (January 1976).

Mckenzie, Edna B. "Remark at Marker Dedication, 5/11/91." (unpublished paper) Historical Society of Western Pennsylvania, Pittsburgh.

———. "Doctor, Editor, Soldier: On Pittsburgh's Very Own Martin R. Delany." *Post Gazette*, February 5, 1992.

Meier, August. "Afterward: New Perspectives on the Nature of Black Political Leadership during Reconstruction." In *Southern Black Leaders of the Reconstruction Era*, ed. Howard Rabinowitz. Urbana: University of Illinois Press, 1982.

Miller, Floyd J. "The Father of Black Nationalism: Another Contender." *Civil War History* 17 (December 1971).

Newby, Idus. "Historians and Negroes." *Journal of Negro History* 54, no. 1 (January 1969).

Olsen, Otto H. "The Ku Klux Klan: A Study in Reconstruction Politics and Propaganda." *North Carolina Historical Review* 3 (summer 1962).

Painter, Nell I. "Martin R. Delany: Elitism and Black Nationalism." In *Black Leaders of the Nineteenth Century*, ed. Leon Litwack and August Meier. Urbana: University of Illinois Press, 1988.

———. "Martin R. Delany: A Black Nationalist in Two Kinds of Time." *New England Journal of Black Studies* 8 (1989).

Pease, William, and Jane Pease. "The Negro Convention Movement." In *Key Issues in the Afro-American Experience*, ed. Nathan Huggins, Martin Kilson, and Daniel Fox. Vol. 1. New York: Harcourt Brace, 1971.

Phillips, Ulrich B. "The Central Theme of Southern History." *American Historical Review* 34, October 1928.

Rankin, David C. "The Politics of Caste: Free Colored Leadership in New Orleans During the Civil War." In *Louisiana's Black Heritage*, ed. Robert R. Macdonald et al. New Orleans: Louisiana State Museum, 1979.

———. "The Origins of Negro Leadership in New Orleans During Reconstruction." In *Southern Black Leaders of the Reconstruction Era*, ed. Howard N. Rabinowitz. Urbana: University of Illinois Press, 1982.

Rosenfeld, Louis. "Martin Robison Delany (1812–1885): Physician, Black Separatist, Explorer, Soldier." *Bulletin of the New York Academy of Medicine*, 2nd series, 65, no. 7 (September 1989).

Sajna, Mike. "Martin Delany: Father of Black Nationalism." *Greensburg Tribune-Review*, February 25, 1990.

Simkins, Francis B. "The Ku Klux Klan in South Carolina, 1868–1871." *Journal of Negro History* 12, no. 4 (October 1927).

———. "The Ku Klux Klan during Reconstruction: The South Carolina Episode." *Journal of Negro History* 49 (January 1964).

Stuckey, Sterling. "A Hymn of Freedom: South Carolina." *Journal of Negro History* 50 (January 1965).

———. "Twilight of Our Past: Reflections on the Origins of Black History." In *Amistad 2: Writings on Black History and Culture*, ed. John A. Williams and Charles F. Harris. New York: Vintage Books, 1971.

Tebeau, C. W. "Some Aspects of Planter-Freedmen Relations, 1865–1880." *Journal of Negro History* 21, no. 2 (April 1936).

Townsend, Belton O'Neall. "The Political Condition of South Carolina." *Atlantic Monthly*, February 1877.

———. "South Carolina Morals." *Atlantic Monthly*, April 1877.

———. "The Result in South Carolina." *Atlantic Monthly*, January 1878.

Wesley, Charles. "Lincoln's Plan for Colonizing the Emancipated Negroes." *Journal of Negro History* 4, no. 1 (January 1919).

Whipper, William. "Nonviolence to Offensive Aggression." *The Colored American*, September 16, 1837.

Woody, Robert H. "South Carolina Election of 1870." *North Carolina Historical Review* 8 (1931).
———. "Franklin J. Moses: Scalawag Governor of South Carolina." *North Carolina Historical Review* 10 (April 1933).

DISSERTATIONS/THESES

Burton, Orville Vernon. "Ungrateful Servants? Edgefield Black Reconstruction: Part One of the Total History of Edgefield County, South Carolina." Ph.D., Princeton, 1976.
Ford, Lacy K. "One Southern Profile: Modernization and the Development of White Terror in York County, 1856–1876." M.A., University of South Carolina, 1976.
Graham, Glennon. "From Slavery to Serfdom: Rural Black Agriculturalists in South Carolina, 1865–1900." Ph.D., Northwestern University, 1982.
Griffith, Cyril E. "Martin R. Delany and the African Dream, 1812–1885." Ph.D., Michigan State University, 1973.
Miller, Floyd J. "Search For a Black Nationality: Martin Robison Delany and the Emigrationist Alternative." Ph.D., University of Minnesota, 1975.
Pope, Ida W. "Violence As a Political Force in the Reconstruction South." Ph.D., University of Southwestern Louisiana, 1982.
Powers, Bernard E. "Black Charleston: A Social History, 1822–1885." Ph.D., Northwestern University, 1982.
Shirley, William H. "A Black Congressman during the Democratic Resurgence in South Carolina: Robert Smalls, 1876–1882." M.A., University of South Carolina, 1970.
Simmons, Adam D. "Ideologies and Programs of the Negro Anti-Slavery Movement, 1830–1861." Ph.D., Northwestern University, 1983.
Simpson, Donald. "Blacks in Ontario." Ph.D., University of Western Ontario, 1971.
Walton, Jonathan W. "Blacks in Buxton and Chatham, Ontario, 1830–1890: Did the 49th Parallel Make a Difference?" Ph.D., Princeton University, 1979.

INDEX